DIASPORAS WITHIN AND WITHOUT AFRICA

Dynamism, heterogeneity, variation

Edited by

Leif Manger and Munzoul A.M. Assal

Nordiska Afrikainstitutet, Uppsala 2006

Indexing terms:

Migration
Internal migration
Migrants
Human relations
Africans
Identity
Diaspora

Cover illustration:

Oil on canvas by an unknown artist, bought for the Library of the Nordic Africa Institute in 1999 at the Longacre Market in Lusaka, Zambia.

Index: Margaret Binns
Language checking: Elaine Almén
ISBN 91-7106-563-6

Printed in Sweden by Elanders Gotab AB, Stockholm 2006

Contents

Acknowledgements

An earlier version of the introduction written by Leif Manger and two of the papers (Bangstad, Assal) were first presented at a workshop held in Bergen 6–8 September 2001. The title of the workshop was "The Concept of Diaspora and the Theorising of Diaspora". Several papers presented at that workshop dealt with non-African cases and do not appear in this collection. But we do thank all the participants for valuable discussions and contributions.

Our meeting was organised jointly with a separate workshop, entitled "Contested Realities: An International Workshop on Epistemological Issues in Qualitative Research about Visible Minorities in Occidental Urban Settings". This workshop was organised under the umbrella of the IMER-programme (International Migration and Ethnic Relations) at the University of Bergen and dealt with empirical studies of migrants and ethnic minorities in Western metropoles. We thank the organisers of that workshop, Professor Yngve Lithman and Dr. Polit. Mette Anderson for smooth collaboration.

We also thank the Norwegian Research Council, the Faculty of Social Sciences and the Department of Social Anthropology for financial and logistical support for the workshop.

The paper by Roqaia Abusharaf is a chapter of her published book entitled "Wanderings. Sudanese Migrants and Exiles in North America" (2002) and we thank the publisher, Cornell University Press, for permission to use the chapter in our volume.

Bergen and Khartoum, May 2006

Leif Manger and Munzoul A.M. Assal

Diasporas within and without Africa – Dynamism, heterogeneity, variation

Leif Manger and Munzoul A.M. Assal

Diaspora in contemporary social science

Advocates of the usefulness of the concept of diaspora argue that it opens up promising avenues for understanding processes in the post-modern world, a world of transnationalism, of travelling, of cross-culture borrowing and of mixed, hybrid cultures. The increased attention given to this concept during the last decade relates to ongoing discussions within contemporary social science on globalism, traditions, issues of nationalism and of religious resurgence. This new reality, it is argued, requires a rethinking of basic concepts. The basic concepts that need to be rethought are those that belong to an earlier theorizing about communities and societies and cultures as bounded wholes, of local groups as units of study, isolated from their environment, and of movement of people conceptualised in paradigms of clearcut identities, of ethnicity and race, of minorities and majorities, adaptational strategies characterised by assimilation and so on. Those who do not like it argue that it is part of the post-modern rhetoric and undermining of earlier attempts at understanding movement, identity and social imagining. Members of this camp would rather continue exploring the analytical possibilities of those basic concepts mentioned above.

We think such a discussion is important and it is not difficult to agree on the need for advances in our social science theorizing in order to better understand the tension between globalization and identity, between homogenizing trends and reinforced cultural heterogeneity, between "flow and closure", "flux and fix". However, we also see some problematic areas. On the most general level we find it necessary to warn that in spite of all the criticism of earlier Western social science conceptualisations, many of the critics seem to return to a dichotomisation of the world, of modernity and pre-modernity, of modernity and post-modernity, and the local and the global. Added to this is the fact that the outcome of such meeting-points are seen to be either cultural homogenization, or a totally random post-modern flow of patterns. To us the debate whether globalization leads to cultural homogeneity or heterogeneity is false. There is no in-built drive towards either of the poles, but rather regional and local variation and possibilities. Hence, an important conclusion put forward here is that there is a need to test all claims about the new post-modern world against concrete empirical material in which micro-processes are demonstrated so that we are allowed to get a clearer picture of whether these dynamics are really found, or whether they are assumed by the researcher. The present contribution takes its starting point from the realization that unless the various processes contained within the concept of diaspora are developed and theorized on the basis of specific empirical material it may easily end up being as tricky, and as likely to lead into reified and essentialised types of analyses, as those that it was meant to challenge and replace.

Many "African diasporas"

The contributors to this volume all want to look at and analyse the formation and reproduction of diasporic dynamics relating to different people and communities living in Africa. In some papers we see communities placed in Africa, but with diasporic links outside the continent, in others we see diasporic communities outside the African continent, but with diasporic relations back home to African countries. The book is therefore not about what has conventionally been termed the "African diaspora", which might be said, together with other diasporas, such as the "Jewish diaspora" or the "Armenian diaspora" to represent one of the paradigmatic examples of diaspora. This African diaspora emerged from the Atlantic slave trade, and resulted in the various communities established in America and the Caribbean in which different forms of diasporic memories and consciousness emerged. A huge international literature exists on this type of diaspora, and the contributors to this volume are certainly inspired by it. But the aim of the present volume is not to add another publication to this vast literature. Rather, we want to look at other diasporas relating to Africa, both outside and inside the continent. The choice is a conscious one, and is made for two reasons that will be further explored in this introductory chapter. First, we want to provide empirical cases of other types of diasporas that have been of importance in African history in order to show how much variation is hidden behind terms like "diaspora" and "Africa". Second, we want to use the empirical cases and the variation presented to reflect on the concept of diaspora itself, to contribute to the ongoing attempts to develop a more precise understanding of what analytical use a term like diaspora might have.

First to the point about empirical variation. Looking at the movement out of Africa, the slave trade across the Atlantic certainly marked a very significant forced movement of people who ended up in America and the Caribbean. This is obviously of great importance and it represents a defining moment in African history. But it is also evident that this Atlantic focus tends to hide other historical developments that also came to have profound effects on African societies. If we look towards the east, instead of west, we will see the Indian Ocean, not the Atlantic. In that region we will also see a movement out of Africa, with communities of Africans emerging in Arabia, the Persian Gulf, India and elsewhere in Asia. But the Indian Ocean history also provides examples of people moving into Africa. These movements relate to a history of slavery as well, but a slave business in which Arabs and Muslims were involved, alongside the Western slave traders. But the movement of people was also caused by many other historical events and processes such as more regular trade and also religious missionary activities. The Indian Ocean history thus provides examples of processes of Islamization as much as the processes of Christianization that are tied to the Atlantic history. Three papers in this book deal specifically with this side of the story. Sindre Bangstad discusses the Cape Malays in South Africa, who came as slaves within a system of Dutch colonialsm, Leif Manger discusses the settlement of Hadramis and the building of a Hadrami diaspora of small traders in the Sudan, whereas Anne Bang provides a case that shows the settlement of Hadrami religious scholars along the East African coast. The three papers provide specific examples of a general historical development that resulted in communities along the eastern coast of Africa of Omanis, Yemenis and Indians, and of Indians and Malays in South Africa. Through these discussions we see examples of African communities of Malay and Hadrami descent with diasporic ties outside Africa and with a diasporic consciousness producing an Africanness that is not necessarily identical to what is found in communities originating in the Atlantic world mentioned above. At the same time the cases provide examples of how diasporic communities are internally organised and how they relate to homelands, to colonial administrations and to nation states, thus providing much needed historical depth to contemporary developments in the diasporic communities under discussion.

The book also carries examples of a contemporary African diaspora that is now being formed as a consequence of the ongoing crises within many African states. The papers present examples of how internal oppression, sometimes developing into civil wars or wars between nations, accounts for the present forced migration leading to internal displacement and refugee migration that brings Africans to areas with better security, both inside and outside the continent. Three papers focus on these results of the decay in the contemporary African post-colonial state, Bettina Conrad analyzing Eritrean refugee communities in Germany, Rogaia Mustafa Abusharaf presenting a portrait of Southern Sudanese in the USA and Munzoul Assal discussing Somali and Sudanese refugees in Norway. All three papers show that the euphoria of political independence from colonial rule in Africa was not necessarily accompanied by economic independence and prosperity. The result was rampant political chaos, civil wars and an increased modern out-migration by Africans, caused by the Africans themselves. The political dimension of diasporas relating to Africa is thus also clear and the emerging Eritrean, Somali and Sudanese diasporas in Europe and North America speak directly to the very contemporary challenges that face the post-colonial state in Africa.

The discussions in the various chapters also show that a discussion of diasporas cannot be limited to one single diaspora by itself. The focus must be broadened to a wider canvas in which processes of migration and transnationalism must be seen in a historical perspective through which we see how diaspora formations are interlinked with wider processes of local, regional and global scale. Various political contexts, colonial, imperial or that of nation-states, are important for the way diasporas develop. But so are other contexts, such as other, non-diasporic groups with whom diasporic populations interact. All the papers contain specific discussions of such contexts, but perhaps the ones dealing with the Sudanese diasporas in Europe and the USA touch most explicitly on such global contexts. Thus the cases of Sudanese refugees presented by Abusharaf and Assal refer to the contemporary situation in which refugees and migrants find themselves in the West. The cases show a global picture in which a complex set of contexts must be understood in order to grasp the dynamics of the situation, contexts that bring us outside the narrow view of African-related diasporas as such. In the contemporary Western world that is the focus of these papers the diasporas under discussion are seen as a mixture of suffering individuals and a group of people representing a direct threat to the nation states. The result is a mix of humanitarian organisations and human rights groups representing various non-governmental efforts to deal with the situation and a government run apparatus based on a complex legal system dealing with quotas and visa categories based on immigrant, refugee and asylum statuses. Many of these groups are African Muslims, and they are affected by the 11 September events and the way these events resulted in new realities that are moulding world politics into directions that might have far reaching implications on the Muslim presence in the West.

But refugees are not only Muslims. Many other religions are represented, as local, national, regional and global crises come and go. Hence, in addition to the contemporary drama surrounding Muslims in the diaspora, and the political relationships between the West and Middle Eastern and Asian Muslim countries, some basic issues will remain important to discuss, in order to deal with this general situation of increasing diversity. A general focus on the uneasy relationship between diaspora and the state is thus of general importance, as it dramatizes how nationalist ideologies place immigrant groups in a position as an anomaly, dramatizing the link between identity and place in the contemporary world, leading to a distrust towards certain types of movement and home-making that challenge a certain type of Western social order. This also shows that the problem of diaspora is not only about the migrating population but also about the populations in the countries in which the migrants settle and also about political and bureaucratic systems and their dynamics. Restricting immigration possibilities, sealing borders and checking on those who are within borders are some of the measures taken to control immigrant populations. The issue of multiculturalism is part of this in that multiculturalism is an attempted answer to the challenge of how to allow people to maintain individual identities as members of minority groups while at the same time allowing them to feel they are part of a wider society. The question of citizenship also belongs here, whether citizenship can have foundations other than a national collective, thus opening for a broader understanding of the relationship between particularistic identities and universalized rights. Judging from what we see at the time of writing it is difficult to be optimistic, and it seems that a further development towards the erection of transnational borders is as likely as a further development and acceptance of transnational loyalties.

The central concern of this volume is thus to bring together papers that focus on different types of migrations in and out of Africa, and to make use of the case studies to reflect critically on the concept of diaspora. What we see in the various chapters is that diasporas within and outside Africa represent different historical experiences and instances that took place at different points in time and for different reasons. But although there is empirical variation, the variation does not mean that the concept of diaspora cannot help us untangle the processes presented in our cases. In all of them we see diasporas as sites of multiple identifications and intersectionalities, sites of consciousness, as well as forms of personal experiences and histories. We see diasporas as providing important political and economic resources and a basis for redefining people's identities and forms of belonging. For some people, diaspora is an enabling space to remake their self and overcome ascribed difficulties or inhibitions. But then diasporas also entail challenges of adaptation and coming to terms with new configurations of social reality. And we see that in the same way as ethnic identity is relational, diasporic identity is also relational. A dialectical relationship develops between the different nodes people relate to. How people relate to their homeland and the host societies in which they live depends on both the homeland and the surrogate home country as well as the ease in various communication systems which enables contemporary migrants to remain in touch with their homeland in ways that were not possible just a few decades ago. What comes out of our efforts then, we believe, is a reminder of the complexity of the African continent, and that what we understand by the terms Africa and the Africans is contextual and bounded in time and space.

What is diaspora?

Diaspora communities are, according to William Safran, "expatriate minority communities:

1. That are dispersed from an original centre to at least two peripheral places;
2. that maintain a memory, vision, or myth about their original homeland;
3. that believe they are not – and perhaps cannot be – fully accepted by their host country;
4. that see the ancestral home as a place of eventual return, when the time is right;
5. that are committed to the maintenance or restoration of this homeland;
6. and of which the group's consciousness and solidarity are importantly defined by this continuing relationship with the homeland" (Safran 1991:83–84).

Safran's attempt at a definition is echoed by others. James Clifford, in an influential article on the Jewish and African diasporas (1994:305), takes the main features of the diaspora to be: "a history of dispersal, myths/memories of the homeland, alienation in the host country, desire for eventual return, ongoing support for the homeland, and a collective identity importantly defined by this relationship". And Robin Cohen (1997), with a much broader, comparative agenda than Clifford, follows up with similar formulations – diasporas are about dispersal and scattering; collective trauma; cultural flowering; troubled relationship with the majority; a sense of community transcending national frontiers; promoting a return movement.

Several issues of clarification come out of such attempts at defining the phenomenon of diaspora. Relating to the first point, of dispersal, it is important to move beyond the dominant case of the Jewish diaspora, which, together with the African diaspora we have already labelled as "ideal type diasporas". Both, however, have emerged through rather special historical circumstances characterised by a forced dispersal of a population. But other diasporas may be seen as a result of voluntary migration and the diaspora itself as a location of hope and opportunities, without people having any clear vision of wanted return. Robin Cohen (ibid.) tries to answer some of this criticism by introducing a further typology of diasporas, pointing at "victims diaspora", "labour diaspora", "imperial diaspora", "trade diaspora" and "cultural diaspora" as types of diasporas that cover more ethnographic variation than the single, ideal-type one. This is clearly a basis for better comparative studies of the phenomenon although such attempts at typologizing can never cover all possible aspects of diaspora reality, nor does such typologizing save us from the need for further theorizing of diasporic dynamics.

Instead of developing more and more detailed typologies of various forms of diaspora we agree with Roger Sanjek's (2003) suggestion that we put diaspora in a general context of other types of human movements in history. Sanjek argues for the view that

> human migration might be disassembled into a set of seven processes – expansion, refuge-seeking, colonization, enforced transportation, trade diaspora, labour diaspora and emigration. These processes are sequential in historical appearance and cumulative in impact, each continuing to occur after each later process emerged. (Sanjek 2003:318)

We certainly sympathise with Sanjek's point that our understanding of the social and cultural effects of human movement must be understood on the basis of all these processes, that human movement is not new, and that the consequences of particular movements must be understood within this broad context of movement. Or, in the words of Sanjek again:

> American Indians arrived in the New World via expansion, as did Polynesians in Hawai'i; Africans arrived in the 13 colonies by enforced transportation, and Spaniards in Mexico and Puerto Rico by colonization. In contrast to the present-day legal categories of state-regulated immigration, a broader anthropological view of human migration may help to improve upon current distinctions of "immigrant and involuntary "minorities"or "immigrants and established residents" and illuminate deeply-rooted political sentiments existing in contemporary multiethnic, multilingual settings. (ibid.:318–19)

Within this broader canvas the term diaspora as used by Sanjek takes on a different meaning from the attempts at definition discussed above.

> The process of diaspora, as I [Sanjek, editors' note] will use the term, occurs when people voluntarily leave their home area from distant regions within or beyond the state in which they reside, and continue to remain in contact in various ways with their point of origin. "Almost always ... migration is followed by a counter stream moving back to the migrants' place of origin" (Anthony 1990:897–8).
>
> Moreover, unlike expansions, diaspora are spatially discontinuous, with distances and other peoples separating their component population clusters. And unlike refuge seeking, diaspora involves continuing and relatively unimpeded ties to places of origin. Unlike don't-look-back emigration, diaspora includes occasional, frequent or long-postponed returns home. And unlike colonization, diaspora involves no dominion over or dispossession and enforced transportation of others, although diasporas often do follow in the wake of other peoples colonisations. Bear in mind that diaspora here is one process of human migration, not an enduring characterization of a particular ethnocultural group. Diaspora thus may mark a phase in a particular group's history, with other migration processes preceeding or succeeding it. (Ibid.:323–4)

What is important here is not to agree or disagree with every detail of Sanjek's argument. Rather, what we find promising is the general direction of Sanjek's thinking, by putting diaspora in a broader context of human movement and analysing the implications of such movements. At certain times such movements appear as organised in ways we may term diasporic, in other periods this is not necessarily the case. This starting point allows empirical realism and dynamism that is not available if the starting point is a totalizing view of diaspora as a special type of society, different from other types. This latter approach leads towards a search for an ideal type-diaspora such as the Jewish one or the African one, mentioned above.

Thus our quest for understanding should not be biased towards diaspora, ethnic groups, and types of associations or other types of groups. Rather, the quest should be broadened to one of understanding *general social identities*. Such identities are of different types. We cannot assume that one particular type of identity, such as one based in kinship or in ethnicity, or in diaspora for that matter, will necessarily be dominant. Nor is a starting point focusing on groups necessarily where we want to go. Identities are bounded only to a limited extent, and people may cross the boundaries between them and there is little mutual reinforcement among them. Hence, rather than start with properties of groups, we should start with more basic and enduring patterns of social relationships and how such relationships are organised and acted out in daily life. What we need then, is not a noncommittal "multiple voices" type of approach, but rather systematic models of diversity and inequality that assume that everything is culturally construed, and that people realize cultural meanings through their practice of social relationships. Such meanings are always evaluative and our task is to see how such systems of meaning are constructed and how people understand the unequal distribution of prestige, power and privilege. This also means understanding why actors do not achieve their aims, the structural condition of action and the unintended consequences of action.

Another issue arising from Sanjek's discussion is the role of history in diasporic studies. Although the cases of diasporas presented in this book certainly show that the meeting point between the various diasporas relating Africa and the West is important, it is also clear that the papers contain enough evidence to state that diaspora studies should not be limited only to the study of Western models for cosmopolitan life, or reactions towards Western ways of life. It would serve our aims better, we think, if we also focus on phenomena that contain similar characteristics, but that have taken place in non-Western contexts and also at earlier times. The point we are raising here is that we need to establish diaspora discourses in specific histories in which diasporic subjects may be examples of not-so-modern, transnational, intercultural experience. Historicised in this way, diaspora becomes a field of study that shows how such processes have been going on under different circumstances, in different contexts, and hence with different effects of the people involved. In this there is a call for comparisons not only in space, but also in time.

Conceptualizing diasporic identity

Through their discussions all the authors are concerned to show that diasporic dynamics are not homogeneous phenomena, but are characterised by variation and historical specificity. This conceptual fact comes out clearly if we focus on the issue of diasporic identity. Again, a comparison with the literature on the paradigmatic African diaspora might provide a useful avenue through which to approach our point. The literature we are referring to privileges the construction or re-construction of "an African identity" or "a black identity" in the diaspora. Many such studies take as their starting point assumptions about "collective consciousness" and "primordial attachments" as defining characteristics of peoples of African origin. Primordial attachment and collective consciousness are certainly part of the diasporic communities' life-courses but the discussions in the contributions to this volume also show that neither primordial attachments nor collective consciousness necessarily constitute the main defining characteristics of a homogeneous African identity. For example, and drawing from the examples in the papers, what is common between an African-American in New York, a descendant of a pre-nineteenth century slave, and a Somali refugee in Oslo? Or what is common between a die-hard Eritrean nationalist sitting behind a computer keyboard in Germany and a staunch Sudanese religious conservative in the same country? They may all have links to their home countries, and have a diasporic consciousness but probably not in identical ways. Which leads to the simple point that even if the phenomenon of diaspora may be global this should not lead to an obliteration of differences produced within the same phenomenon.

A second tricky point relates to the notion of homeland. Although the notion of homeland is clearly part of the diaspora, it is important not to make diaspora a special type of society, only defined by its ancestral roots in a particular homeland. Diaspora populations have other concerns as well, and relationships that cannot be reduced to those towards the homeland. Furthermore, the will to restore the homeland should not be taken only to mean restoration in the sense of creating a nation state, or even to a desire for physical return. The homeland may remain part of an imagining, without any direct political ambition behind it, nor will the people in question ever return. What should be avoided, then, are the reification and essentializing of concepts like homeland, diaspora and diasporic community. Rather, we should seek an understanding of the many and varied spaces that are relevant for the diasporic population, not in order to arrive at clearcut definition of what they are, but to understand what they do to the people who live their lives within them. In such a perspective the importance of the homeland may vary. Several papers show for instance that the identity based on attachment to a homeland may fade away, and a Muslim identity takes over as dominant, both to the diasporic population and the host population. Any analysis must allow for such flexibility and have conceptual underpinnings that can handle such variation and dynamism.

Apart from privileging links to the homeland, the papers also show a need to problematize the tendency to give privileged attention to the view that African diasporic identity is always set against the nation states in which Africans live. Contributions by Stuart Hall (e.g. 1991) and Paul Gilroy (e.g. 1993) are brilliant examples of this type of argument. Hall discusses identity politics among black people in the British metropole and asks how the

> politics of representation has to do with an awareness of the black experience as a diaspora experience, and the consequences this carries for the process of unsettling, recombination, hybridization, and cut-and-mix. (Hall 1992:258)

Gilroy's seminal book *The Black Atlantic* (1993) presents the history of the West as seen through the works of black intellectuals like Du Bois and Richard Wright, writers whom Gilroy sees as having inhabited "contested "contact zones" between cultures and histories". In both cases diaspora appears in contradiction to the nation state in such a way that a national identity rooted in the nation state is juxtaposed against a diasporic identity which is transnational and constructed on a world scale rather than within any nation state. Our papers show that the nation state plays a key role, but they also show that we must not assume that the nation state – diaspora relationships are given through some underlying dynamics. We believe this type of thinking might lead us towards a dichotomization of the world that should be avoided. This bias is particularly evident within the culturalist perspective on diaspora and it seems in this perspective that the diasporan subject has replaced the anti-hegemonic heroism of the earlier working class and subaltern subjects. Diasporan populations and cosmopolitans are now seen as liberating agents, as heroes of the post-nationalist era. And in this lies its potential (feared or celebrated) for destabilizing the nation-state. This may be true in some cases, but not in all and we need pespectives that also open up for other possibilities, for instance that diasporic groups might be important in defining the nation state itself, or that diasporic groups interact with nation states in ways that do not lead to a dichotomization but rather to a two-way process through which both nation state and diaspora, or nationalized space and de-territorialized practice are constituted in the process. Variation and differentiation within both nation state and diaspora are as likely outcomes as is their homogenization.

The problem relates to the tendency to see diaspora as a type of identity totally different from the type of identity based on the notion of the nation state. Nation states are bounded, diasporas are unbounded, nations are national, diasporas are trans-national. An intriguing idea perhaps, but it is an idea which points towards simplistic dichotomizations rather than towards the complex relationships of many factors, and the possibility of the nation state and diaspora actually reinforcing each other. It also plays down the historical facts and the diasporic effects of human migrations before the nation state became a dominant political form. Supra-local identities (diasporic, refugee, migrant, national etc.) have never been spatial and temporal extensions of a prior, naturally given identity rooted in "locality" and "community", nor do we have to see the global as a new, artificially imposed, or inauthentic type of identity. We should rather see any identity as being "constructed" and our aim should be to study such processes of identity formation as they unfold within different contexts. The aim should be to avoid models of integrated local systems and to focus on the unbounded, de-territorialised character of such communities, without sacrificing our ideal of uncovering basic patterns and dynamics. In a world of overlapping social networks with crosscutting boundaries and flows of meaning, which historically was the case in certain communities and which in the contemporary world seems to have a more global reach, people's experiences have been touched by what might be termed "global" social processes. But at the same time, people's interpretations of such processes have varied a lot and produce a variety of localized adaptations and responses. And it is precisely this variation that we need to understand.

There is thus a need to focus more explicitly on the complexity of the diaspora concept by paying more attention to the intersectionality of many processes, not only of transnational movement and the assimilation processes taking place within nation states. Diaspora is about relationality, which means that diasporas should be situated both against their own internal differentiation as well as in their relationship to each other, thus focusing on the economic, political and cultural specificities of such relationships. This involves concrete histories, in addition to narratives of individual memories as well as collective ones. The dynamics of the diaspora are not fixed or pre-given, they are constituted within the materiality of everyday life, in the everyday stories told individually and collectively and they relate to issues such as gender, race, class, religion, language and generation (see e.g. Brah 1996, Anthias 1998). In this sense diaspora space is a contested space, and the collective "we" must be problematised. This means that we need to look at institutions, discourses and practices rather than assume ahistorical constructs. Thus we need to look not only at one group against a host community, but at many groups together, how they are constructed vis-à-vis each other. Several papers in this book show that the ways people relate to a diasporic identity may vary within the same group, some embracing such an identity, others not. Participating in organised diasporic life, for instance through associations, will provide arenas in which a shared diasporic history may be learnt and celebrated and will promote a feeling of togetherness for some. Other members of the same group may disappear into a host population through processes of assimilation. Such different developments must be discovered empirically, they cannot be derived from any theoretical position.

Conceptualizing diasporic consciousness

Understanding diasporic processes requires specific historizations, not only of general systemic forces but also of a history of people living their lives. Rather than looking for causality, we should be more interested in seeing the various ways through which historical processes provide material for various *interpretations* among people and lead to discussions of change. This point relates directly to an understanding of the formation of diasporic consciousness. Movement between homelands and diaspora spaces, whether physical and real or cognitive and imagined, is exercised through a myriad of networks, including kinship, trade, and religious networks and is affected by technologies of travel and communication. But the diasporic reality may also be established through literature, or be displayed in museums. Or it may only be available in associations in which diasporic links are celebrated. It is important to explore the conditions or circumstances under which collective consciousness develops but it is also important to avoid reifications. And again, our argument is to approach the issue not by making diaspora consciousness a special type of consciousness, but to discuss it in the context of broader processes through which consciousness and meaning are established. Some narrate the present as a configuration of the past; others argue that the flux in the present is novel and that old things cannot be taken for granted. It is not possible to predict how such debates will surface, nor what the specific topics will be. These remain empirical questions and make it impossible to decide any privileged level of analysis. But they do relate to the existence of different *modes of historicity* which makes necessary a focus on a group's self-definition. A shared history, i.e. the past, is part of this common interest. Our best way to approach this shared interest, and hence shared identity, is through narrative, through which we can see the group memory evolve, and at the same time also see how such claims to historical truths are being debated. Narratives come in addition to other elements like ritual, song and dance in establishing a people's past. Narratives allow us to establish what types of truths local people believe in, rather than engaging in "what really happened" types of history writing (Ricoeur 1984). Narratives are then not about *preserving* memories, but rather about *reconstructing* them (Halbwachs 1980). Individual actors play a role in such processes of reconstruction of memories but the contexts are also important, such as the technological context. Many technologies may be involved in the narration, from oral story telling to writing, from books to the Internet. The ease in communication brought about by globalisation and information technology thus adds new dimensions to diaspora studies. Globalisation, or Harvey's so-called "compression in time and space", made it possible for people to connect with wider spaces and maintain networks that transcend geography and political borders. As a result of the ease in communication, people can organise and mobilise in ways that have never been possible before. Of particular interest is the use of cyberspace, or the establishment of Internet sites that bring people of different political orientations and goals together. But these Internet forums are also contested spaces for different loyalties and opinions. Our argument, then, is that we need to expand our perspective to also include the various technologies available for transmitting memory more generally, in different societies, thus looking at the *institutional conditions for the production of various social knowledge* (Asad 1984). This requires a broad exploration, not only of ideas, but of the historical context within which such ideas are produced, reproduced and changed. Memory is a narrative which is discursive, through oral or printed means, but it is also incorporated and habitual. There is thus a case for arguing for the interaction between space, time, narrative and group memory. A comparison between the ways the Hadrami Alewis handle their group history through religious networks, travelling and personal meetings (Bang) and the use of Internet among Eritreans in Germany (Conrad) is illustrative and shows how different technologies affect the knowledge that is being produced.

But these examples also point at another important lesson. Such narratives and understandings of the diaspora may not be shared by everyone. Within the same group a diasporic history may be important to some, ignored by others. Hence, our point about variation is also valid here. Such variation may be class based – an economic or political elite of a population may live a life as diasporic cosmopolitans thus experiencing the reality of the diaspora as a site of possibilities, whereas another segment of the same group may be at the bottom of the ladder of stratification, experiencing life in diaspora as defined by discrimination and exclusion. A disporic consciousness may also be dependent on participation in specific arenas, such as associations. Those who frequent such associations may embrace a diasporic identity and treasure a diasporic memory, whereas others place themselves outside such contexts. Diaspora may thus be different things to different people. To some it is real life, to others it is being imagined and to some its very existence may be contested. Diasporic history and events are not isolated points on a temporal line, but in themselves make up socially constituted time. People live their lives in several times, past present and future, represented by real life events, dreams, fears, stories etc. Clearly this entails looking into actors' interpretations, practices and sacred symbols, imagery in terms of which social status and groups are presented.

The individual contributions

The individual papers relate to and develop the points raised here in different ways and from different angles and we conclude this introductory chapter by pointing at some key elements in those contributions as well as indicating their historical specificities. The first paper, by *Sindre Bangstad*, covers many of the issues we have raised. The paper takes the "re-discovery" of diasporic links between the Muslim community of Cape Town, South Africa, and Muslim communities in Malaysia and Indonesia as a starting point. Looking at this community as a diasporic community Bangstad seeks to demonstrate how the notion of diaspora is not a static notion, but must be understood on the basis of specific historical trajectories. Although the origin of what came to be known as the Cape Malay community in South Africa relates to Dutch colonialism and its main agent, the Dutch East India Company in southeast Asia, it is a fact that the group of people eventually called "Cape Malays" and "Cape Muslims" is a heterogeneous one. Which is precisely the point made by the author. Bangstad stresses the fact that the self-understanding is produced by the activities of individuals and elite groups and is not essentialized cultural traits that people have carried with them. The notion of a 'Malay diaspora' and a self-understanding as Cape Malay developed through the years of segregation and apartheid and was a strategy by leaders to deal with the classification of this particular group as part of the coloureds. The emergence of the notion Cape Muslim is also tied to broader processes in South Africa and beyond and due to the failure of a Malay identity in solving the problems people had within the social stratification defined by apartheid, the Muslim identity often operates as a minimal common denominator. In the twilight days of apartheid Islam came to provide an overarching source of identification through which people preferred to be seen as "Cape Muslims" or simply "Muslims" to emphasise that it is their religious adherence, not an imagined ethno-geographical origin that distinguishes them from other coloureds. As a consequence, the ulema (religious men) in the Cape Muslim community tend to identify more with Saudi Arabia, Kuwait, Egypt and Pakistan, all representing areas in which the *ulema* received their training and subsequent material and spiritual support, rather than relating to Malaysia and Indonesia which make up the original ethno-geographical homelands of many of them. But the paper also shows that there are processes at work through which a sense of "Malayness" is re-appearing. The period after 1994, which was the end of apartheid, has seen a resurgence of notions of Malayness, but Bangstad argues that this is not only a process linked to developments in South Africa. The author also demonstrates how Malaysia and Indonesia actively seek to encourage this type of diasporic consciousness for their own nationalist reasons, thus making this also an example of the cultural resurgence of the globalized world of the 1990s. But again, although the paper gives examples of individual efforts to establish such links, through the establishment of museums and other cultural means, it remains an activity involving the few. The overall conclusion is that the heterogeneity of the community of people with Malay descent cannot easily be reduced to any clearcut identity. Various notions of diaspora come and go, and cannot be said to represent any overall self-identification for people. And the notion of Malayness does not imply any longing for return to the geographical homeland of the Malays. The processes discussed by Bangstad are firmly rooted in South African realities and the political and social commitments are firmly grounded within the confines of South African territorial space.

The chapter by *Leif Manger* focuses on the Hadrami diaspora in the Sudan. The Hadramis come from South Yemen and they represent a long history of migration throughout the Indian Ocean. Different groups of Hadramis have migrated, from powerful groups of traders and religious scholars who were instrumental in Islamizing the areas in which they settled, to poorer groups of tribals, sailors and local fishermen, who ended up at the bottom of the various communities they lived in. Manger's discussion shows two sorts of diasporic dynamics relating to Hadramis in the Sudan. One is the historical migration of people who managed to set themselves up as small traders and run small businesses in the Sudan, exploiting the different opportunities provided by policies of commercialization in the country, both as an Anglo-Egyptian colony and as an independent country. As Arabs and Muslims they had no problems in settling in, and had no problem of acceptance in the Sudanese communities in which they came to live. The second dynamic relates to the modern political developments in the Sudan as an Islamic state, and the involvement of the regime with Usama bin Laden during the 1990s. Through the case of Usama bin Laden who is of Hadrami origin, Manger shows how the identity as a Hadrami is of little or no importance, but that the identity as Muslim becomes crucial. Usama only lived in the Sudan for a few years in the 1990s, but his presence there illustrates a development in the Hadrami diaspora from the earlier "small traders, small businesses" type of Hadramis who came to settle in the Sudan to a situation in which some Hadrami individuals like Usama bin Laden came to play a role in a wider field of interaction in the post-modern world in which a rising trend of violent radical political Islam increasingly became a rallying point for anti-colonial and anti-imperial struggles against powerful Western, American and Jewish enemies. To explain this development the general context of Hadrami migration must also be expanded into an explanation of how the Hadramis came to be part of a diaspora in which some of them came to play important roles in various cases of Muslim resistance against Western colonialsm and imperialism. Manger puts Usama bin Laden into this historical context, thus showing how a religious mission can play a role in the resistance against empires with global aims, generated from a diaspora that also has become global, but which also is significantly shaped by alliances with various nation states sharing its aims. In this case the alliance was with the Islamist regime in Kharotum.

Anne Bang also provides a case that is based in the Hadrami diaspora. Bang's paper takes a family history as a point of departure and by detailing the personal biographies of two Hadrami religious scholars living in Zanzibar and the Comoro Islands we get a glimpse of the part of the Hadrami diaspora that geographically was focused on the East African coast, that was based on the religious mission of the *sada* Alewi, and that was organised around the networks of religious scholars who played key roles both in Islamizing the areas in which they live and, as in Bang's case, also played key roles in relating to colonial and national authorities. The major focus of the paper is on the life story of Umar bin Sumeit, son of Ahmad bin Sumeit whose life was discussed in an earlier study by the author (Bang 2003). Taken together the life stories cover a period from the end of the 19th century to the early 1970s, and demonstrate how people maintained links through individual and family connections and networks that related back to the homeland of Hadramaut but that also brought together diasporic areas like Zanzibar, the Comoros and Madagascar, without involving the homeland. Circumstances both in the homeland and diaspora thus affected the kind of networks Umar bin Sumayt maintained. Equally significant is the fact that Umar was placed in a network that was built by his father before him, thus showing the importance of the geneaological connections within the Alewi *sayyids* of Hadramaut. But Anne Bang's aim is not only to show continuity in an Alewi tradition, re-played through the generations. Rather, it is also to show that although the links are based on such family links, they are formed and shaped by the various ways they interact with the broader patterns of social and political contexts of which they were part. Comparing the networks of father and son, the author demonstrates similarities in family and scholarly religious networks, and in patterns of travels to the homeland and in colonial employment as *qadis* in Zanzibar. But there are also differences. Whereas the father was mostly based in Zanzibar, the son was more involved with the communities in the Comoros. The implication of this is shown to be a closer association with sufi groups in the Comoros, a closer association with the French colonial administration and a clearer identity as a Comorian in Zanzibar at a time when the British colonialists put increasing emphasis on racial and ethnic belonging. With the appearance of modern associations in the 20th century, people tended to be organised more along professional and organisational lines than before. The author argues that the formation of associations in the twentieth century in the Comoros drew people like Umar more closely to the Comorian community than was the case of his father. Umar's life also brings us into the period of nation states in East Africa, showing how the religious groups of Muslim leaders adapted to these changing circumstances, not least to the increased emphasis on the differences between an Arab and an African identity. Certain groups sought to exploit an Arab identity in order to avoid the various forms of stigmatization attached to the African identity, others engaged in forms of religious reform movements in which the ethnic aspect was less prominent. Apart from elucidating important parts of how a certain Yemeni and Hadrami diaspora evolved in East Africa the paper also shows the importance of detailed empirical specifications of such evolving processes. Anne Bang's concern here is to warn against simplistic historical continuities and replaying of tradition, and to argue for an analysis and understanding of diaspora based in thick ethnographic descriptions. Anne Bang's chapter is a case that clearly shows the dynamics of diaspora, and how its understanding must be based on an exploration of interactions between different variables such as genealogy, kinship, religion and relationships with colonial authorities, where individual biographies and life histories can be linked to the questions of belonging, identification and nation-state.

Bettina Conrad's chapter provides an interesting case of Eritrean real and cyberspace interactions among the Eritrean diaspora communities in Germany. The paper shows clearly that there is more to the Internet than increased speed and tendencies towards homogenization. Conrad shows that the existence and use of Internet among the Eritreans vary over time. In the beginning, in the early 1990s, the emergence of the first Eritrean web-site coincided with Eritrean independence and this early web-site clearly played a national role, being focused on issues of nationbuilding at home. In a sense the Internet was used to continue the flow of information previously generated within the networks of the political and military mass organisation from the civil war period, particularly the EPLF and ELF. In this sense the Internet helped structure the diasporic communties along familiar Eritrean lines. The second phase coincided with the Ethio-Eritrean war in 1998, and was characterised by a virtual explosion in Eritrean online activities, most of which had nationalistic overtones and aimed to counter Ethiopian "propaganda" about the war. But the phase also shows an opening up of the Eritrean web-pages to audiences that were not involved before, leading to a series of other issues also being brought up and discussed. This proliferation was impossible for the regime to control, thus also leading to a democratisation in the information flow. This development continued into a third phase which appeared in 2000, and brought a more lively debate among the Eritreans themselves, formulating political differences, pro- and anti-regime positions and and an increasing degree of polarization and fragmentation. This also led to a further increase in different sites and chat rooms, built around specific political positions, including that of the regime itself, developing different rhetorical styles and ways of symbolizing their belonging to Eritrea. Bettina Conrad shows how these phases are not only relevant for the virtual communities on the Internet, but also reflect on real world communities, thus making the point that Internet can only be understood as a communicative tool put into use by real world people, and that any analysis must take such an interaction into consideration. By focusing on a specific Eritrean diasporic group in Frankfurt and its site on the web, the paper shows this interaction in empirical detail. Such a linking with the real world also shows the limits to the effects of the Internet, from the lack of infrastructure and computer illiteracy in a poor country like Eritrea, to the necessary command of relevant languages used on the sites. Rather than bringing all diasporic Eritreans together in a shared sense of Eritreanness this development creates segmentation among groups and serves political fragmentation as much as unity. It also creates a situation of interpretation, in which those who actively use the Web spread information about what is going on among those who are not able to use this technology. This creates a situation in which the Internet links bring together local Eritrean groups in different countries with each other, thus promoting a more trans-national dynamic among the users, and the face to face and orally based interactions in which the messages from the Internet are further spread and interpreted. "Cyber-Eritrea" thus not only represents a deterritorialised Eritrean nationality, but also provides room for competing sub- and intra-national models of Eritreanness which emerge in processes that cannot be reduced to Internet dynamics alone.

The chapter by *Roqaia Abusharaf* takes as its starting point the civil war in the Sudan and offers an overview of the complexity of ethnic and religious dimensions that have become part of the political crisis in that country. The north-south dimension of the civil war is extended into an ethnic boundary between Arab and African people and a religious one of Muslim, Christian and animist communities. The boundaries have become increasingly conflict ridden through the policies of an Islamist regime in Khartoum. Civil war, slavery and oppression have resulted. But Abusharaf shows also that although these are all possible and relevant factors, they are also a part of a political rhetoric that tends to hide other possible boundaries. For instance that both the north and the south are themselves divided internally along similar lines as those characterizing the alleged boundary between north and south. The particular focus of the paper is Southern Sudan and it mentions in particular the ethnic tensions between Dinka and Nuer that led to a civil war situation between the two groups, producing waves of refugees both within southern

Sudan and outside. The last thirty years have seen an increasing rate of out-migration from southern Sudanese communities, with serious consequences for local adaptations, local groups and in particular women and children and local culture. Migration to northern Sudan has created pressures towards Arabization and Islamization. Migration to neighbouring African countries, for instance Egypt and Uganda, brings a life in unemployment, overcrowding and homelessness, representing the suffering of a different type of "war", one of practical difficulties as well as being stigmatized as "criminals" by the host population. All this produces a wish to migrate out of Africa, and chances to go to various Western countries produce hope and optimism. But these expectations are rarely fulfilled. Based on fieldwork and interviews of Christians from southern Sudan Roqaia Abusharaf presents a number of life stories of southern Sudanese in the USA. The author weaves together such individual stories into a tapestry of shared causes for migration, types of suffering and diasporic trajectories, trying to escape war, political and religious oppression and balancing the trauma of exile with the hopes for new opportunities in the diaspora. But the search for a better future does not mean that the people have forgotten the homeland. Remittances are sent back home, and concern for the future of the homeland is expressed, individually and in joint political action, in the US. But the understanding of the homeland varies between a hope for an end to war to build a united Sudan, to a hope that the war will lead to an independent South Sudan. Nor is life in diaspora without problems, as is seen from the early meetings in the USA between refugees and the system of social and health workers, to later stages of adaptation in which language, relations to landlords and employers emerge as important factors for a successful adaptation. Variations among refugees also add to the problems, with differences in education affecting chances in the labour market, whether families arrive together or whether the refugees are made up of groups of individuals torn away from their families. Dealing with lonely minors and juveniles adds to the challenge.

The book ends with a chapter by *Munzoul Assal* which also focuses on the Sudanese diaspora, but in Assal's paper we see a comparison between the Sudanese and the Somali diasporas. The discussion focuses on how Somali and Sudanese refugees in Norway organise themselves as diasporic communities and how such means of organisation mediate the various internal ethnic, political and religious divisions within the communities themselves, as well as mediating the cultural differences with the host society of Norway. The paper offers details about the clan and lineage based Somali society back home and seeks to show how the organisations in the diaspora are organised in ways that reinforce such a segmentary and regional organisation in new settings. But this particular dimension of Somali organisations and a Somali collective identity largely goes unnoticed in Norway. It is their identity and organisation as Muslims that make them most visible to Norwegians, thus making them part of a Norwegian discourse on the tense relations between the West and Islam and Muslims. The Sudanese are similar to the Somalis in that at home they are also organised along tribal lines. But this segmentary aspect of their organisation is not reflected in the same way in the diaspora. In Norway the organisation among Sudanese is mostly in organisations reflecting the north-south divide, thus reflecting the history of long-lasting civil war in the home country. And this also leads to a different perception of Sudanese in Norway, with the northerners being conceived as Arab and Muslim, and joining the Somalis in Norwegian perceptions as part of a somewhat threatening population, whereas the southerners are seen as Africans and Christians, and are met with sympathy as "victims" of the civil war. Information on the internal heterogeneity in the groups is not known to Norwegians, and the fact that individuals differ in their religiosity or their involvement in the war at home, has little effect on the formation of Norwegian stereotypes. In conceptual terms Assal raises an important point directly relating to our discussion of diaspora in this book, that we need to avoid homogenizing the diasporic population and reducing diasporic dynamics to a two-way process between a homeland and a diasporic community, and an interaction in the diaspora between a clearcut diasporic identity among the refugees and a clearcut national identity of the host society. Assal shows that the identities as Somalis and Sudanese and their many possible sub-categories are not primordial and given but contextual and contested. And so are the ethnicities in Norway. The understanding of boundary processes can therefore not be understood as their being based solely on identities of origin (nor of class or gender, for that matter). The homelands of Somalia and Sudan are contested territories, and what goes on in Norway is not an unproblematic meeting between a "deterritorialized ethnicy" of the refugees or a homogeneous ethnicity of the Norwegian nation state. And all attention is not towards the homeland either. Given the history of dispersal the Somalis and Sudanese in Norway have important links to diasporic communities elsewhere in the diaspora, thus making the links and the longing for the homeland only one of several possible dynamics that help form a diasporic community and the diasporic consciousness. Rather than homogenizing complexity, Munzoul Assal argues for studies of complexity, of internal debate and contestation in all the communities involved, within the communities themselves, between the communities as well as within the research community trying to understand these processes.

References

Abusharaf, Roqaia M., 2002, *Wanderings: Sudanese migrants and exiles in North America*. Cornell: Cornell University Press.

Akyeampong, Emmanuel, 2000, "Africans in the diaspora: The diaspora and Africa", *African Affairs*, 99:183–215.

Anthias, Floya, 1998. "Evaluating diaspora: Beyond ethnicity", *Sociology*, 32(3): 557–580.

Appadurai, A., 1996, *Modernity at Large. Cultural Dimensions of Globalisation*. Minneapolis: University of Minnesota Press.

Asad, T., 1984, *The Idea of an Anthropology of Islam*. Center for Contemporary Arab Studies, Occasional papers series. Washington: Georgetown University.

—, 1993, *Genealogies of Religion: Discipline and Reasons of Power in Christianity and Islam*. Baltimore: John Hopkins University Press.

Assal, M.A.M., 2004, *Sticky labels or rich ambiguities: Diaspora and challenges of homemaking for Somalis and Sudanese in Norway*. Bergen: BRIC/The University of Bergen.

Bang, A.K., 2003, *Sufis and Scholars of the Sea. Family networks in East Africa, 1860–1925*. London: Routledge Curzon.

Barth, Fredrik, 1969, "Introduction", in Barth, Fredrik (ed.), *Ethnic groups and boundaries: The social organisation of culture difference*, pp. 9–38. Oslo: Universitetsforlaget.

—, 1989, The Analysis of Culture in Complex Societies, *Ethnos*, 54 (I–II).

Bentley, 1993, *Old World Encounters: Cross-Cultural Contacts and Exchanges in Pre-Modern Times*. New York: Oxford University Press.

Bernal, Victoria, 2004, "War and Diaspora in the Digital Age: Citizenship, the Public Sphere and the (Re)Imagining of Eritrean Nationhood". Paper presented at workshop on (Post) Conflict and the Remaking of Place and Space: Economies, Institutions and Networks Khartoum, 1–2 September 2004.

Bowen, J. and R. Petersen (eds), 1999, *Critical Comparisons in Politics and Culture*. Cambridge: Cambridge University Press.

Brah, A., 1996, *Cartographies of Diaspora. Contesting Identities*. London: Routledge.

Chartier, R., 1988, *Cultural History. Between History and Representations*. Cambridge: Polity Press.

Clifford, James, 1994, "Diasporas", *Cultural Anthropology*, 9(3):302–38.

—, 1998, *Routes. Travels and Translation in the Late 20th Century*. Cambridge, MA: Harvard University Press.

Cohen, R., 1997, *Global Diasporas: An Introduction*. London: University College London Press.

Connerton, Paul, 1989, *How Societies Remember*. Cambridge: Cambridge University Press.

Farah, Nuruddin, 2000, *Yesterday, tomorrow: Voices from the Somali diaspora*. London and New York: Cassell.

Featherstone, M., S. Lash, and R. Robertson (eds), 1995, *Global Modernities*. London: Sage.

Friedman, J., 1994, *Cultural Identity and Global Process*. London: Sage.

Gilroy, P., 1993, *The Black Atlantic*. London: Verso.

Griffiths, David J., 2000, "Fragmentation and consolidation: Contrasting cases of Somali and Kurdish refugees in London", *Journal of Refugee Studies*, 13(3):281–302.

Grønhaug, R., 1978, "Scale as a Variable in Analysis: Fields in Social Organisation in Herat, Northwest Afghanistan", in Barth F. (ed.), *Scale and Social Organisation*. Oslo: Norwegian University Press.

Gupta A. and J. Ferguson (eds), 1997a, *Culture, Power, Place: Explorations in Critical Anthropology*. Durham: Duke University Press.

— (eds), 1997b, *Anthropological Locations. Boundaries and Grounds of a Field Science*. Berkely: University of California Press.

Halbwachs, M., 1992, *On Collective Memory*. Chicago: University of Chicago Press.

Hall, S., 1991, The Global and the Local: Globalisation and Ethnicity, in King A. (ed.), *Culture, Globalisation and World-System*. Binghampton: Department of Art History, State University of New York at Binghampton.

Harris, Joseph, 1982, "Introduction", in Harris J. (ed.), *Global Dimensions of African Diaspora*. Washington: Howard University Press.

Harvey, D., 1989, *The Conditions of Postmodernity. An Inquiry into the Origin of Cultural Change*. Oxford: Blackwell.

Humphrey, Michael, 2002, "Humanitarianism, terrorism and the transnational border", *Social Analysis*, 46(1):118–124.

Huntington, S., 1996, *The Clash of Civilzations and the Remaking of the World Order*. New York: Simon and Schuster.

Issawi, C., 1998, *Cross-Cultural Encounters and Conflicts*. Oxford: Oxford University Press.

Jenkins, R., 1996, *Social Identity*. London: Routledge.

Kymlicka, W., 1995, *Multicultural Citizenship. A Liberal Theory of Minority Rights*. Oxford: Clarendon.

Lash, S., 1999, *Another Modernity. A Different Rationality*. Oxford: Blackwell.

Mandalios, J., 1999, *Civilization and the Human Subject*. Lanham, MD: Rowman and Littlefield.

Manger, L., 1999, "Introduction", in Manger L. (ed.), *Muslim Diversity. Local Islam in a Global Context.* London: Curzon Press.

—, 2001, "On the Concept of Diaspora and the Theorising of Identity". Paper presented to workshop "On the Concept of Diaspora and the Theorising of Identity". Organised by the Department of Social Anthropology and the International Migration and Ethnic Relations Program (IMER), 5 September 2001.

—, 2002, "September 11 and October 7: From human tragedy to power politics", *Social Analysis*, 46(1):143–147.

Ricoeur, P., 1984, *Time and Narrative*, vol. 1. Chicago: University of Chicago Press.

Safran, W., 1991, "Diasporas in Modern Societies: Myths of Homeland and Return", *Diaspora*, vol. a, no. 1.

Sanjek, R., 2003, "Rethinking migration, ancient to future", *Global Networks*, 3(3): 315–336

Van der Veer, P. (ed.), 1995, *Nation and Migration: The Politics of Space in the South Asian Diaspora.* Philadelphia: University of Pennsylvania Press.

Van Hear, N., 1998, *New Diasporas. The Mass Exodus, Dispersal and Regrouping of Migrant Communities.* Seattle: University of Washington Press.

—, 2002, "From 'durable solutions' to 'transnational relations': Home and exile among refugee diasporas", in Fredriksen, B.F. and N.N. Sørensen (eds), *Beyond Home and Exile: Making sense of lives on the move*, pp. 232–251. Occasional paper no. 23. Roskilde: International Development Studies.

Vertovec, S., 2000, *The Hindu Diaspora. Comparative Patterns.* London: Routledge.

Diasporic Consciousness as a Strategic Resource – A case study from a Cape Muslim community

Sindre Bangstad

You have found your blood brother(s) after 300 years!
Datuk Abdul Razak, Defence Minister of Malaysia,in a speech to a Muslim audience at the Tercentenary of Shaykh Yusuf's arrival at the Cape in 1994

We have moved through several worlds without losing our roots
Muslim informant, Cape Town 2000

Introduction

The concept of 'diaspora' appears to have become increasingly popular in social anthropology in the course of the last decade. The processes of 'globalisation' – by which I mean to refer to the intensified flows of people, capital and information (Tambiah 2000:164) between different states, and international finance capital's global destabilisation of national political and economic agendas and priorities, has served as an impetus for the 're'-discovery of transnational links. As several analysts have pointed out, globalisation does not necessarily entail cultural and/or ethnic homogenisation (the 'Americanisation' of society to which sceptics of globalisation often refer), but also a simultaneous process of cultural and/or ethnic heterogenisation (see for instance Appadurai 1990:295, Friedman 1990:311 and Hall 2000:215). Globalisation is of course by no means a novel phenomenon, but merely an intensification of its ever-present effects that marks our day and age.

The paper on which this essay is based was first presented at a workshop on "The Concept of Diaspora and the Theorising of Identity", at the University of Bergen on 5 September 2001. I would like to thank the participants, and Professor Leif O. Manger in particular, for constructive comments.

The nation-state may have weakened, but its mirror image in the so far most globalised of historical eras, the diaspora, appears to attract all the more interest. Definitions of the concept of diaspora vary, but it has in the literature often been linked to 'expatriate minority communities' (Manger, chapter 2) maintaining a notion that their country of origin (or 'imagined country of origin') – the 'homeland' – "has a claim on their loyalties and emotions" (cf. Cohen 1997:ix). For the purposes of this article a minimal definition of the concept will be the guideline. I therefore adopt Anthias' definition of diaspora as "a connection between groups across different nation-states whose commonality derives from an original but maybe removed homeland...[...]..." (Anthias 1998:559–60). The main reason for doing so is that alternative definitions of diaspora based on general criteria ('ideal-types') run the risk of essentialising our approach to it. Only a few diasporic communities would for instance meet the criteria often deemed typical of it, namely the desire for a literal return to their country of origin (Tambiah op.cit.: 169). If one argues that the stability of nation-states depends on the citizens' commitment to the political community of the same state (as for instance Parekh 2000 tends to do), the 're'-discovery of diasporas will be seen as entailing increased strains on the nation-state, due to an assumption that the loyalties and identifications of diasporic communities having rediscovered their 'roots' are somehow problematic.

However, the 're'-discovery of diasporas has clearly been a phenomenon largely generated in and by national and trans-national elites (Friedman 1997:88). To an increasing extent, geographical mobility has become a marker of high social status. Indeed, Friedman implies that the social logics by which 'diasporic consciousness' and 'chosen hybridity' are generated by the "highly educated world travellers of the culture industries" (ibid.:84), are quite different from the social logics developed in the underclass neighbourhoods of multicultural societies (ibid.:83–4). For the former, the diaspora is a source of liberation and empowerment, "liberation from the oppression of the nation-state, of modernity, of mass capitalism" (and) "... a source of real power, both political and economic, in the world system". For the latter, it is still largely related to an exposure to social processes of exclusion and stigmatisation from the majority population in the countries of the diaspora's abode, in spite of the optimism of multicultural claims. It is only recently that the term diaspora has come to have positive connotations even for the trans-national elites (Kessler 1999:40).

The methodology of social anthropology, with its historical insistence on spatial localisation in a restricted, fixed 'field' (the 'community'), seemed at the outset ill prepared for the study of trans-local links, such as those of diasporas old and new (Gupta and Ferguson 1997:3). But it should be recalled that the myth of isolated, virgin territories dissipated quite rapidly from the horizons of modern social anthropology, and that ethnographies have reflected globalisation for a long time. Bearing this in mind, it may be argued that it is precisely the 'spatial practices' of social anthropology, which make it suited for the study of 'diasporas'. Even so, it has been argued, it requires an 'opening up' of the methodological practices traditionally associated with social anthropology, or, as Gupta and Ferguson state a focus on 'location' rather than a focus on 'the local' (ibid.:5).

This article is premised on a trans-disciplinary approach that combines empirical data generated by traditional fieldwork with primary and secondary data regarding state agents' actions and perceptions, as well as historical data.

I have borrowed the concept of 'diasporic consciousness' from Vertovec (2000). For Vertovec 'diasporic consciousness' is "a particular kind of awareness said to be generated among contemporary trans-national communities. Its particularity is described as being created by various dimensions of dual or paradoxical nature. This nature is constituted negatively by experiences of discrimination and exclusion, and positively by identification with a historical heritage ...[...]... or contemporary world cultural or political forces" (ibid.:146–47). Brah (1996:196) is opposed to a conceptualisation of diaspora based on the idea of a 'transcendental diasporic consciousness'. But 'consciousness' as I understand it for the purposes of this article, is not 'transcendental', existing "absolutely, independently of social action and invention or of the contingencies of the lived" (Malkki 1995:240), but rather constituted "within the crucible of the materiality of everyday life" (Brah op.cit.: 183).

This paper approaches the study of 'diasporic consciousness' through the study of social and/or genealogical memory. By social memory, I mean referring to memories of past historical events that are structured by culturally defined patterns of meaning as well as the social context in which they are generated (cf. Werbner 1998:106). I will be using the term 'social memory' rather than 'collective memory' in order to underline that memories vary individually and contextually, i.e. so as not to create the impression that we are dealing with homogenous and holistic processes in which memories are collectively shared rather than individually variable. The individual members of a group differ in the intensity with which they remember, and how far back they remember (Halbwachs 1980:48, 124). Social memory can be 'real' or 'constructed' precisely because the methods by which trans-national historical links are reconstructed in a local community do not necessarily accord with the demands of academic history. If it is the case that "our memory truly rests not on learned, but on lived history" (ibid.:57) then it is clear that the further an individual gets from his or her lived or experienced history, the more drastically the 'truth-value' of his or her social memory is reduced. However, the historical accuracy of the social memory contributing to a 'diasporic consciousness' need not concern us here. What matters in people's everyday lives is not historical 'facts', but the perception of these 'facts'.

Also, more important for this analysis than what 'diasporic consciousness' might be is the issue of what it actually does, as read from its articulation in a local community, such as the Muslim community in the Cape Town township of Mekaar.

The local setting

Mekaar[1] is a township community located in the Cape Peninsula south of the city of Cape Town. It has an estimated population of 30,000, most of whom are coloureds. Mekaar was established as a township for coloureds forcibly removed from nearby areas declared as white under the Group Areas Act of 1950 in the period from 1968 to 1978. Among the places from which the present residents of Mekaar originated was the small town of Bayside. Residents in Mekaar have historically been employed in the secondary sector, but in recent years there has been a shift towards relatively low-paid work in the tertiary sector. There is reason to believe that the level of unemployment was somewhere between the estimated national average of 30 per cent and the national coloured average of 24 per cent in 2000. The average level of education is relatively low, as of now there are probably less than 10 residents attending South African universities. Approximately 13 per cent of the population of Mekaar are Muslims. Most coloured Muslims in Cape Town are nominally

1. The names of all places and persons have been altered, in order to protect the anonymity of informants. There are however two notable exceptions in this regard: Mr. Erefaan Rakiep, presented further below, appears under his real name, as I have reason to believe that he would have preferred it so, and as he was a public figure known from local media, there does not appear to be any reason to alter his name. The same applies for Mr. Hashiem Salie. I would like to express my appreciation for their generous co-operation.

adherents of the Shafīʾī school of law (or *madhab*). The coloured population of Cape Town is a 'motley crue', to quote the British colonial traveller Lady Anne Barnard (1750–1825): they are the descendants of colonial slaves, 'free blacks', the indigenous Khoi and San groups etc. (cf. Marais 1938). The variety of phenotypical traits in the coloured population also attests to historical processes of intermixture between whites and coloureds, whites and black Africans, coloureds and black Africans, and coloureds and Indians. However, this should not be taken to mean that *all* coloureds are of 'mixed' origins. The coloured Muslim community of Cape Town is in terms of its ritual practices, strongly influenced by Sufi practices, which the popularity of visits to saint's tombs, *mouloet* [ar. mawlid] and *ratiep* [ar. rātib] demonstrate.[2] However, increased contact with Muslims in the Arab world after the petroleum crisis of 1973, have resulted in increasing conflict and contestation between Muslim religious leaders (*oelema* [ar. 'ulamā') oriented towards a more 'shari'a-centric Islam' and Sufis in Cape Town.

The imaginary homelands of apartheid

Social agents act within a socially and historically constituted space of possibilities and constraints (Bourdieu 1977). Ideologies outlive their phases of realisation in terms of the material practices of the present. The ideology of apartheid imposed a highly selective interpretation of the past origins of its citizens to serve its pipe-dream of ethnic, cultural and sexual purity. The racial categories of apartheid proved socially effective because they were based on common-sensical assumptions about social status rather than biological essence, and this goes a long way towards explaining their afterlife in post-apartheid South Africa (Posel 2001).

2. Mouloet refers to the annual celebration of the prophet's birthday that take place in local communities during weekends throughout the 'mouloet season'. On the first day, females gather in the mosque for the *rampie-sny*, the cutting of the orange leaves, which is accompanied by recitation, *dhikr* [ar. dhikr]. On the second day, local men and visiting choirs gather for *dhikr*. *Ratiep* is a ritual practice of Sufi-origin related to the Rifaiʾī tarīqa or brotherhood, and is practised for instance in Iraq, Zanzibar, Aceh and Sulawesi in Indonesia, as well as in South Africa. It involves *dhikr* and dances to the music of drums whilst initiates force swords and skewers against or through their own skin in order to 'test their faith'.

Please note that in line with anthropological practice, I have applied an approximation to local transliterated spellings for Arabic and Arabic-derived terms.

Underlying 'separate development', which became one of the core themes in apartheid thinking from the 1950s,[3] (Posel 1991) was the idea that all ethnic groups (for most purposes conveniently conflated with 'race') had separate origins and belonged to different 'nations', which rhetorically of course were 'separate, but equal', even if they had blatantly unequal civil rights under apartheid legislation. In apartheid reasoning, not only were there separate 'nations' (which for 'their own good' needed to be kept apart through strict segregation), these 'nations' belonged in distinct geographical areas of South Africa.[4] Apartheid policies encouraged the indulgence in tribal fantasies of imaginary homelands as a strategy of divide and rule – the 'Bantu Education Act' of 1953 provided education in one's mother tongue and skills geared to the 'forms of labour' deemed appropriate for 'Bantus' (black Africans) (an euphemism for a servant's education), the 'Bantu Authorities Act' of 1951 culminated in the declaration of independence of the national 'homes' of black Africans (Saunders and Southey 1998:19). A programme for 'repatriation' of Indians to their 'home' in India was developed.

The design of 'separate development', however, left South African coloureds as a 'matter out of place'. At the same time, coloureds represented living testimonies of the arbitrariness of apartheid's 'racial' classifications and thereby made the limited implementability of 'separate development' visible (Norval 1996:10). Clearly, as most of them had arrived at a time which made their 'repatriation' unimaginable for the apartheid state, and had no discernible 'national homeland' within the territory of South Africa to which they had historically had exclusive rights (the small and partly assimilated San-population of the Northern Cape being the only existing exception in this regard), declaring a 'national homeland' for coloureds was out of the question

3. A central proponent of 'separate development' was the Volkeskunde-anthropologist Van Eiselen, secretary of state in the 'Native Affairs Department' under Verwoed, who later became prime minister. Van Eiselen had a background as 'Volkeskunde'-anthropologist at the University of Stellenbosch in the Western Cape. 'Volkeskunde' was an Afrikaaner-dominated brand of anthropology which defined 'culture' in deterministic terms in the form of a theory of the 'ethnos'. Even if 'ethnicity' and 'race' were conflated in public discourse under apartheid, Van Eiselen as well as Verwoed made a point of the analytic distinction between the two concepts at an early stage (Dubow 1995:278).

4. It was naturally not a coincidence that most black Africans were regarded as belonging in the most destitute and barren areas of South Africa, which later became the 'bantustans' or 'homelands' such as Transkei and Ciskei. The rural/urban divide thus accentuated represents one of the greatest challenges of the post-apartheid state (Mamdani 1996:297–98).

(even if some apartheid ideologues seem to have favoured this option in the early 1950s). It was however regarded as crucial to separate coloureds from black Africans so as to prevent the development of broader social alliances against white domination. The apartheid system opted for what it termed 'parallel' rather than 'separate' development for coloureds. The Western Cape was declared a preferential area for coloureds and stricter influx controls and labour market regulations imposed in order to prevent black African settlement west of the so-called 'Eiselen line'.[5] The policy was termed the 'Coloured Labour Preferential Policy' (CLPP), and went hand in hand with the undermining of coloureds' political and civil rights (Goldin 1987:86–91). A remaining question is then how the coloured Muslims fitted into apartheid's social engineering.

The 'Cape Malays': The cunning of 'Volkeskunde'

In 1944, a local publisher in Cape Town brought out a book titled ' The Cape Malays'. It was written by Izaak David du Plessis, an Afrikaaner poet and University of Cape Town (UCT) academic, who was later to become secretary of state in the 'Coloured Affairs Department' and honorary chancellor of the coloured University of the Western Cape (UWC) in Bellville outside of Cape Town. Du Plessis, an ethnomusicologist by training, had by then been involved for over a decade in the establishment and promotion of 'Malay' choirs or *nagtroepe* in Cape Town (Martin 1999:24). The Muslims of Cape Town had a long tradition of popular music going back to the era of colonial slavery, for instance in the form of *nederlandsliedjies* and *moppies* (ibid.:26). Nederlandsliedjies are popular songs considered to be of Dutch origin, whereas moppies are comic songs, improvised for a certain occasion.

It is doubtful whether the term 'Malay' had been used at all prior to the 19th century (Jeppie 1988:7) (in which case it would have been used as a colonial designation for slaves and 'free blacks' with origins in the Malaysian archipelago). Slaves with origins in what was then Dutch Batavia (parts of present-day Indonesia) were known as 'Bugis' or 'Buginese' at the Cape

5. Due to strong opposition to the measures from black Africans, the policy did not prevent a substantial increase in the black African population of Cape Town in the decades before the abolishment of influx controls in 1986. The preferential treatment of coloureds relative to black Africans on the labour market and in terms of communal housing has long since been abolished, but there is still a lot of discrimination of black Africans on the labour market of the Western Cape, both in the private and the public sector.

(ibid.:7), and less than one per cent of slaves imported to the Cape had origins in Malaya (Malaysia) (ibid.:7). It seems however, that by the early 19th century 'Malays' had come to be used in reference to all Muslims at the Cape (ibid.:8). The term 'Cape Malays', then, was hardly du Plessis' own invention.

Du Plessis was well aware of the extremely diverse origins of the coloured Muslim population in Cape Town (cf. ibid.:4, du Plessis et al. 1953:45), but in his works the 'Malay' component was emphasized to such an extent that 'Malay' and 'Muslim' for all means and practices became indistinguishable.[6] This was 'ethnos-theory' in the style of 'Volkeskunde'-anthropology:

> "The 'pure' Malay of the East is small in stature (average height just over 5 feet) with an olive skin which is sometimes yellowish, light brown or cinnamon-coloured, has a flattish face, high cheekbones, black (slightly slanting eyes, hands and feet small and delicately formed, thin legs, coarse, straight black hair and a sparse beard" (ibid.:3). Furthermore, "he is introspective, polite, kind towards women, children and animals, inclined to speak slowly, to be passive and indolent. *When aroused he may lose all self control and run amok*" (ibid.:3, my emphasis).

Lest I overstate my case here, let it be said that du Plessis was what in the later stages of apartheid was to be described as a 'verligte',[7] and advocated a policy of nominal "equal opportunity for all, irrespective of race, creed or colour" (ibid.:86–87), even if this was to be achieved, if necessary, through "drastic measures against individuals or groups of individuals who are found to be acting against the interest of the community as a whole" (ibid.:87).

Du Plessis regarded the 'Cape Malays' as an elite in the 'coloured' population of Cape Town and its surroundings, despite his admittance that "many Malays have only a small income, and live on or below the poverty datum line" (du Plessis 1953:69). The idea that 'Cape Malays' were an elite had been established during the era of colonial slavery, when slaves with Asian origins (more specifically the 'Buginese' slaves) fetched the highest prices on the slave market in Cape Town, locally born slaves excepted (Shell 1994:50). Cape

6. Du Plessis largely left Cape Town's Muslims of Indian origin out of the picture (1944:1).

7. In Afrikaans 'verligte' denotes 'enlightened'. The antonym is 'verkrampte', 'rigid', 'cramped', 'extremely conservative'. In analyses of apartheid, 'verligte' came to refer to the more liberal sectors of the ruling Nationalist Party, and 'verkrampte' to the hardline conservatives (Silva et al. 1996:770–771), divided particularly by their divergent views on racial segregation. The terms were first used in public discourse by William de Klerk, an older brother of Fredrik W. de Klerk, State President from 1989 to 1994.

Muslims perceived 'elite status' is still a source of self-pride for many Cape Muslims. Du Plessis, in a paternalistic and patronising mode, was clearly concerned with the impact of modernization in the Western mode on 'Cape Malays' culture:

> Modern Western society has caused the Cape Malay to be caught between the upper and nether millstones of two conflicting cultures, *and it is incumbent on us to circumvent wherever possible the evil results of this conflict.* (du Plessis 1953:67, emphasis mine.)

The "us" of du Plessis' preceding paragraph were whites in positions of political influence and authority, whom du Plessis clearly considered as responsible for the prevention of "the infiltration of groups which can not be assimilated into their [i.e. the 'Cape Malay's'] system" (ibid.:67). If other white politicians of his day were not prepared to assume this 'responsibility', du Plessis certainly was. To the chagrin of a large number of the areas' Muslim and non-Muslim population, Bo-Kaap or Schootsche Kloof was renamed 'The Malay Quarter' and declared a 'Cape Malay group area' in 1957 (Western 1996:115). At the very same time, preparations were being made to evict coloureds, including 'Cape Malays', from residential areas in central Cape Town, such as District Six. If anything, District Six and Bo-Kaap were at the time areas in which 'Cape Malays' had long since learned to live with the supposedly 'conflicting cultures of a 'modern Western society.'

'Malayism', in the style of du Plessis' local version of 'separate development' bore the promise of a special relationship between the white apartheid authorities and the 'Cape Malays': the investment by the local Muslim elite in this relationship was not finally abandoned before the implementation of the Group Areas Acts in the 1960s and 70s had brought to evidence that ordinary coloured Muslims had little to gain from it and Black Consciousness' appeal for unity among the oppressed attracted important sections of the social and political elites in South Africa's coloured population. For the coloured Muslim intellectuals of the 1970s, 'Cape Malay' became an insult to which they reacted very strongly. They preferred (and in most cases still do) the term 'Cape Muslim' or simply 'Muslim' in order to draw attention to the fact that it is their religious adherence, and not an imagined 'ethno-geographical' origin that distinguishes them from other coloureds. Furthermore, in the politicised arena of the late 1970s, to be 'Muslim' also meant to be part of what they perceived as a global anti-colonial movement led by Muslims, and inspired by such examples as the 1979 Islamic revolution in Iran, which had significant impact even on the largely Sunni Muslims of Cape Town.

Post-apartheid: The resilience of the past

A multicultural society is a society that includes two or more cultural communities (Parekh op. cit. 6). The term multicultural refers to a factual cultural diversity, the term multiculturalism to a normative response to this fact (ibid.:6). Multiculturalism "references the strategies and policies adopted to govern or manage the problems of diversity and multiplicity which multicultural societies throw up" (Hall op. cit. 209).

If apartheid South Africa was multiculturalism writ large and abused, post-apartheid South Africa is multiculturalism revised. Apartheid may be dead, but the corpse of its specific brand of multiculturalism refuses to lie down and be buried in the past. Social inequalities are as present as ever, and these social inequalities more often than not follow lines established in the past, even if the black African middle and upper class have increased substantially since 1994 (Nattrass and Seekings 2000). Most South Africans continue to live in segregated enclaves and interaction is hindered by a perception of others based on fears and stereotyping. Voting patterns largely appear to follow established 'ethnic lines' (see Johnson and Schlemmer 1994 for this view, and Seekings and Eldridge 1996 for a critique), and neither the ANC-led government nor the opposition are strangers to the contextual shifts to a political discourse premised and focused on the concept of 'race'. *Plus ça change, plus c'est la même chose.* There has been a shift from the group-based rights of apartheid law-making to individual rights as guaranteed in the liberal constitution of 1996. This liberal constitution is premised on individual rights, but various sections, and in particular those relating to alternative personal law systems, open up a limited space in which group rights are seen to take precedence over individual rights (Gloppen 2000:178). Concessions of group rights have been deemed necessary in order to achieve societal stability since 1994 – polygynous marriages among black Africans have been legalised, and Muslim Personal Law (MPL) is about to be incorporated into the legal framework in the foreseeable future. This will in all probability make polygynous marriages legal for South African Muslims for the first time in South African history. The issue as to whether this really is compatible with the principles of gender equality enshrined in the 1996 Constitution's Bill of Rights, which takes precedence in the case of conflict with laws passed at later stages, remains contentious. Comaroff, citing Wallerstein, claims that the development of 'ethnic consciousness' often is a result of a loss of privileges (Comaroff 1992:165). I believe however that this statement is too mono-causal – only in rare instances will one find this to be the only possible explanation for the 're'-emergence of ethnic consciousnesses. But it is a fact that coloured Muslims, as well as other coloureds, in many cases are ambivalent about the new political regime. Coloureds of low socio-economic status particularly seem to fear loss of employment due to competition from local black Africans.

The problem with instrumentalist theories of ethnicity such as Comaroff's is often that they have a circular quality characteristic of the 'seek, and you shall find ethnicity' approach. If one accepts the increased occurrence of for instance pilgrimage and regular ritual practice as an index of Islamisation, then a process of Islamisation is what the Muslim community in Mekaar has experienced during the last decade. I find it hard to believe, however, that perceived or actual threatening of privileges should be the only causal factor in this process. The increased availability of individual funds likely to be used for purposes such as pilgrimage (due to processes of restructuring and retirements at nearby industrial plants), a greater institutionalisation of Islam in the form of Islamic high schools, seminaries and a proliferation of mosques and increased access to religious education among younger members of the community have probably been of far greater importance.

A celebrated master trope in post-apartheid South Africa has indeed been 'diversity' (as in 'unity in diversity', the 'rainbow nation', and in the case of Cape Town: 'one city, many cultures' etc.). Partly a prerequisite for national reconciliation after the bitter and divisive years of violent apartheid repression of the 1980s, this master trope has served as an encouragement for the 're'-discovery of 'roots' and allegiances, not seldom wrapped up and served as 'local culture' for foreign visitors by the local tourist industry. Analysts have pointed out that the evolving discourse of diversity in post-apartheid South Africa rests on primordial notions of 'culture', "in which culture is seamlessly constituted by a traceable purity or demonstrable authenticity" (Rasool 2000:8). This process has of course not been without its contradictions and problems, as the balancing act between a diversity of divergent and at times mutually contradictory interests attests to.

In recent years the metaphor of the 'African Renaissance' has attracted the attention of the political elite. African roots, it seems, are perceived as being in need of discovery, since the ANC, according to its own understanding, has brought South Africa 'home' and into the fold of African nations. Prinsloo (1997), quoting Hendricks (1997), phrases it this way:

> "The political discourse of multiculturalism also necessitates the reframing and solidifying of identities. If rights are to be determined by culture, then those [perceived as being without] roots...[...]... need to 'reposition' themselves and reclaim their stake in order to access resources, or be doomed [to] perpetual marginalisation" (Prinsloo op. cit. 22). This problematique is particularly acute for coloured South Africans, since populist African nationalist discourses that have had some resonance within the ANC, historically have tended to brand 'coloureds' as 'non-indigenous' and as a 'people without culture' due to the coloured population's very heterogeneity.[8]

Some coloured Muslims for their part have turned back to the discourse of 'Malayism'. During fieldwork I witnessed a highly flexible and contextual use of terms such as 'Cape Malays' and 'Muslims' among Muslims in Mekaar. The term 'Cape Malays' was often used with substantial pride when referring to oneself, even though it was most frequently used during festival occasions such as the mouloet (annual celebrations of the birth of the prophet) and when talking about food and 'customs'. When 'culture', however defined, appears to be the issue in conversations, the tendency to phrase one's identity with reference to 'Cape Malayism' appears to be strong. On the whole, I found few who reacted to the designation 'Cape Malay', even if many informants were well aware of the historical inaccuracies inherent in the concept. The distinction between Cape Malay/Cape Muslim in emic discourse is not rigid. This has to do with the fact that the distinction between what is regarded as 'culture' and as 'religion' is fluid. It varies for instance according to the social position of the informant. For example, quite a few practitioners of or individuals sympathetic to the practice of *ratiep* claim that this is part of their religion. For a literalist, this point of view comes close to the abhorrent, as the *ratiep* for them at best is 'culture' (and as such, simply to be disregarded), or at worst, innovation [ar. bid`ā] (and therefore to be opposed).

8. Such sentiments were reflected in the statements of Blackman Ngoro, a Zimbabwean-born media advisor to the ANC mayor of Cape Town, Nomaindia Mfeketo, who after facing popular outrage was fired from his position in August 2005 after alleging that 'Africans' [i.e. black Africans] are 'culturally superior' to coloureds (Kassiem 2005). By no means representative of the ANC, his statements nevertheless point to the existence of a substratum of racialised and populist African nationalist discourses within the ANC. At a popular level, the existence of such discourses is also confirmed by the salience of the derogatory Xhosa term *aMalau* for coloureds, a term which implies that coloureds are lost and without any tradition (Ramphele 1993:61).

The *ratiep* attracts the larger part of its following from the working class in the community of Mekaar.

But in general the likelihood of phrasing one's identity as a 'Muslim' instead of 'Cape Malay' increases when religion strictly defined is the matter under discussion.

The Tercentenary of Shaykh Yusuf's arrival at the Cape in 1994,[9] which occurred in the run-up to the first democratic elections, illustrated the extent to which 'Malayism' had gained new-found acceptance among local Muslims. Even the academic Achmat Davids, a social historian supportive of the ANC, who in the past had been extremely critical of the whole 'Cape Malay' concept (quite likely due to its abuse by apartheid strategists) came out of the closet as a 'Malayist' during the proceedings, to the astonishment of local Muslim intellectuals like Jeppie (1996a: 81).[10] Local guests appeared in Malaysian-styled *sarongs* and *sangkok* headgear, which is rarely, if ever, seen among Muslims in Cape Town (ibid.:80). The Malaysian Defence Minister, representing a delegation of 250 Malaysian political and business executives welcomed the 'Cape Malays' back to the 'Malay' fold. His dramatic and high-pitched speech and its reception by the Muslim audience present in the Good Hope Centre in Cape Town outshone the future State President Nelson Mandela, who was also present as an honorary guest. The Defence Minister, Datuk S.M.N.T.H Abdul Razak, was verging on tears when closing his high-pitched and sentimental speech:

> "...[...]... You have found your blood brother(s) after 300 years ... after 300 years we have found each other ... we will never let go of each other...(and) as brothers

9. The Tercentenary in 1994 commemorated 300 years of Muslim presence in Cape Town. Generally recognised by Cape Muslims as the founding father of Islam in South Africa, sheikh Yusuf of Macassar arrived with a retinue of 52 followers aboard *De Voetboog* in 1694. He was a royal banished to the Cape for having taken part in an uprising against the Dutch in Bantam. It should be noted, however, that among the *Mardijkers*, slaves assigned with the task of protecting the Dutch colonial settlement against attacks from the Khoi-Khoi, who arrived as early as 1658, there were in all probability Muslims. For more on the Mardijkers, see Shell 1995.

10. It is difficult to ascertain what might have motivated David's statements in this context. He passed away in 1999. David's academic works attest to remarkable skills in the balancing act between serious academic scholarship and communal interests. Former friends of Mr. David's have however confirmed to me that he felt that there were limits as to what he could say in the communal context. His statements during the Tercentenary might therefore simply have been contextual pragmatism amidst general euphoria.

we will help you in every possible way ... you will go down in history as freedom fighters!"

Needless to say, the Tercentenary in 1994 seems to have involved a certain degree of posturing for the Malaysian and Indonesian visitors on the part of local Muslim elites. Most of the oelema present had far stronger links to for instance Saudi Arabia, Kuwait, Egypt, India or Pakistan (where many of them had been educated) than to Malaysia and Indonesia, in spite of appearances in this context.

One year later a Malaysian and an Indonesian consulate was opened in Cape Town. This created new opportunities for local cultural entrepreneurs, as soon will be depicted. It is at this point that the local enters the global. But first, a few words about what might have motivated the strong interest in the 'Cape Malays' on the part of the Malaysians.

The idea of a Malay 'diaspora'

The interest in the idea of a Malay diaspora and its promotion on the part of the Malaysians grew out of the internal political situation of Malaysia. Approximately thirty per cent of the population of Malaysia is Chinese (Stier 2001), and as in Indonesia, this Chinese diaspora tended to dominate economic enterprises. Affirmative action programmes initiated by the Malaysian state in the 1970s under the then President Mahathir Mohamed sought to empower the largely rural Malay population, and many within the ANC in South Africa saw these policies as a possible blue-print for black economic empowerment (BEE) in post-apartheid South Africa. The Malays of Malaysia are largely Muslim, and anthropologists have noted that Islam has become a key symbol of Malay identity in Malaysia since the 1970s (Peletz 1996:40). As part of the Malaysian regime's attempts to circumvent Chinese influence in Malaysia proper through an emulation of the vast Chinese diasporic network, the 're'-discovery of the Malay diaspora had turned into an important priority for the Malaysian regime in the 1990s. The concept of a 'Malay diaspora' had been explored by intellectuals affiliated to *Gappena*, the Malay writers' association (Watson 1996:12), and its chairman, Mr. Ismail Hussein had established a network of links with Muslim 'Malays' in 'diasporas' all over the world, including in South Africa (ibid.:12). On the back of these initiatives followed a steady stream of Malaysian businessmen, anxious to explore business opportunities in post-apartheid South Africa. They could draw on the useful links to the state of some of the South African Muslims empowered by the transformation policies of the ANC. By 1997, Malaysia was second only to the USA as far as foreign direct investment (FDI) in South Africa was concerned (Padyachee and Valodia 1997:23). The strong Malaysian presence at the Tercentenary was therefore no coincidence, nor was the subsequent visit of Mahathir Mohamed to Cape Town in 1995.

Furthermore, in the reconstitution of 'Cape Malayism' it was important that the ANC, in its appeal to Cape Muslim voters in the period after 1994 seemed to focus part of their attention on the 'Cape Malay' strand of thinking.[11] The South African Malayu Cultural Association was visited by Ben Ngubane, state secretary in the Department of Culture. The Department of Culture sponsored trips to Indonesia. It also bears mentioning that the ANC prior to the elections in 1994 received extensive funding from the Indonesian state.

The relations between 'Malays' and 'Cape Malays' have however not been without their paradoxes. There is no small amount of essentialism at play on the Malaysian side of the equation – a curator at Iziko Museums in Cape Town recounted how a Malaysian television crew who had come to Cape Town to make a documentary about Cape Muslims in 2005 had astonished museum staff by excitedly labelling every single Cape Muslim they were shown in historical photographs from Cape Town as 'Malays'. There is a strong denial of heterogeneity on the part of these Malaysians, as well as among some of their local interlocutors. Apart from that, 'Malays' have come to realize that in terms of ritual practice, the 'Cape Malays' sometimes differ markedly from them. A year after the Tercentenary an official Malaysian delegation, headed by Mahathir Mohamed resolutely walked out en masse during an official reception in protest against a *ratiep* performance by a local *ratiep* group. The supreme irony, which did not escape local Muslims, was of course that the reception during which the Malaysian delegation walked out, was hosted by the then Speaker of Parliament, Frene Ginwala, of the ANC, and was attended by the then Deputy President, Thabo Mbeki. By including the performance of this ritual, the organisers had successfully managed to offend the religious sensibilities of both Malaysians and the more literalist among Cape Muslims.

11. According to the election results only the coloured and Indian Muslim upper and middle-class appears to have voted to a significant extent for the ANC prior to the 2004 local and provincial elections.

Diasporic consciousness: The case of Muneez

On 9 September 1999 a local museum in Bayside south of Cape Town received a curious fax. It was from a middle-aged Muslim man they knew very well. In fact, the museum, which contains memorabilia of the coloured community in Bayside, from which Mekaar's residents had been forcibly removed in the period between 1968 and 1978, had been established a few years previously largely as a result of ideas and input from this man. His name was Muneez.

The fax was addressed 'To all South Africans', and faxed from a hotel in the city of Sumbawa Basar on the Indonesian island of Sumbawa. Another fax received a few days earlier was introduced by "Att. The rainbow nation of South Africa".

In the second fax, Muneez claimed to have found the village from which a man he believed to be his ancestor, Imam Sharaf, came. He claimed that this ancestor had been brought in chains to the Cape by the Dutch East India Company (VOC) in 1786. At the Cape, Muneez was convinced, the Sumbowan *bandiet* (colonial Dutch designation for prisoners banished to the Cape for political reasons) Sharaf, married a local woman and settled in Bayside. In fact, according to Muneez, Sharaf must have been the first imam in Bayside.

Muneez is a man in his fifties. He left school after standard 7, and has spent the most part of his life working as a cook aboard South African ships. During the international sanctions of the 1980s he was aboard South African ships that sailed under false registration in order to break the sanctions. He has never been married, and admits that part of the reason for this may be that he in his youth was, as his family would say, on the 'wild' side. Muneez was born in Bayside, but after the Group Areas Act of 1968 his family was dispersed. A substantial number of them now reside in Mekaar. In Bayside his family 'clan' had been among the most numerous and most influential in the community. They considered themselves (and were indeed considered by others) as an educated elite in the Muslim community there.

In 1997, Muneez claimed to have been visited in his dreams by his late father, who called upon him to 'look into the affairs of his family'. He decided to research his family's history more closely at the Cape Archives and in the Deeds' Office in Cape Town, the former being a public archive containing official documents dating back to colonial times, the latter a register of publicly registered property sales in Cape Town.

The model for Muneez' research was the research undertaken by a Mr. Erefaan Rakiep. Mr. Rakiep, a man then in his late seventies,[12] had been a tailor in Hanover Street in District Six in Cape Town before the proclamation of District Six as a white area in the 1960s forced him to move to Bridgetown in Athlone. In his spare time, Rakiep had spent countless hours in the Cape Archives in order to substantiate his claim to be a descendant of Tuan Guru, the imam of the first mosque in Cape Town, the Auwal Mosque in Dorp Street in the Bo-Kaap, from its establishment in the early 19th century. Tuan Guru had two sons, Abdolrauf and Abdolrakiep, and they founded two of the most influential imam dynasties in Cape Town.

In his capacity as a descendant of Tuan Guru, Mr. Rakiep had been in Indonesia twice, the first time as early as in the 1970s, when it was extremely difficult for a South African, let alone a coloured South African, to get a permit to visit Indonesia (the Soeharto regime being opposed to the apartheid regime, and a prominent member of the Non-Aligned Movement). Mr. Rakiep had taken great care in substantiating his claims through thousands of pages of copies of archival records regarding Tuan Guru and his descendants. For a period, Muneez visited Mr. Rakiep frequently, but their relationship soon soured, as Mr. Rakiep expressed his scepticism and demanded unambiguous evidence of the claims brought forward by Muneez. Back in 2001, a friend and co-researcher of Mr. Rakiep's characterized Muneez claims as a 'myth' on a local Muslim radio-station, the '*Voice of the Cape*' (personal correspondence, Mekaar informant).

In the fax to the museum, Muneez described his experiences in the Sumbowan highlands:

> "By passing the right village...[...]...I could feel the presence of someone in the bus so strong I cried" (and on his arrival in the *kampung*) "...[...]...I met my 'uncle' in the road about 10.00 a.m. Without looking at the document [i.e. the document which he had brought with him in order to substantiate his claim that he was related to an ancestor from this village] he told me later he knew I was family of his and that I was related to Imam Sharaf...[...]...Only when we were seated in his home and he spoke directly to me ... I cried, someone was present, but by then I knew he was my family. He also cried. Later in the afternoon he took us to the kramat (burial site for a Muslim saint) on top of the hill, to his ancestor, the brother of Imam Sharaf [where] while kneeling and making duah (a prayer of supplication) the loose *messang* (tombstone) shook in the presence of both. I mentioned the name of Imam Sharaf and put my hand on top of the

12. Mr. Rakiep passed away in 2005.

messang, and it stopped moving. By then I knew that the kramat in Bayside was that of Imam Khaleed, son of Imam Sharaf".

Muneez appears to have created much ado in the Sumbowan village. He had brought a handy-cam, and a videotape of no less than three hours which he returned with shows him as he is being crowned as a prince, dressed up in a *sarong* and Indonesian headgear, and being treated to a *slametan*, a communal meal, by the village elders. Municipal authorities produced stylishly framed certificates in which they confirmed that he was indeed the descendant of Imam Sharaf, certificates which upon his return to Cape Town were granted pride of place in the modest living rooms of Muneez' close relatives in Mekaar. He was received at the Sultan's old palace in Sumbowa. Back in Cape Town he received a substantial amount of attention from the local media. The '*Leadership Magazine*' (a large South African business magazine) carried a feature article about the discovery of his roots. He attracted attention from academics at the University of Cape Town involved in the work on local cultural conservation programmes. The local museum in Bayside dedicated a whole wall of its exhibition to his trip. A museum curator from the Tropenmuseum in Amsterdam in the Netherlands decided to devote a section in an exhibition on South African families to Muneez' and his family's story. The following year Muneez was included among prominent local politicians, bureaucrats and performers from the South African Malayu Cultural Association[13] who spent a month in Indonesia on a programme of cultural exchange sponsored by local businesses, the South African state and the Indonesian government. In Indonesia, he was among those organizing an exhibition of 'Cape Malay' memorabilia at a local museum. A Cape Muslim curator also present noted that Indonesian schoolchildren seemed to know very little about *Africa Selatan*. A female South African novelist was reported to be working on a novel on the story of his ancestor (the novel never materialised). Muneez familiar-

13. The South African Malayu Cultural Association, established under the leadership of Mr. Hashiem Salie of Crawford, Cape Town in 1990, regularly appears at social functions in Cape Muslim communities, performing various dances, songs and rituals believed to have been practised by Cape Muslims during the time of colonial slavery. It has also initiated courses in Bahasa Malayu for local students. Even though Salie was unwilling to disclose the sources of the association's funding to me during my interview with him in 2000, sources in the community suggest that the association has received extensive funding from Malaysian and Indonesian donors, and that Mr. Salie himself has profited from involvement in business deals with Malaysian counterparts. According to Mr. Salie, the association was established after extensive 'consultation' with the Malaysian ambassador to Great Britain in 1990.

ized himself with the staff at the Indonesian consulate in Cape Town, and was invited to stylish diplomatic receptions.

Being of a rather intense disposition, he launched a wide array of initiatives – he requested the Indonesian department of Culture to support an application to the South African National Monuments Council to have the kramat on the hillside above Bayside declared a national monument (later apparently granted), forwarded a request that the South African government declare Imam Sharaf a 'national hero' (like Shaykh Yusuf, the mythical founding father of Islam in South Africa, who was brought to the Cape from Bantam in 1694) (which apparently met with no response), applied to the Bayside municipality to have Imam Sharaf and his son honoured with a plaque, made a video documentary, initiated public meetings, and proposed to create exhibitions on local history in Mekaar.

Implications of diasporic consciousness

Foucault has been quoted as stating that social agents "know what they do, frequently know why they do what they do; but what they don't know is what they do does" (as quoted in Dreyfus and Rabinow 1982:187). This points to an existential ambiguity – as social agents we may have very clear intentions about what our actions are supposed to mean or bring about, but the actual implications may be in stark contradiction with those intentions. Likewise, stated intentions are often in contradiction with intentions expressed through specific actions. Two aspects of Muneez' actions and the responses to these actions will be explored – firstly the communal aspect, and secondly the familial aspect.

The local museum to which Muneez was affiliated, and had contributed many artefacts and much material, was established in 1998. The establishment had come about as a result of the owner's long involvement in the work on an exhibition on the forced removals under the Group Areas Act from Bayside from 1968–78, which had taken place at the historically white museum of Bayside, a few hundred metres away. She had worked closely with coloured residents of Mekaar, but realized that they were extremely reluctant to contribute personal artefacts, photos and materials because they had a basic distrust of a museum which had been run by whites, and which had so far only preserved local white history. She recalled being asked the rhetorical question as to which interest the museum staff had taken in them at the time during which they [i.e. the coloured residents of Bayside] were removed, and in the thirty years that had passed since then. At the same time, the land restitution programme initiated by the ANC had opened up an opportunity to get back the property belonging to her late father, a prominent coloured politician in Bayside before the advent of the Group Areas Act, as this property was vacant. The property at which the museum was established, was the first property returned to coloured owners in Bayside. She must have felt that she was making a claim to historical coloured space in Bayside as well, much as I have reason to believe that Muneez did when he requested that the kramat on the hill be declared a national monument. The twin of diasporic consciousness is in this case a reclaiming of land. Representatives of the Muslim community of Cape Town have since 1994 been actively involved in the reclaiming of what it defines as 'Muslim spaces' in Cape Town, for instance by temporarily blocking development of school property in formerly white residential areas (in Zonnebloem, formerly District Six in Cape Town, where local Muslims believed that the property to be developed had been used as a Muslim cemetery, and contained the graves of Muslim saints. Two archaeological excavations under the co-ordination of Abdulkader Tayob, a Professor of Religious Studies at the University of Cape Town failed to substantiate this).

In order to be granted state funding for a museum, a museum in post-apartheid South Africa must be regarded by relevant authorities as contributing to the preservation of more than one particular ethnic and/or religious community's history. The new museum of Bayside has not been granted such funding. Visitors will undoubtedly notice the extent to which Muslim artefacts and memorabilia dominate the exhibition of the museum, in spite of the owner's stated intentions to the contrary (Bayside was a mixed community prior to the Group Areas Act, with white, coloureds and black Africans). In fact, the museum was established with a name that connoted Muslim exclusivity, and it was later changed to a more inclusive name. The owner however expresses clear intentions to correct the imbalances in the future, and there have been significant developments towards this in the years after my fieldwork. The main focuses of the exhibition are religious and cultural events, such as Muslim marriages, going on pilgrimage, mouloet, *ratiep* a. s. f. Du Plessis, who in his time was instrumental in establishing the Bo-Kaap Museum in central Cape Town (aimed at preserving 'Cape Malay' cultural and religious traditions), would probably have been pleased.

What then was the community's response to Muneez' initiatives?

The number of visitors to the museum in Bayside is limited. My general impression is that most of the visitors from Mekaar are Muslims. But a majority of Muslims in Mekaar have never been to the museum, even if the distance between Mekaar and Bayside is short. A public meeting called at the initiative of Muneez and the museum at the end of my fieldwork, attracted a limited audience. The intention was to establish a committee that was to work for the preservation of the coloured community of Bayside/Mekaar's history. Less than twenty local residents appeared for the meeting in the mosque *madressa*. It was pointed out that if one wanted to include non-Muslims as well, it was a bad idea to hold the meeting at the madressa. The residents present at the meeting were for the most part middle-aged and older members of middle-class families of Bayside. If this was 'diasporic consciousness' actualized, it was decidedly an elite phenomenon. The imam of Mekaar, who had been called upon to support the initiative, was not present, even though he expressed his support after prayers about a week later. The people present were more concerned about the use of a *kietap* (here: a religious book) in Muneez' possession than about the initiative that was being launched. The kietap had been written by a former imam in Bayside and in it he had registered most of what was happening in the Muslim community in Bayside about a hundred years ago. Those present were clearly concerned that some of the darker secrets of their ancestors (Muslim children born out of wedlock etc.) would now become public.

I now turn to the familial aspects involved in this case of 'diasporic consciousness'. It is a commonplace in anthropology that social and/or genealogical memory can serve as strategic resources in the attempts by individuals or groups to achieve or to confirm higher social status (Eickelman 1981:178). As mentioned, Muneez' family had historically been influential in Bayside, and is known to have had many educated males in its ranks. However, there had been a significant number of inter-religious marriages (i.e. marriages between Muslim and non-Muslim partners, in which case the non-Muslim partner in most cases converts to Islam, even if frequently this does not happen) in the family. Muneez' mother was a Christian. The implications of having a relatively high frequency of intermarriages (and marriages not resulting in conversion to Islam, or even worse, conversion from Islam) in your immediate family are clear in the Muslim community of Mekaar – it may lead to a reduction of social status (see also Bangstad 2004).

Muneez' research on his family's 'historical roots' can therefore be seen as an attempt at achieving familial and communal reconciliation – which he himself readily admits. Indeed, the wording of some of his documents that are in my possession suggests a certain spill-over from the national South African discourse of 'truth and reconciliation' so prevalent at the time at which he wrote them.

Local residents however, for the most part treated Muneez with indifference. The intensity and excitement revealed by his speech patterns was made into an object of humorous remarks. People knew, or assumed that they knew, about his 'wild past' in contradiction to the tenets of Islam. Muneez complained that they would always bring up that issue some way or the other. Sarcastic remarks about Muniz "wanting to be a royal" were common. They saw a discrepancy between this newfound status as a royal, and his modest financial means. It appeared that his narrative came up against the egalitarian ethos which the circumstances of deprivation in Mekaar had ingrained in local Muslims over the years.

A few days before I was leaving the field, he told me that he had decided to 'put the work in the hands of others' and signed up for several months at sea again. My impression was that he was frustrated with the limited resonance he had found in Mekaar.

Hybrid histories and the limits of 'diasporic consciousness' in the Cape Muslim community

The way in which we name and describe phenomena in the social world has consequences for the way in which the world is constituted as well as experienced (Foucault 1998:38). Discourse structures, empowers and represses (ibid.:30). Bourdieu and Wacqant are among those who caution us against the frequently excessive nominalism of academic discourse. They regard the discourse on globalisation and multiculturalism as restrictive and restricting in as much as it makes social inequality disappear from the academic point of view, and naturalises trans-national relationships of power (Bourdieu and Waquant 1999:42). Several analysts have pointed to the limitations inherent in the concept of 'diaspora' (see for instance Anthias op. cit.). A social anthropological critique of the concept should therefore take the limitations that the concept imposes on our empirical data, as the starting point.

The idea of a 'diaspora' presupposes an idea of a stable geographical referent, the imaginary homeland, however construed. It is in this sense we may say that the 'diaspora' is the mirror image of the 'nation-state', and increasingly so in a globalised world. But it need not imply any ideas about an eventual return. I also think that it is safe to assume that it presupposes a perception among a minority whose historical origins lie in another part of the world than the country in which they currently reside, that they in some way or another are, or have been, sidelined as a result of social and/or political processes in the country of their abode. So far about the usefulness of the concept of 'diaspora'.

The problems inherent in the concept however concern the privileging on a monochrone, unilinear and teleological history, actualised in the present identity of the 'diasporic' 'nation', as if the process by which the 'diasporic nation' as such was constituted is not more a result of processes in the present (constructivism), rather than the way in which the 'diasporic nation' has 'been' since time immemorial (essentialism). For poststructuralist thinkers, such as Brah (1996), Clifford (1994), Hall (1990) and Gilroy (1993), for whom the notion of diaspora has come to denote social conditions particularly compatible with postmodernity and globalisation, and a critique of modernistic essentialisms inherent in concepts such as 'ethnicity' and 'the nation', it must be a paradox to find that imagined communities of 'diasporic nationalism' are no less imagined than the imagined communities of 'nationalism' (cf. Anthias 1998:560, 558), and, perhaps more significantly, no less essentialised than its precursors, 'the ethnic group' or 'the nation'.

In the case of the Cape Muslim community, the identities of local Muslims are marked by a fundamental heterogeneity – theirs are the ideal-typical hybridized or hyphenated identities so celebrated by poststructuralist thinking (Caglar 1998:172). They are most certainly neither the 'Cape Malays' of apartheid strategists nor the 'newborn Malays' of the Malaysian regime. The Cape Muslim community is extremely diverse, both in terms of ritual and cultural practices, and phenotypic traits – Sufi practices abhorrent to the literalists (the Sufi revival of recent years) exist side by side with a highly political Iranian-inspired Islamism (in the form of Qibla), Deobandi asceticism (in the form of the reformist missionary organisation, the Tablīg Jamāt), and Wahhabi/ Salafi conservatism (the dominant orientation among oelema affiliated to the Muslim Judicial Council, the largest oelama body in Cape Town); their skin colour straddling all shades of white, brown and black. This is the case in Mekaar as in the wider Cape Muslim community. For Cape Muslims Muslim identity often operates as a minimal common denominator – apart from this commonality of identification and identity, they often differ significantly over outlook and ritual practice. To the extent then that 'diasporic consciousness' is dependent on an essentialised 'diasporic nation' fixed with reference to an imaginary 'national homeland' (as in the discourse of 'Cape Malayism') it cannot attain hegemony within the Cape Muslim community, precisely due to the Cape Muslim community's *essentially* heterogeneous and hybrid character. As in many 'diasporic communities' in the world, the trans-ethnic is here more significant than the trans-national (Anthias 2001:632). The Cape Muslim community has historically been located on the periphery of developments in the Muslim world – even if there appears to have been more or less regular contact with Muslims in East Africa and the Middle East from 1850 and onwards (da Costa 1992:8, Jeppie 1996b).

It was noted by visitors to Cape Town in the 19th century that for Cape Muslims the pilgrimage to Mecca meant a partial reorientation of allegiances (cf. Mayson 1963). Presumably, it exposed them to varieties of Middle Eastern Islam which in many respects were distinct from what they were used to from Cape Town. The first Cape Muslim to have undertaken the pilgrimage was Gastordien, also known as Carol Pilgrim, from 1834 to 1837. He became an imam upon his return to Cape Town (Jeppie op.cit.: 144). But given that most Cape Muslims formed part of the urban underclass, very few had the means to go on pilgrimage (ibid.:145), or for that matter, acquire higher Islamic learning at institutions in the Middle East. This does not necessarily imply that there was no universal discourse of Islam among Muslims in South Africa prior to the onset of apartheid (1948–1990), as Tayob (1999:118) seems to suggest, but it would at the very least seem to imply that the discourse of Islam that existed bore a heavy imprint of the notions and understandings of Islam prevalent in the areas from which Cape Muslims historically originated, as well of the local context. As the pilgrimage has turned into a commodity attainable for the Cape Muslim masses (the South African Hajj and Umrah Council registered over 7,500 South African pilgrims in 2000) in recent decades, and the number of youngsters going to Egypt, Saudi Arabia or Pakistan for higher religious education has increased markedly with the influx of Arabian petrodollars, chances are that an imposition of an idea of homogenous 'Malay diaspora' has long since been rendered impossible by developments in the Cape Muslim community.

Since 1994, there has been a flourishing of interest in genealogy and history in some sections of the Cape Muslim community. More often than not, this interest is expressed as an interest in tracing one's ancestors, and entails the construction of links with apical ancestors, whose surnames happen to be similar to one's own. Given that the written historical records on the lives of individual early Cape Muslims are scant, that the names individual Muslim slaves were given by their masters were often arbitrary, and that a person's name for various reasons could change over the course of a lifetime without there being historical records to that effect, the archival terrain on which this flourishing of interest is played out is bound to be uncertain and contested, as indicated by Muneez' case.[14] In spite of an increasing number of members of the Cape Muslim elite visiting Malaysia and/or Indonesia, or going there for educational or business purposes, it remains a fact that extremely few (if any) Cape Muslims are likely to define any of these countries as their 'home'. Their political and social commitments are firmly grounded within the confines of South African territorial space. Local notions of 'home' in Mekaar point to a 'rootedness' in Cape Town's geographical space. Ethnographic studies of social memory among coloureds in Cape Town have demonstrated the extent to which collective identities are constructed on the basis of embeddedness in a concrete, physical landscape (cf. Bohlin 1998, 2001). If "'home' is also the lived experience of a locality" (Brah op. cit. 192), then most Cape Muslim residents of Mekaar perceive Cape Town, if not necessarily Mekaar, as their 'home'. Brah (ibid.:197) claims that from an analytical point of view, we must distinguish between 'feeling at home' and declaring a place as one's 'home'. But my point here is precisely that for most people, privileged intellectuals excepted, there is no such distinction: 'feeling at home' is synonymous with 'being at home': morality and the attachment to a specific place are intertwined (cf. Malkki op. cit. 1). Furthermore, a 'Cape Malay diasporic consciousness' in the case of the Cape Muslims does not hold the instrumental promise of strengthening local Muslims' demands for multicultural recognition of their distinctiveness by the post-apartheid South African state – it is Islam, defined as a global community of believers, yet expressed in the localised Muslim community of South Africa, which is presented as the basis of the demands for such recognition. Even so, the discourse on 'Cape Malays' as a 'Malay' diaspora is likely to subsist as one of multiple strands in Cape Muslims' reflections upon their historical origins in a globalised world, at least as long as Malaysians and to a more limited degree, Indonesians, are willing to foot the bill for their 'diasporic' imaginings. If the reader has gained the impression that my approach to the issues at hand are in line with Barth's original formulations of his theory of ethnicity (1969), transferred to the issue of 'diasporic consciousness', the impression is entirely appropriate. 'Diasporic consciousness' has been analysed as an instance of mobilisation for largely instrumental purposes – be those of an economic, political or social nature. Unlike Barth however, I am not proposing this model as a general

14. I would like to thank Ms. Jackie Loos for providing me with some insight into the problems involved in genealogical research on Cape Muslims.

model – only as a model of how 'diasporic consciousness' might be analysed given this specific context.

References

Anthias, F., 1998, "Evaluating 'Diaspora': Beyond Ethnicity", *Sociology* 32(3)1998.

—, 2001, "New Hybridities, Old Concepts: The Limits of 'Culture'", *Ethnic and Racial Studies* 24(4)2001.

Appadurai, A., 1990, "Disjuncture and Difference in the Global Economy", in Featherstone, Mike (ed.), *Global culture: Nationalism, globalisation and modernity*. London: Sage.

Bangstad, S., 2004, 'When Muslims Marry Non-Muslims: Marriage as Incorporation in a Cape Muslim Community", *Journal of Islam and Muslim-Christian Relations* 15(3)2004.

Barth, F., 1969, "Introduction", in Barth, F. (ed.), *Ethnic Groups and Boundaries*. Oslo: Scandinavian University Press.

Bohlin, A., 1998, "The Politics of Locality: Memories of District Six in Cape Town", in Lovell, N. (ed.), *Locality and Belonging*. London: Routledge.

—, 2001, "Places of Longing and Belonging: Memories of the Group Area Proclamation of a South African Fishing Village", in Bender, B. and M. Winer (eds), *Contested Landscapes: Movement, Exile and Place*. Oxford: Berg.

Bourdieu, Pierre, 1977, *Outline of a Theory of Practice*. Transl. R. Nice. Cambridge: Cambridge University Press.

Bourdieu, Pierre and Loïc J.D. Wacquant, 1999, "On the Cunning of Imperialist Reason", *Theory, Culture and Society* 16(1)1999.

Brah, Avtar, 1996, *Cartographies of Diaspora*. London: Routledge.

Caglar, Ayse C., 1997, "Hyphenated Identities and the Limits of Culture", in Modood, Tariq and Pnina Werbner (eds), *The Politics of Multiculturalism in the New Europe – Racism, Identity and Community*. London: Zed Books.

Clifford, James. 1994, "Diasporas", *Cultural Anthropology* 9(3)1994.

Cohen, Robin, 1997, *Global Diasporas – An Introduction*. London: UCL Press.

Comaroff, John L., 1992, "Ethnicity, Nationalism and the Politics of Difference in an Age of Revolution", in Wilmsen, Edwin and P. McAllister (eds), *The Politics of Difference – Ethnic Premises in a World of Power*. Chicago: University of Chicago Press.

Dreyfus, Hubert L. and Paul Rabinow, 1982, *Michel Foucault: Beyond Structuralism and Hermeneutics*. Chicago: University of Chicago Press.

Da Costa, Yusuf, 1992, "Assimilatory Processes amongst the Cape Muslims in South Africa during the 19th Century", *South African Journal of Sociology* 23(1)1992.

Dubow, Saul, 1995, *Scientific Racism in Modern South Africa*. Cambridge: Cambridge University Press.

Du Plessis, Izaak David, 1944, *The Cape Malays*. Cape Town: Maskew Miller.

Du Plessis, Izaak David and C. A. Lückhoff, 1953, *The Malay Quarter and Its People*. Cape Town: A.A. Balkema.

Eickelman, Dale F., 1981, *The Middle East – An Anthropological Approach*. Englewood Cliffs, NJ: Prentice-Hall.

Foucault, Michel, 1998, *Diskursens Orden [The Order of Discourse]*. Trans. Espen Schaaning. Oslo: Spartacus Forlag.

Friedman, Jonathan, 1990, "Being in the World – Globalization and Localization", in Featherstone, Mike (ed.), *Global Culture: Nationalism, globalization and modernity*. London: Sage.

—, 1997, "Global crises, the Struggle for Cultural Identity and Intellectual Porkbarelling: Cosmopolitans versus Locals, Ethnics and Nationals in an Era of De-homogenisation", in Modood, Tariq and Pnina Werbner (eds), *Debating Cultural Hybridity*. London: Zed Books.

Gilroy, Paul, 1993, *The Black Atlantic*. London: Verso.

Gloppen, Siri, 2000, *South African Constitutionalism: The difficult balancing act of the Constitutional Court in South Africa 1994–2000*. Unpublished Ph.D. Thesis in Comparative Politics. Bergen: University of Bergen.

Goldin, Ian, 1987, *Making Race: The Politics and Economics of Coloured Identity in South Africa*. London: Longman.

Gupta, Akhil and James, Ferguson, 1997, "Discipline and Practice: 'The Field' as Site, Method and Location in Anthropology", in Ferguson, James and A. Gupta (eds), *Anthropological Locations: Boundaries and Grounds of a Field Science*. Berkeley: University of California Press.

Halbwachs, Maurice, 1980, *On Collective Memory*. Trans. Francis J. Ditter and Vida Yazdi Ditter. New York: Harper and Row.

Hall, Stuart, 1990, "Cultural Identity and Diaspora", in Rutherford, James (ed.), *Identity: Community, Culture, Difference*. London: Lawrence and Wishart.

—, 2000, "The Multicultural Question", in Hesse, Barnor (ed.), *Un/settled Multiculturalisms: Diasporas, Entanglements, Transruptions*. London: Zed Books.

Hefner, Robert W., 2000, *Civil Islam – Muslims and Democratization in Indonesia*. Princeton, NJ: Princeton University Press.

Hendricks, Cheryl E., 1997, "Creating, Consolidating, Contesting and Re-negotiating Coloured Identity." Unpublished seminar paper. Cape Town: Human Sciences Research Council.

Jeppie, Shamil, 1988, "I.D. du Plessis and the 're-invention' of the 'Malay' c. 1935–1952". Unpublished seminar paper. Cape Town: Centre for African Studies, University of Cape Town.

—, 1996a "Commemorations and Identities: The 1994 Tercentenary of Islam in South Africa", in Sonn, Tamara (ed.), *Islam and the Question of Minorities*. Atlanta: Scholars Press.

—, 1996b " Leadership and Loyalties: The Imams of Nineteenth Century Colonial Cape Town, South Africa", *Journal of Religion in Africa* 26(2)1996.

Johnson, R.W. and L. Schlemmer (eds), 1994, *Launching Democracy in South Africa: The First Open Election, April 1994*. New Haven, CT: Yale University Press.

Kassiem, Ayesha, 2005, "Ngoro may face Equality Court as row over website race comments grows", *Cape Times* 22.07.2005.

Kessler, Clive S., 1999, "A Malay Diaspora? Another Side of Dr. Mahathir's Jewish Problem", *Patterns of Prejudice* 33(1)1999.

Malkki, Liisa H., 1995, *Purity and Exile: Violence, Memory and National Cosmology among Hutu Refugees in Tanzania*. Chicago: University of Chicago Press.

Mamdani, Mahmood, 1996, *Citizen and Subject: Contemporary Africa and the Legacy of Late Colonialism*. Princeton, NJ: Princeton University Press.

Marais, Johannes Stephanus, 1938, *The Cape Coloured People 1652–1937*. Johannesburg: Witwatersrand University Press.

Martin, Denis-Constant, 1999, *Coon Carnival: New Year in Cape Town, Past and Present*. Cape Town: David Philip Publishers.

Mayson, John Schofield, 1963 [1861], *The Malays of Cape Town*. Cape Town: Africana Connoisseurs Press.

Nattrass, Nicoli and Jeremy Seekings, 2000, "Two Nations? Race and Economic Inequality in South Africa Today", *Dædalus* 130(1)2000.

Norval, Aletta J., 1996, *Deconstructing Apartheid Discourse*. London: Verso.

Padayachee, Vishnu and Imraan Valodia, 1997, "Malaysian Money: Sustainable Investments?", *Indicator South Africa* 14(2)1997.

Parekh, Bhikhu, 2000, *Rethinking Multiculturalism: Cultural Identity and Political Theory*. London: Macmillan Press.

Peletz, Michael G., 1996, *Reason and Passion: Representations of Gender in a Malay Society*. Berkeley: California University Press.

Posel, Deborah, 1991, *The Making of Apartheid 1948–1961: Conflict and Compromise*. Oxford: Oxford University Press.

—, 2001, "What's in a Name? Racial Classifications in Apartheid South Africa and Beyond", *Transformation* 47.

Prinsloo, Rachel, 1997, "Disintegrations: The Politics of Coloured Identity", *Indicator South Africa* 14(3)1997.

Ramphele, Mamphela, 1993, *A Bed Called Home: Life in the Migrant Labour Hostels of Cape Town*. Cape Town: David Philip.

Rasool, Ciraj, 2000, "The Rise of Heritage and the Reconstitution of History in South Africa", *Kronos* 26.

Saunders, Cristopher and Nicholas Southey, 1998, *A Dictionary of South African History*. Cape Town: David Philip Publishers.

Seekings, Jeremy and Matt Eldridge, 1996, "Mandela's Lost Province: The African National Congress and the Western Cape Electorate in the 1994 South African Elections", *Journal of Southern African Studies* 22(4).

Shell, Robert Carl-Heinz, 1994, *Children of Bondage – A Social History of Slavery at the Cape of Good Hope 1652–1834*. Johannesburg: Witwatersrand University Press.

—, 1995, "The March of the Mardijkers: The toleration of Islam at the Cape, 1633–1861", *Kronos* 22.

Silva, Penny et al., 1996, *A Dictionary of South African English on Historical Principles: South African Words and Their Origins*. New York: Oxford University Press.

Stier, Ken, 2001, "Malaysia: Back to the Future", *Newsweek Web Exclusive* at <http://www.msnbc.com/news/547887.asp>. Accessed 24.03.01.

Tambiah, Stanley J., 2000, "Transnational Movements, Diaspora and Multiple Modernities", *Dædalus* 129(1)2000.

Tayob, Abdulkader, 1999, "Southern Africa", in Westerlund, D. and I. Svanberg (eds), *Islam outside the Arab World*. Richmond, Surrey: Curzon Press.

Vertovec, Steven, 2000, *The Hindu Diaspora: Comparative Patterns*. London: Routledge.

Watson, C.W., 1996, "Reconstructing Malay Identity", *Anthropology Today* 12(5)1996.

Werbner, R., 1998, "Beyond Oblivion", in Werbner, R. and T. Ranger (eds), *Memory and the Postcolony: African Anthropology and the Critique of Power*. London: Zed Books.

Western, J., 1996, *Outcast Cape Town*. 2nd ed. Berkeley: University of California Press.

A Hadrami Diaspora in the Sudan – Individual life courses in regional and global contexts

Leif Manger

The first Hadrami – "small traders, small businesses"

I met Ahmed Abu Bakr Bajabr in Mukalla in 1994. Or rather, he met me. He heard me talking Arabic to someone in a Government office, noticed my Sudanese accent and came over to find out what strange incident had given a «*khawaja*» such an accent. And as Ahmed was in fact based in the Sudan he came to represent a special case for me too. It turned out that he was visiting from Port Sudan, trying to establish a chicken-farm in the area, which was his way of joining the boom of investments going on in Mukalla at the time. Hadramis abroad, particularly from Saudi Arabia and the Gulf, had started to invest heavily both in business and in housebuilding after the Yemeni Unification in 1990. And my first meeting with Ahmed Bajabr was actually in an office dealing with land sales connected to this investment boom. The boom itself lasted until the civil war in 1995, which demonstrated to the Hadramis in the diaspora that the unification might not run as unproblematically as they had thought. But that is another story. We shall return to Ahmed and his life story.

He was born in Andel, near Hureida, Hadramaut, in about 1934. His father died when he was two years old. He has three sisters, two in Andel, one in Mukalla. As the eldest in the family he was supposed to contribute to the family's income. His father had been a local farmer, with small means, so there was not much to do in Andel. He did however attend Islamic school in Andel for a period. But at the age of 11, in about 1945, he left with his uncle (FaBr). They travelled by boat from Mukalla to Jedda, stayed 6 months in Jedda before they decided to go to Sudan, also by boat. In the Sudan they came first to Suakin, where they were involved in trade. Then they left for Aroma, in the Gash Delta near Kassala, where he got further schooling.

Ahmed was not the first Bajabr to settle in Sudan. In 1925 another FaBr Mohamed Omer BaJabr was the first from his family to leave Andel for Sudan. He established himself trading in Suakin, but later left the Sudan to go back to Hadramaut, where he died. Mohamed Omer had married both in Hadramaut and in Sudan (one wife from the Hadrami community and one local). His sons also married girls in Hadramaut as well as in the Sudan (Port Sudan, Aroma), which meant that when Ahmed arrived he met his family.

Even before the Bajabrs there were Hadrami families in Sudan. Names such as al Amoudi, Ba Hayder, Bin Said and BaGouffa were common. They all come from Wadi Dua'an. These early settlers lived in Suakin, with Turks, Saudis, North Yemenis, and a few Jews. According to Ahmed other people were involved as carriers and in fishing but the Hadramis stuck to their traditional vocation – trade. Some of this trade was to Saudi Arabia, to Jedda, when this was still a small town. Some Hadramis from Suakin went south to Eritrea and to the border town of Aqiq. There they were involved in trade in agricultural products and animals, which also brought many of them into close contact with the Beni Amer, the dominant group in the area.

Ahmed himself married while he stayed in Aroma. His wife was a Beni Amer girl with her father from Eritrea. His first son went to school in England and eventually married a girl from Wales. The son is dead, but the wife and daughter visit Port Sudan from England where they live. The second son, Badr Ahmed BaJabr, is involved in his father's business. Actually I met the two together in Mukalla, where he had come from the family business in Sana'a. Two daughters live in Saudi Arabia, and one in Sudan. Both she and her mother travel with Ahmed when he goes to Yemen, which he does for a number of months every year after the Yemeni unification.

Ahmed has been involved in a number of occupations. First in trade from 1949 to 52. In 1952 he was in Omdurman where he established the hotel "*Funduq al Felah*" ("Hotel Peasant"), and worked it until the 1960s. In 1969 he established a new hotel. He also went to Jedda and stayed for a short while in the 1950s, but he did not like it and returned to the Sudan. In 1971 he established a hotel in Port Sudan, also "*Funduq al Felah*" which he ran until 1984. Then he established "*Funduq al Riadh*" ("Hotel Riadh"). He ran a business in *Hai el Arab* The Arab quarter) in Port Sudan, where he had an office and a compound of 1000 sq.m. where he kept his main trade items, iron and wood. In 1979 he went to Saudi and stayed in Jedda for three years. He came back and farmed in Gereif. Although he travels around, Ahmed's base is in Port Sudan, where he owns two houses and some land.

His involvement in Yemen goes back to the late 1980s when the ambassadors of North Yemen and South Yemen had been to Port Sudan to discuss possibilities for opening trade between Sudan and the then two separate countries. Ahmed acquired a Yemeni passport and he first started in Sana'a with a shop selling fast food. After unification in 1990 he went to Aden and Mukalla, and is now trying to get land to establish chicken feed production. Among his workers in Mukalla is another Sudanese Hadrami, by the name of Hamoudi. He is the son of Abdalla Al Mahamoudi who is a *qabili* (tribesman) from Wadi Hamoudi near Mukalla. Abdalla had worked as a lorry driver between Tokar and Port Sudan. Other relatives from the same family went to Kenya and Somalia. Abdalla had 6 sons. Apart from the one working with Ahmed the others are now also in Mukalla. One is a millionaire from working in the land market after the unification when land prices exploded during the investment boom.

A Hadrami diaspora in the Indian Ocean

Ahmed's story is one illustration of the long history of Hadrami migration throughout the Indian Ocean region, linking the homeland of Hadramaut to various diasporic communities in the region. Before we deal with the specific link between Hadramaut and the Sudan, we shall present some broader contexts of this migration history. The region we are talking about is defined by the old trade routes around the Indian Ocean. Such routes were governed by the monsoon winds which took small ships to areas on the Indian coast, to East Africa, to South East Asia as well as to the islands of the Indian Ocean like the Comoros, the Maldives and Madagascar. The region of the Middle East, of which Hadramaut is a part, shows very old contacts indeed, and evidence indicates that economic contacts in this region ranged over a very large area even several thousand years before the first urban based states appeared and that such links were a constant source of political troubles as many ancient empires tried to control trade routes. With such a general background in mind we should not be surprised that our focus on the Hadramis in the Indian Ocean also displays patterns of early contacts and interdependencies, of spatially and temporally shifting relationships. These links go back to antiquity (Reade, ed., 1996), and relate mainly to trade in luxury items like frankincense and myrrh. Significant developments of these contacts relate to the periods after the rise of Islam in the region, particularly after 1000 (Chaudhuri 1990, Risso 1995). Starting from the Middle East (Palestine and

Syria) trade routes were developed through the Abbasid capital, Baghdad, before diverting in two directions. One route went overland through Persia, again splitting either towards Central Asia or towards India. The second diversion was towards the south, down the Tigris to the Persian Gulf and eventually to the Indian Ocean. Further north, another major overland route developed linking Turkey, the Black Sea and the Caspian Sea areas, Central Asia and China. Our interest here is in the southern route, along which Muslim traders and navies sailed to India, starting the Muslim encounter with the Indic civilisation in Sind and Punjab in the west and Bengal in the east. The decline of the Mongol Empire in Central and Western Asia constrained the development of some of these formerly important routes and opened up for the Indian Ocean to become an important arena for travelling, trade and learning. The western part of the Indian Ocean was dominated by Muslim merchants and ship-owners operating from the Arabian coastal towns; a middle region connected the Indian coast with the Hinduised Southeast Asian regions of Sumatra and Malaya, and an eastern circuit linked Java to China, thus bringing Muslims into the realm of Buddhism and Confucianism. By the end of the 13th century city states appeared in Malay-speaking Southeast Asia, spreading Islam and at the same time providing Europe with spices. Two centuries later Islam started penetrating the interior of Java, not meeting European traders as competitors as they did in the coastal towns, but a Hindu-Buddhist civilisation. Similar processes brought Islam to Africa, via the trans-Saharan trade between North and West Africa, via trade routes across the Red Sea to the Sudan, and across the Indian Ocean to the Swahili coast, and the Nile Valley. After the fall of Baghdad, Cairo took over as the main Muslim city, and the seat of the Mamluk dynasty. This brought interaction between Arabs and Muslims throughout the Sudanic world, and also among the Bantu on the Swahili coast. The trade that provided the dynamics into these links was luxury goods such as ivory, rhino horn, frankincense and slaves in return for Arabian and Indian handicrafts, and spices from the east (Curtin 1984, Abu Lughod 1989).

The post-1500 story of the Indian Ocean was also affected by the appearance of the European imperial powers in the region (Curtin 2000). Being a major commercial area the Indian Ocean first caught the interest of the Portuguese in the 16th century, looking for trade routes as well as taking over the most profitable trade, e.g. in gold. In the following centuries Ottoman Turkey also emerged as a competitor for influence in the region as did the French, the British and the Dutch. All these powers became of importance to the developments in Hadramaut. The Ottomans and British as direct occupants in South Yemen, the French and British in constant competition in India, the British East India Company providing contexts for Hadrami settlements there, the Dutch as a colonial power in Southeast Asia, of importance to the significant Hadrami community on Java. In 19th-century Africa, Germany also entered into the picture as a colonial power in Zanzibar and on the Tanzanian coast, in competition again with the Omani Sultanate on Zanzibar. But in spite of political and economic competition the early centuries of European presence were not characterized by their dominant position, but rather by the ways they were swallowed up by the Indian Ocean world. By this I mean that for two centuries the Europeans carried out their trade, and adapted to realities in the region alongside all other groups. They were not dominating. The traces of this history are most vividly present in the various trading towns with their peculiar intermixing of cultures, identities and ideas that were linked through cultural forms, kinship relations, business circuits and travel trajectories, as well as through loyalty to the religious centres of the diaspora. This medieval world of the Indian Ocean and the Red Sea has been termed "the Geniza World", due to the outstanding contribution by S.D. Goitein, the historian of transnational cultures based on manuscripts found in the *geniza*, the store-room of the synagogue at Fustat (Old Cairo)(see e.g. Ghosh 1992, Clifford 1994:305).

However, by the second half of the 18th century and into the 19th century the pattern changed. This period represents a change in European interests in the region from trade to territory. Through this we enter the period of colonialism and imperialism. Various centres were being subjected to Western rule and exploitation, the mechanisms being trade as before, but also plantation agriculture, mining, cash cropping and intensified forms of slavery (Bayly 1989). Hadramis maintained various forms of links to power-holders and elite groups, and were indeed in many places part of such ruling elites.

This general pattern lasted until the post-colonial period, in which the new nation-states emerging provided yet new dynamics. The struggles for independence in Southeast Asian countries and in India were of great importance as they provided inspiration for nationalist thinking in Hadramaut. The end of British rule in India in 1947 ended the special links between Hadramaut, South Yemen and India. Rather, the British Colony of Aden grew in importance as the political centre of southern Yemen, a development which lasted until the South Yemeni war of independence that was successfully completed in 1967. The developments within South Yemen itself have also been characterized by major upheavals. The war of liberation, the subsequent socialist regime in the People's Democratic Republic of Yemen (PDRY), trying to eradicate the existing social and economic structures of the past, and then the collapse of the Communist world, and the subsequent unification between North and South Yemen and the outbreak of a civil war only a few years after the unification are just some major events. This recent period is also characterized by the emergence of Saudi Arabia and the Gulf states as nation-states and as major oil producing countries, providing avenues for labour migration from Hadramaut. This is today of great significance to development in Hadramaut itself. The collapse of South Yemen and its unification with North Yemen in May 1990 provided a situation in which Hadrami migrants who had left during the Communist reign (1967–90) could return to their home country to reclaim their property and start investments protected by the new open market economy. This development was temporarily halted by the short civil war between North and South Yemen in 1994, but the investments and links, particularly to the Hadrami communities on the Arabian peninsula, continue. A second pattern in this period is the migration towards the Western countries of Australia, Europe and the USA, bringing the Hadramis, although not in large numbers, into contact with contemporary developments regarding immigration, employment-unemployment policies and the unfolding of racism.

Hadramis in the Sudan – a Red Sea tale

Returning to Ahmed's story at the beginning of this paper, it turned out that it was rather representative for a number of Hadramis in the Sudan that I came to meet later in Mukalla, in Port Sudan and in Khartoum. The migration to Sudan did not start with the Bajabr but was initiated during a period of profound change, not only in the Red Sea region but all the way down to the Swahili coast further south. The contexts are the commercial developments, particularly related to the opening of the Suez Canal, but also to the political competition among regional powers such as Egypt, Ethiopia, and the European colonial powers such as Britain, France, Italy and Germany, eventually leading to Britain's colonization of Egypt in 1882 and Sudan in 1898.

Let us start at the northern end of the area, in the Red Sea and the two coastal towns of Suakin and Massawa. It was here that Khedive Ismail Pasha of Egypt (1863–1879), inspired by his grandfather Muhamed Ali, dreamed of establishing an African empire. The proximity of the three towns of Suakin-Massawa-Jedda linked Africa to the Hijaz and the Muslim pilgrimage traffic and trade. Ever since the time of the Wahhabi revolt, that he was asked to suppress, Muhamed Ali had also been interested in these towns. Egypt gained control of the towns in 1811, and Muhamed Ali made his son Ahmad Tusun Pasha Governor of the *Vilayet* of Jedda. After the Wahhabi revolt was over in 1827 the towns reverted to Ottoman Turkish rule, but they were left for Egypt to dominate during the lifetime of Muhamed Ali. Muhamed Ali got involved in the Yemeni coffee trade, and set up a monopoly in the 1830s. He had already occupied Sudan in 1821, and with his Syrian campaigns starting in 1831 Muhamed Ali appeared as a ruler of importance. Britain watched these developments with concern. The regional developments were certainly part of the considerations when they occupied Aden in 1837. From Aden the British could also keep an eye on Ethiopia, especially the important trading town of Massawa.

Muhamed Ali died in 1849 and his two successors, Abbas (1849–1854) and Sa'id (1854–1863) were not particularly interested in developing the expansionist policies in Africa. But this changed with Ismail Pasha, who ruled Egypt from 1863 and who wanted both to restore an empire like that of his grandfather, and also to safeguard the territories won earlier in the Nile Valley (Talhami 1979). After Egyptian control was secured a series of administrative reforms and experiments were started. Administrative structures shifted between organizing Suakin, Kassala and Massawa in one province or three, with one or three governors, with independent powers from Khartoum, answering directly to Cairo, to being controlled by the Governor-General in Khartoum. Plans for transport links, for telegraph and other types of communication were started. Water works were developed, as were health services, schools, mosques and general housing. New tax systems and new local administrative systems were developed. The leading administrators, Mumtaz and Munziger operated with considerable independence, but also at times ended up in conflict with Cairo. There were also conflicts with the local populations, over issues such as taxes and forced labour. Economic development was also promoted. Increased cotton and dhura production was a priority in areas that allowed for irrigation. Market oriented cash crops appeared. Tokar was such an area, as was the Gash and Aqiq in the south. Cotton was a definitive priority in order to exploit the available market shares left open by the American Civil War. Mining was another activity. Salt was important and was sold in Jedda to be resold to Indian boats. Minerals were also sought. To reach relevant markets improved communication between Sudan and Egypt became another priority. Work started on the Aswan-Khartoum railway link (towards the Berber-Suakin link), bringing in British engineers to work on the problem of the cataracts in the Nile. Although many successes were reported, the policy was a drain on the Egyptian economy. Egypt could not alone carry the expenses the development policies entailed, and depended heavily on foreign borrowing. But what really stopped the Egyptian attempts at developing Massawa and Suakin was the war with Ethiopia in 1875–76. The war was fought over territory and Egypt lost. The defeat created discontent among the high officers and added further burdens on an already weak economy. Local opposition also increased, as did Egyptian – Ottoman conflicts. The defeat also brought Britain more actively into the regional politics of the Red Sea, both as an arbitrator after the Egyptian-Ethiopian war, and also as a direct actor in the Sudan. The area was increasingly being focused on by the Europeans as an area in which European supremacy should replace "African", "Muslim" and/or "Turkish" chaos. And due to Egypt's debts Britain was more directly involved in Egyptian affairs. Ismail was deposed, and Mohamed Tawfiq took over. A nationalist initiative by Urabi Pasha and other Circassian officers was also contained. With the Mahdist Revolution (1881) and the British take over of Egypt and Sudan (1898) the areas were increasingly run by the British. Suakin, regarded as the only Egyptian territory that escaped Mahdist control, was no exception (Talhami 1979).

It is in this general environment that we find the early Hadramis (Ewald and Clarence-Smith 1997). The Hadramis migrating in this area came from inland of Hadramaut, particularly Wadi Daw'an, travelling to Aden, the Red Sea and Egyptian ports of Jedda, Suakin and Cairo. With the development of railway tracks and roads the interior was opened to trade and migration also in Ethiopia, Somalia and Kenya. Shipping was also an important activity, particularly the pilgimage traffic. Slave trading was also common, and slaves were frequently found as crew on ships. Trade in coffee to Egypt was important as was the arms trade to Djibuti. Less dramatic trade items were represented by items such as millet and sesame from Somalia to Hadramaut (Alpers 1983), hides, millet and camels out of Massawa. Moneylending was also common, in which the Hadramis competed with the Indians and by 1930 the Hadramis had placed much capital in property. They were also involved in the politics of the *Sharif* of Mecca, and they operated as soldiers under various leaders.

The Hadrami diaspora in the Sudan

But our story of the Hadramis in the Sudan really takes off in the first half of the 20th century. This is a story in which the Sudan is run by the British and also a story dominated by the development of Port Sudan as the dominant city in Eastern Sudan, replacing Suakin. Port Sudan became the major market in the region, and as Sudan's major port, it has been of crucial importance to the capital, Khartoum, and the nation as a whole. It has also been a gateway eastwards, into the Red Sea and Gulf of Aden areas, and hence, to the Indian Ocean (Perkin 1993).

After the British decided that Suakin, the old urban centre on the western shore of the Red Sea, was no longer a suitable harbour for 20th century Sudan, the development of Port Sudan became a major concern for the British colonial rule. Its story begins in 1904, when it was founded by the British at *Shaikh Barghuth*, the burial place of a Muslim saint. The place for the new city was chosen because of the area's suitability as a harbour that could facilitate the type of shipping that existed at the turn of the century. Once established, the population of Port Sudan grew fast, with inhabitants of varied origins. There were groups of Sudanese, Egyptians, Arabs, Ethiopians, Syrians, Persians, Somalis, Eritreans, Indians, Italians and Greeks, in addition to the British themselves. In this situation the British followed a policy of land allocation based on race and class, with first class plots allocated to commercial elites of European origin, down to the quarters (*daims*), i.e. undeveloped areas for local Beja people. Over the decades the accommodation of an increasing Beja population has been a constant challenge to city planners, as have the problems of the inhabitants' sanitation, education and public safety.

The development of Port Sudan over time became an increasing drain on the region's marginal resources and constitutes major developmental problems in the area to this day (Manger et al. 1996). One such issue is the solution of the city's water problem by bringing water from *Khor* Arba'at. The increasing demand for wood as fuel is another. The establishment of irrigated agriculture in the water carrying areas in order to provide vegetables and fruits for the city dwellers is a third. The need for labour, particularly in the port, has also constituted a major issue during Port Sudan's history. As there was not enough labour coming from the local groups, it was considered necessary to import labour from outside; mainly from Upper Egypt and Yemen. This particular problem directly involved the Yemenis. Ali Yahia al Yamani arrived from Aden in 1906 and became a famous recruitment agent for such labour. The recruitment agents were powerful people, and Ali remained dominant into the 1930s. During the 1920s Sudanese agents challenged his hegemony, and tried to enlist the support of the British to engage more Sudanese labourers, in competition with the Yemenis brought in by Ali. The British were reluctant, however, as the local labour supply among the Beja pastoralists fluctuated with the climate in their home areas. During droughts they willingly came forward, but in years of sufficient rainfall they withdrew to their pastures. An initiative to bring in labourers from Western Sudan also triggered British concern, as the solution would mix groups from Western and Eastern Sudan. The two regions made up the core areas of support for the two major religious movements and political parties in the Sudan. These were the Khatmiyya and the DUP in the East, the Ansar and the Umma in the West and the authorities were worried over possible political unrest. The local solutions to the labour issue in Port Sudan thus related to international relationships across the Red Sea and to Egypt, as well as to basic national concerns within Sudan itself.

These labour issues related as much to Northern Yemenis as they involved Hadramis. Hadramis, as Ahmed Bajabr said, were involved in trade. But they were certainly part of the picture in Port Sudan and Eastern Sudan. Judging from sources from the 1930s (Ingrams 1937) there were important Hadrami settlements only in Eastern Sudan. At Port Sudan there was an important Hadrami merchant (of the Safi family) who had offices in Port Sudan and Suakin. The Acting Commissioner stated on request from Harold Ingrams, the Resident Advisor to the Quaity sultan, that colonies of Hadramis existed at Port Sudan, Suakin and Tokar, with small groups at Halaib, Aqiq and Karora. Approximate figures were said to be as follows: Port Sudan 180, Suakin 228, Tokar 294, Halaib 4, Aqiq 30, Karora 6, making a total of 742 (Ingrams, ibid.). The Hadramis in the Sudan at that time were of two categories: those permanently settled, who had been in those parts since the old days of Suakin, and had practically severed their connections with Hadramaut; and the visitors, who would normally spend about three years in the Sudan between visits of about a year's duration to their homes. The division between the categories was said to be roughly half and half. In the towns, the Hadramis were primarily shopkeepers or shop assistants. A few made their living as cooks, bakers and labourers, and in the Tokar Delta many had taken up cultivation. Some became allottees of Government land, thus becoming land owners. Others worked as '*nusf*' cultivators, that is they worked other people's land in return for half of the profits and hoped in due course to become allottees themselves. There does not appear to have existed any extensive Hadrami community in the interior of the Sudan. Only one person was reported to be permanently settled in Khartoum (running a cafe there) and two in Omdurman (two from the Hadramaut and six from places like Nisab and Balhaf on the western borders of the Hadramaut).

The British estimated that about a third of the Hadramis in the Sudan had definitely severed their connections with the Hadramaut, but they did not coalesce to any noticeable degree with the local population. The settled Hadramis principally intermarried among themselves, although the visitors occasionally intermarried with local inhabitants, particularly the girls of the Beni Amer. The majority either had wives in the Hadramaut or were unmarried. But the British also noted a surprisingly large number of bachelors. For instance, none of the 30 residents of Aqiq was married, which over time led to a stagnation in the number of Hadramis. Commercial relations with the Hadramaut were at that time said to be negligible if not non-existent.

Compared to the situation in the 1930s a survey made in the 1990s (with Samia al Naqar al Hadi) gives the general impression of an overall integration and of considerable economic and social success of the Hadramis in the Sudan. Thus the period from the 1930s until today seems to have brought further integration into the Sudanese society, a movement of Hadramis to the towns of Central Sudan, to engagement in new occupations, and marriage strategies both among themselves and with the Sudanese in ways that allow for a steady increase in numbers of the Hadrami community, not the stagnant one depicted by the British commissioner.

There are differences in the extent the Hadramis intermarried into the Sudanese society, and also the extent to which they in certain places maintain close ties among themselves as Hadramis. Generally however they show a history of integration, of involvement in the economic development of the Sudan, taking advantage of the possibilities opened up through the establishment of irrigated agriculture, of mechanised farming, and of opportunities offered by the Sudanese educational system. At the economic level, government intervention in the Red Sea area since the colonial period consisted mainly of sponsoring two agricultural schemes (Gash and Tokar), opening a number of mines in the region and construction of the railway (1920s) and tarmac road (1970s) linking the port with the interior of the country.

Hadramis have been part of all these developments. Mining in the Red Sea hills achieved little economic success and the small scale of investment and lack of the required technical skills have denied the local population any substantial job opportunities except for a few seasonal manual jobs. On the other hand the rail and road lines have opened up new possibilities in the transportation sector and in the needs of hotels and restaurants and other services. Important also are the two agricultural schemes, Tokar and Gash, in which the Hadramis could engage as not only scheme owners, but also as suppliers of the basic necessities to the various groups of people who flocked to the areas for employment. This history represents the major part of Ahmed Bajabr's story with which we started the chapter. The family histories collected confirm this general pattern. The Hadramis came to the Sudan through Suakin and later Port Sudan, then went on to work in farming in places like the Tokar and Gash Schemes, where first the Egyptians and later the British launched irrigated cotton farming. They invested in businesses like hotels and similar ventures in the expanding urban areas of Port Sudan, Omdurman and Khartoum and sent their children to schools and universities. These children later appeared as leading and highly respected professionals in the Sudan. Marriages were both within the Hadrami group and also within various Sudanese families. The early operators in Tokar married Beni Amer women, more established families later married into the riverine families. Hadrami identity in the Sudan seems to be without problems, and the maintenance of this identity did not create conflicts with other types of identities. They have integrated into the culture of Eastern Sudan, also influencing it through their prestige as Shafi'i Muslims, with an important history of Islamic teaching in their home areas in Hadramaut (Tarim etc.). Some of them joined the Sufi-movements of the Eastern Sudan, particularly the Khatmiyya. Furthermore, developments initiated by the British during the period of Anglo-Egyptian Sudan as well as by various governments in independent Sudan seem to have provided platforms on which the Hadramis could build careers in trade, in the professions and as leaders also in the opposition against the British (e.g. Bakhreeba, a trade union leader in the Gezira Tenants Union).

Also within cultural life we find Hadramis such as the poet Ahmed Jiritli, Elrayah Elaydarus, Abelaziz Alkabli, and later Hussein BaZaraa and Naji Elqudsi. During the 1990s, i.e. after the unification of the two Yemens, a new trend of opening up links with their home area in Hadramaut has developed. Several Hadrami families, or individual family members have decided to return to Hadramaut to work, start businesses and to start a life there.

Another type of Hadrami – "financial tycoon, global jihadist"

The second Hadrami in my story I have never met. Nor was he a lifelong resident in the Sudan. But he did live in Sudan at the time when I met Ahmad Bajabr in Mukalla. But as Ahmad represented a typial Hadrami living in Sudan, with a typical career as a small trader this other Hadrami was a financial tycoon, and his career as a global jihadist certainly made him a more famous representative of the diasporic world of which Ahmad was part. This Hadrami is Usama Bin Laden. Usama himself is a Hadrami born in the diaspora, namely in Saudi Arabia. His family comes from Wadi Du'an, one of the tributaries to the main Wadi Hadramaut, and his father moved to Saudi Arabia in the 1950s, where Usama was born in 1957.

As the main international "terrorist" the life of Usama Bin Laden is of course surrounded by myths and speculations, and I shall not engage in this mythmaking here. But it is possible to isolate certain features of Bin Laden's activities that show how he as a person, and his activities represent a different type of "diaspora" than that of Ahmed. While Ahmed Bajabr is the typical representative of a historical Hadrami diaspora in the Sudan, the story of Usama begins in the same diasporic world, but develops into the global, Muslim diaspora that we have seen unfold since the 1970s. This type of global, Islamic diaspora is increasingly defined against the Western world, interpreted as American imperial culture and Israeli aggression, but the same developments also have links to developments in the Sudan and the Horn of Africa (e.g. de Waal, ed., 2004).

We need therefore a discussion of those specific contexts in which Usama's activities should be placed in order to provide a comparative view of this diaspora compared to the diaspora of Ahmed Bajabr and the other Hadramis described in this chapter. We should also point out that in the history of Hadrami migration throughout the Indian Ocean we find several examples of Hadramis prominent in movements of resistance against Western traders and colonialists.

Usama then stands in a long line of individual Hadramis who have used their position in the diaspora to fight representatives of imperial and colonial powers. In Usama's case the understanding of the traditional Hadrami diaspora takes us part of the way in explaining how his particular story evolved. First of all, the migration of the Bin Laden family signifies the most recent historical wave of migration of Hadramis, to Saudi Arabia and the Gulf. Many of the families that ended up in Sudan followed the same route. The father developed links to the Royal House in Saudi Arabia and built himself an economic empire in the construction business. In this the Bin Laden family was a very successful, but not atypical example of Hadrami adaptations in Saudi Arabia.

But here Usama's life story takes a significant turn and must be interpreted against regional and global political events. Israel, the USA and the West make up one important context. From an initial restoration of Arab self-respect through the Yom Kippur war in 1973, the effects of the oil boom of the 1970s brought wealth to the conservative oil countries, allowing for the import of the latest technologies available, but also increased travel to the West, for leisure or education, as well as a local life style that many interpreted as a threat to Islam. This situation led to many types of tensions and reactions. In Saudi Arabia the assassination of King Feisal by a "Westernised" Prince is part of the picture. Anwar Sadat's flirting with the USA and Israel was proof of the same decadence. These developments were debated among young people in the Middle East, also in the Saudi universities where Usama studied. But there were also other political developments that helped form the career of Usama Bin Laden and others of his generation. Khomeini's Iranian revolution is one Islamic reaction to what went on in the Middle East during the 1970s. And the seizure of the Grand Mosque in Mecca in 1979 in order to "save Islam" brought new developments to the Saudi territory. Another shock came when the Soviet Union invaded Afghanistan, putting Muslims under Communist rule. And this event was actually what made Usama Bin Laden go to Afghanistan, to volunteer in the Afghan *jihad* against the invaders. This was also a period during which he maintained close links to the Royal House in Riyad. But as we know, this was to change and his fall-out with his father's old friends led to the loss of his Saudi citizenship.

It is at this point that the Sudan becomes of direct importance to our story. Sudan had recently, in 1989, been taken over by a new regime based on the Islamist groups around strong-man, Hassan Turabi, and the early years of the 1990s saw a phase in which radical Islamist policies were pursued, and in which an ideologically inspired policy dominated over a more realist one. Many examples of this policy can be seen within the Sudan itself. It was a period in which the regime pursued a *jihad* against the rebels in the South and in the Nuba Mountains, and also pursued an active Islamist social policy through "the comprehensive call" programme (*al da'wa al shamla*). The same ideological bent influenced Sudan's foreign policies and, against the advice of many, Turabi declared Sudan's support for Iraq and Saddam Hussein in 1991. This was of course a position that did not go down well in Riyad, and when the Saudi royal house broke their relations with Usama, he and Turabi shared a common enemy. But the alliance was pragmatic. In Khartoum Islamist policies were already in place with the new regime, and new visa regulations in 1990 opened up the country for Arab Islamists. But Usama certainly fitted into the wider agenda for Turabi's policies, an agenda in which Turabi sought to consolidate a position as a leading figure within the Islamists' camp. Usama could operate as part of Turabi's "universal framework for the Islamic movement", based on organsations such as "The Islamic Arab Peoples' Conference" (IAPC) and "Popular International Organisation" (PIO).

But while in Sudan Usama also followed his own agenda. During this period there had been a shift in Usama's thinking, away from a localized anti-Soviet resistance in Afghanistan to an increased emphasis on Islamic resistance both against the West and Westernised Muslim regimes such as the one in Riyad. With Usama now residing in Sudan, the international group of "Afghans" who had fought with him in Afghanistan had a place to go, and they could further develop their organization around their leader. Through the combination of Turabi's policies and Usama Bin Laden's intentions, the Sudan got further entangled in the type of Islamist policies that to an increasing degree also involved violence and terrorism. Usama's personal role is partly as a big trader involved in legal trade and also as a person involved in the activities that went on within various training camps in the Sudan. This combination of personal wealth and direct involvement in political and military activities gives a special profile to Usama Bin Laden's development in the 1990s. His personal wealth of course made him particularly important. One example is the role he played in the period following the collapse of the Bank of Credit and Commerce International (BCCI) in 1991. The collapse of this bank not only created an international financial scandal, but also threatened to reveal important financial structures of the militant Islamist groups since many of them used this bank for money laundering and financing of clandestine operations. After the fall of the bank there was a need to rebuild a financial system for Islamic organisations, and Usama Bin Laden was given the job by Turabi. In the Sudanese security and military-commercial complex Usama found allies that also controlled considerable wealth, and who also shared his visions. These networks operated together in Somalia in 1992, some motivated by a will to spread Islam in Africa, others motivated by their determination to stem American imperial intentions in the Horn of Africa. Whatever the reasons, in 1993 the Americans put the Sudan on their list of states that sponsored terrorism, a move inspired both by events in Somalia and also the bomb explosion in the World Trade Center that year that involved Islamists with links to Khartoum. The accumulated consequences of all this culminated in many ways with the failed attempt to assassinate the

Egyptian president, Husni Mubarak in Addis Ababa in June 1995. This event as well as Sudan's systematic support for Islamist opposition groups in the region made Sudan's neighbouring countries into enemies and further exposed Sudan's links to international terrorism. The situation was serious, and the regime in Khartoum sought to appease the Americans, first by offering Usama to the Americans to show that they did not harbour terrorists, later when the Americans declined, by expelling him from the Sudan in March 1996, allowing him to return to Afghanistan together with many of his followers. But the political crisis for the regime continued and could easily have ended with a total collapse had it not been for the regional consequences of the war that broke out between Eritrea and Ethiopia in 1998.

We shall not speculate on to what extent these structures were involved in the terrorist attacks on American embassies, naval ships and airlines, nor shall we speculate on possible links to Hadramaut and Yemen and to the terrorist attack on tourists in December 1998 in Abyan, or the attack on an American ship outside Aden, carried out by individuals that were said to come from Wadi Duan. The US government certainly thought there were links and directly punished both Afghanistan and the Sudan with missile attacks after the bombing of the US embassies in Kenya and Tanzania. Both countries were counted among the key enemies that had to be dealt with in the American counter-terrorism strategy of the 1990s. The 11 September attack in 2001 removed possible doubts the Americans might have had. The attack brought the terrorist war home to the USA and made clear that there existed an international network of militant Islamists among whom Bin Laden was playing a central role. Both Usama Bin Laden and al Qa'ida became household terms in the West. Bin Laden was now in Afghanistan and there was little doubt that al Qa'ida-type organisations were mushrooming, and that there had developed various links between militant groups, Islamic NGOs and some national governments. The Afghan guerillas had of course played a direct military role in Afghanistan, but were also active in Pakistan and Kashmir. Islamic NGOs had played central roles in Somalia, in the Balkans and in Chechniyya. Links to militant groups in the Phillipines and in Indonesia were also established and made visible through the Bali bombings. Similar developments occurred in Europe, most dramatically illustrated by the Madrid bombings. At the time of writing the Islamic groups operating in Iraq make up the most recent example of a globalised Muslim diaspora in a deadly battle with an Imperial enemy.

It is this contemporary reality that is of interest to our discussion here. It is interesting because it shows the ways in which several historical trends come together to form a new, globalized diaspora, formed around an ideology that put emphasis on the unity of all Muslims within the concept of *umma*, that the *umma* is under threat from non-Muslims and must be defended or must defend itself, and that in this defence all means are allowed. Whatever role Usama Bin Laden has played in this development, his role was not played because he was a Hadrami and belonged to the traditional Hadrami diaspora. Rather, Usama's career shows how that Hadrami diaspora was also part of a broader religious diaspora of Muslims. And this religious diaspora has always produced individuals that have stood out as leaders and spokesmen for the *umma*, some arguing for peaceful co-existence with non-Muslims, others encouraging more violent strategies. Usama's story is also part of this particular development, and his life can be seen as part of that long tradition of continuous Muslim commentary on the world around them, and on events in that world. Such commentaries may be directed at the Western world, but they may also represent a radical Islamic commentary on other, more moderate, Muslim forces that are blamed for no longer behaving like Muslims. Times and places of *jihads* and violent acts certainly vary, but the themes and rhetorics used to justify them show clear continuities. Continuities that are based on a long-lasting historical relationship between Muslim communities of which the Hadramis were a part, and Western Colonial and Imperial forces. Unfortunately this history is too often told from a Western perspective, a perspective that tends to hide important characteristics within the Muslim communities involved. One bias coming out of this is the stigmatization of all Muslims as terrorists, thus placing people like Ahmed Bajabr and Usama Bin Laden in the same group of anti-Western Muslims. It is a central argument in this paper that this is not the case. But in spite of the differences, both individuals belong to a religious and cultural tradition that unites them and that specific tradition is also part of our story. And it is this shared belonging to a tradition we have to grasp if we want to understand how Muslims who are as appalled by the violence as anybody else also seem to understand what the radical groups are trying to do. It is to the general outlining of such a tradition we shall now turn.

Muslim reactions to the Western world

Conventional Western historiography on Muslims in the eighteenth century has portrayed the period as a «dark age», with a focus on the disintegration of the Muslim gunpowder empires (Ottoman, Safavid and Mughal empires) and a general defeat to Western powers. The Western views of Islam came to dominate, portraying Muslim societies as stagnating, as barbaric and so on. Not surprisingly, the situation is more complex (see e.g. Watson 1983, Al-Hassan and Hill 1986 and Tibbets 1981 for counter-examples in the fields of agricultural innovations, scientific knowledge and technology and seafaring and navigation). And the Muslims were not passive observers of the new developments. John Voll (1994) points at four styles of Islamic reactions to the developments in the 18th century. One *pragmatic, adaptionist style* through which Muslims were able to exploit the new opportunities and settle in strange territories; a *conservative style*, in which they were trying to preserve earlier gains; a *fundamentalist style*, in which Muslims looked to the Quran for guidance and emerged as political activists upsetting social stability; the fourth style mentioned by Voll is *the personal acceptance of the religion*, focussed on local holy men, on the Mahdi or the Shi'a Imam as political representations. New theological interpretations that signalled a new fundamentalism were known, for example through the work of Ibn Taymiyyah. Such ideas were also transformed into political action, as represented by al-Wahhabiyy in Arabia. And we see a development of the social organisation of the basic unit in sufism, the *tariqah*. Better organized and more activist *tariqahs* appeared, and became vehicles of revival rather than adaptation. The general economic and political situation developed in ways that made these groups able to mobilize outside the religious platform too. Increased travelling brought these groups in contact with each other. Malay Muslims travelled regularly to Mecca, and it is an interesting fact that some of the leaders behind the Padri movements in Sumatra had been in Mecca during the time of the Wahhabi revolts. It is likely that there were cross-fertilisations between the different Muslim resistances to developments that made them feel marginalised. Scholars travelled widely, being part of transnational networks (Eickelman and Piscatori 1990), often centred on Mecca and Medina, because of the *hajj*, but other centres like Cairo and Damascus were also important. Religion also became the basis for the emergence of new local identities and we find the new types of religious scholars in alliance with new political leaders. The Hadramis were part of these developments and played a role in these networks. They had been travelling to the Gujarati coast and the Malabar coast of India for centuries, and during this period they also established themselves decisively in Southeast Asia. Hadrami families were intermarried with the families of the Sultans in many of the 18th century Malay States. They acted as religious leaders, political leaders and traders. In Indonesia, Hadramis played central roles in Acheh, and there were Hadrami imams in mosques on the islands of Bangka and Madura, in Pontianak in Borneo, in Ternate in the Moluccas as well as the more central towns on Java and Sumatra (Riddell 1997). Their appearance is linked to the central role of South Arabia and Aden during this period, both in trade and as a natural stopping point for pilgrims from the east and south. This was also the context for the early Hadrami migrations to Sudan.

The Muslim reactions to 20th century globalization tendencies are not very different from those mentioned above, but many contextual factors are different. One basic factor that changed in this century is the emergence of nation-states and of nationalism. Early in the century this process was conceived as a threat to Muslim global unity. The issue of the Ottoman Caliphate is one example. This was an attempt to restore the Ottoman sultan as a leader of the Muslims, and also a basis on which to call for a holy war during WWI. Both attempts failed. Rather than a revitalization of the Caliphate, the fight for independence promoted nationalism, and new organisations grew up based on national sentiments expressed in poetry and literature. With independence, reform and modernisation were embarked upon, under different banners such as Arab socialism, signifying a nationalism that was not Western. Egypt's Nasser, Algeria's Ben Bella and Indonesia's Sukarno are examples of such leaders. Muslim leaders usually went along with this development, although associations like the Muslim Brotherhood sprang up before WWII reacting to secularism. Muhamad Rashid Rida (1865–1935) was an important voice in this reaction against modernization. His journal al-Manar became widespread in the Muslim world. Rida argued against secularisation, and for a re-establishment of a Muslim state. Consequently he ended up a supporter of the Saudi state. The radical stance of the Muslim Brothers was just one further continuation of this line of thinking. Other, more moderate trends were also present in the debates. A series of journals and other publications are typical of this period, in which the new ideas appeared, placing Islam against the capitalist West, but also against communism and socialism. All this led to new types of ideological and political syntheses.

But the will for political nationalism was soon counteracted by yet another turn in the process of economic globalization. In the second half of the 20th century a greater geographical mobility of capital, combined with a crisis of the Fordist mass production led to what David Harvey (1989) called a period of "flexible accumulation". His analysis is not that capitalism is changing but that there are financial adaptations to solve the crisis capitalism is in.

But the dynamics within a capitalist system also have political repercussions. In terms of hegemonic power the 20th century is of course characterized by the rise of the USA as a new hegemonic power after the British. Two world wars and economic recession periods which helped destroy the gold standard on which the British financial dominance was built helped bring the USA to its dominant position. The regime of accumulation shifted to one in which multinational companies dominated the world markets. The context has shifted from colonialism to independent nations, with organisations such as the United Nations as foras in which such nation-states should supposedly work out their differences, instead of solving them by war. But the nation-states also became the main vehicle to continue work towards developing the world economy, although the USA dominated. The Bretton Woods institutions, the International Monetary Fund and the World Bank, are as much instruments for American hegemony as they are mediators between independent nation-states. World money was now part of state building developments. And the technological developments have continued, with oil bringing the Arab countries back into the global picture as oil producers, but also as victims of that position, within the current *Pax Americana*. The use of oil has provided a basis for further developments in transportation, with air traffic as the most significant example. Developments in synthetic products also belong to the picture, as does the lowering of production costs by making access to unused areas easier and cheaper. The more recent revolution in information technology is also a part of this, with the decentralization of production processes and the development of finance capital as a key resource. The focus on increased purchasing power in the world economy rather than investment in trade and production, created a crisis and showed the contradiction between the trans-national expansion of American corporate capital and the national basis of US world power. National governments' attempts at control led capital to seek new places which again increased the possibility of the Second and Third World states to pursue their own strategies. Some did succeed, such as the emerging economic giants in Asia, Japan, Hong Kong, Taiwan, Korea, Singapore, Malaysia and Indonesia. The rising importance of the East Asian nations implied that the military centre of the world, the USA, and the world's financial centre, Asia, no longer coincided. And the political consequences of this type of situation are now becoming evident. Not only through increased American willingness to use violence to achieve its strategic goals, but also through increased willingness by certain groups, such as al Qaida, to use violence to oppose these developments.

The attack on the Pentagon and the World Trade Center on 11 September 2001 will of course remain a landmark in modern world history. But so will 7 October 2001, when the Americans started bombing Afghanistan. The first event produced reactions around the world that were mostly humanitarian in tone. People were shocked, and no-one had any problem symphatising with the human suffering involved in the attack. The second event started a series of reactions that were political in nature. The American reaction brought us all back to the realm of power politics, and by that the understanding of 11 September also started to change. Let me illustrate with a few personal vignettes from the autumn of 2001, a period in which I visited Hadrami diasporic communities in Hyderabad in India, and in southern Thailand. Apart from the geopolitical threat of the attack to the region, there was the issue of what effects the bombing would have on the Hyderabadis, Muslims and Hindus alike. Increased tension, was the answer. Tension that led to Muslim riots in the Old City after prayers the following Friday, challenging the right of the Americans to kill innocent Muslims in retaliation for the 11 September victims, and hurt American pride and prestige. Tension that led Hindu newspapers to accuse the BJP-government of being soft and undecisive in their dealing with Muslim terrorists in India, referring to Kashmir of course, but also to the need to control Muslims in a city like Hyderabad, with its history of Muslim-Hindu riots. Ten days later I went to Thailand, and also spent time in the south, where I could observe how the Muslim Malay minority reacted. The criticism against the Americans was now more focussed. Being in Thailand, the expression of the public anger was more subdued than in Hyderabad. But the message was clear. In public rallies the arrogance of American foreign policy was pointed at as a root cause for the 11 September incident. Proof of who was behind the attacks was lacking, said the speaker. Why should anyone trust the Americans and their claims that they had such proof? Chances were that the Americans used Usama Bin Laden in order to make yet another step forward in their quest for total world domination in the post-1989 world. Would it not be a just cause for Muslims to resist such a quest for hegemony?

Conclusion

The above shows how two parties play into each other's hands, creating a situation in which public reactions may provide a basis for new confrontations. Much more could be said about this, but let me now return to my discussion of the Hadramis and conclude with two points. First, the aim has been to present a case of the Hadrami migration to the Horn of Africa, using the migration to the Sudan as an example. The migration of the Hadramis throughout the Indian Ocean region is well described in the literature and we know how the major migration links to India, Southeast Asia and Africa have been established (e.g. Freitag and Clarence-Smith, eds, 1997). In East Africa it is particularly the links to the Swahili coast that have received attention whereas Hadrami migrations to other areas in the region are less known. The Sudan is one of these less known places and my discussion is a contribution to throwing light on this particular chain of Hadrami migration, making up a Hadrami diaspora. Second, the aim has been to illustrate that the Hadrami diaspora is not a product of pre-defined socio-cultural elements. The diasporic communities under discussion cannot be described as a "mini-Hadramaut" in which the basic socio-cultural structures from the homeland are being played out in a new place. Rather, through the contextualization and comparison of the life stories of Ahmed Bajabr and Usama Bin Laden the aim has been to show the dynamic elements of the diaspora and the need to write the history of the diaspora and its links to processes beyond itself. Through such a discussion we see that the Hadrami diaspora cannot be explained as a special type of society, with a special type of social relationships. The relationships of the diaspora are themselves part of historical realities that shape them and make them unfold differently at different times. The history of the Hadramis in the Sudan is but one version of a broader Hadrami diaspora only hinted at in this paper. In the Sudan we see that a shared Arabic and Muslim language and culture made the Hadramis adapt well in northern Sudan, and we see that they are accepted and respected by the Sudanese for their contributions to what was taken as a Sudanese national culture. Our story thus seems to show a harmonious diaspora-homeland relationship. A long history of direct Sudanese involvement in the development of modern education in Hadramaut, with many Hadramis studying in the Sudan and many Sudanese teachers living in Hadramaut, adds further strength to these ties. But the story of Usama Bin Laden also opens up a different aspect of the Hadrami diaspora, as part of a Muslim diaspora in which links between the various diasporic communities are more important than links to the homeland, representing links not only focused at the maintenance of specific types of diasporic identities, or to promote a religious mission or trade interests, but also political links that are forged in opposition to forces that are seen by some as threats to the diaspora itself. In principle little is new in this. Similar links can be established in different historical periods. But it is of considerable interest to establish the ways the various links merge in special ways at particular historical moments and shape the overall development of the diaspora itself. We have seen that through the case of Usama Bin Laden and Hassan Turabi, the Sudan at a certain time came to play an important role in this complexity of inter-relationships. Through the Sudanese example we also see that the links between diaspora and the nation-state are not uni-directional, nor can they always be portrayed as forces opposed to each other. The alliance between Hassan Turabi and Usama Bin Laden represents an example of a type of diaspora-nation-state interaction that at a certain time was characterized by shared pragmatic interests, but that over time brought both parties to pursue strategies that made them drift apart. There was no shared ideological platform between the two to help keep the alliance together. Turabi was following policies that might be inspired by international Islamism but were shaped in a basic way by his position in Sudanese politics. Many local and national concerns that were important to Turabi's choice of action were of little importance to Bin Laden. When such national interests called for an adaptation to the American counter-terrorist policies Usama's days in the Sudan were numbered. And when competing factions within the Sudanese regime found that Turabi's political line was a threat to a more pragmatic line, Turabi himself was sidelined in the Sudanese power struggle in 2000. Usama for his part could never be bogged down by the interests of any one nation-state. He continued his increasingly global quest for Muslim reactions against his enemies by further mobilizing his *mujahidiin*. In this battle the Sudan no longer plays a significant part. The Sudanese peace negotiations and the international presence in the country make it unlikely that what went on in the country during the 1990s can happen again. But Usama continues, perhaps in person, and most certainly as a symbol. If we only look at the violent implications of Usama's acts he probably stands alone in Hadrami history, but if we see him as a case representing Muslim commentaries on the Western world, he fits into a pattern in which there have been many Muslims, and also some Hadramis before him (e.g. Bang 2003, Ho 2004, Manger, in press). They all represent individual cases of reaction and resistance that can only be understood if the dynamics of the diaspora are understood. Some of these dynamics relate to specific times and places, others are not localized in the same way. But they all belong to a history of migration that helped re-shape local as well as global geographies. The history of migration resulted in the emergence of diasporic communities that were tied together not only by ethnic origin but also by religious belonging. The religious dimensions have given the diaspora a global perspective that at certain historical moments has collided with another globalizing tendency, that of the spread of Western capitalism and political ambitions. Diaspora has been pitched against Empire, and the contemporary form of this conflict is but one example of a long tradition.

References

Abu Lughod, J., 1989, *Before European Hegemony: The World System AD. 1250–1350*. New York: Oxford Univesity Press.

Alpers, E., 1983. "Futa Benaadir: continuity and change in the traditional cotton textile industry of Southern Somalia, c. 1840–1980", in *Enterprises et Entrepreneurs en Afrique XIX et XX* (Tome I).

Anderson, B., 1991, *Imagined Communities: Reflections on the origin and spread of nationalism*. London: Verso.

Arrighi, G., 1999, *The Long Twentieth Century. Money, Power, and the Origin of Our Times*. London: Verso.

Bang, A., 2003, *Sufis and Scholars of the Sea. Family networks in East Africa, 1860–1925*. London: RoutledgeCurzon.

Barendse, R.J., 2000, "Trade and State in the Arabian Seas: A Survey from the Fifteenth to the Eighteenth Century", *Journal of World History* 11(2):173–225.

Bayly, C.A., 1989, *Imperial Meridian. The British Empire and the World, 1780–1830*. Harlow: Longman.

Bodansky, Y., 1999, *Bin Laden: The man who declared war on America*. Roseville, CA: Forum.

Bujra, A., 1971, *The Politics of Stratification. A Study of Political Change in a South Arabian Town*. Oxford: Clarendon Press.

Burckhardt, J.L., 1822/1978, *Travels in Nubia*. London: Murray.

Chaudhuri, K.N., 1990, *Asia before Europe. Economy and Civilization of the Indian Ocean from the Rise of Islam to 1750*. Cambridge: Cambridge University Press.

Clifford, J., 1994, "Diaspora", *Cultural Anthropology*, vol. 9, no. 3, pp. 302–338.

Curtin, P.D., 1984, *Cross-Cultural Trade in World History*. Cambridge: Cambridge University Press.

—, 2000, *The World and the West. The European Challange and the Overseas Response in the Age of Empire*. Cambridge: Cambridge University Press.

De Waal, A. (ed.), 2004, *Islamism and Its Enemies in the Horn of Africa*. London: Hurst.

Eaton, R.M., 1990, *Islamic History as Global History. Essays on Global and Comparative History*. Washington, DC: American Historical Association.

Edens, C., 1992, "Dynamics of Trade in the Ancient Mesopotamian 'World System'", *American Anthropologist* 94(1):118–139.

Eickelman, D. and J. Piscatori (eds), 1990, *Muslim Travellers. Pilgrimage, Migration, and the Religious Imagination*. London: Routledge.

Ewald, J. and W.G. Clarence-Smith, 1997, "The Economic Role of the Hadrami Diaspora in the Red Sea and Gulf of Aden, 1820s to 1930s", in Freitag, U. and W.G. Clarence-Smith (eds), *Hadrami Traders, Scholars and Statesmen in the Indian Ocean, 1750s–1960s*. Leiden: Brill.

Freitag, U., 1997, "Hadramis in International Politics c. 1750–1967", in Freitag, U. and W.G. Clarence-Smith (eds), *Hadrami Traders, Scholars, and Statesmen in the Indian Ocean, 1750s-1960s*. Leiden: Brill.

—, 2003, *Indian Ocean Migrants and State Formation in Hadramaut. Reforming the Homeland*. Leiden: Brill.

—, and W.G. Clarence-Smith (eds), *Hadrami Traders, Scholars and Statesmen in the Indian Ocean, 1750s–1960s*. Leiden: Brill.

Friedman, J., 1994, *Cultural Identity and Global Process*. London: Sage.

Gallagher, J. and R. Robinson, 1953, "The Imperialism of Free Trade", *The Economic History Review*, second series, vol. VI, no. 1, pp. 1–15.

Ghosh, A., 1992, *In an Antique Land*. New York: Vintage.

Harvey, D., 1989. *The Conditions of Postmodernity. An Inquiry into the Origin of Cultural Change*. Oxford: Blackwell.

Hill, R., 1959, *Egypt in the Sudan. 1820–1881*. London: Oxford University Press.

Ho, E., 2004, "Empire through Diasporic Eyes: A View from the Other Boat", *Society for Comparative Study of Society and History*, pp. 210–246.

Hobsbawm, E., 1979, *The Age of Capital 1848–1875*. New York: New American Library.

Hobson, J., 1938, *Imperialism. A study*. London: George Allen and Unwin.

Hofheinz, A., 1996, *Internalizing Islam. Shaykh Muhammad Majdhub, Scriptural Islam and Local Contexts in the Early Nineteenth-Century Sudan*. Dr.Philos – thesis, University of Bergen.

Huntington, S., 1993, "The Clash of Civilizations", *Foreign Affairs*, no. 3, pp. 22–49.

—, 1996, *The Clash of Civilizations and the Remaking of the World Order*. New York: Simon and Schuster.

Ingrams, H., 1937, *A Report on the Social, Economic and Political Conditions of the Hadramaut*. London: His Majesty's Stationery Office.

Manger, L. (ed.), 1984, *Trade and Traders in the Sudan*. Bergen: Bergen Studies in Social Anthropology.

—, et al. (eds), 1996, *Survival on Meagre Resources. Hadendowa Pastoralism in the Red Sea Hills*. Uppsala: The Nordic Africa Institute.

—, 1999, "Introduction", in Manger L. (ed.), *Muslim Diversity. Local Islam in a Global Context*. London: Curzon Press.

Manger, L., (in press), *Hadramis in an Indian Ocean World. Diasporic Identities in the Making*. Oxford: James Currey.

Perkin, K.J., 1993, *Port Sudan. The Evolution of a Colonial City*. Boulder, CO: Westview Press.

Reade, J. (ed.), 1996, *The Indian Ocean in Antiquity*. London: Kegan Paul.

Rhoden, D., 1970, "The Twentieth Century Decline in Suakin", *Sudan Notes and Records*, LI, 7–22.

Riddell, P.G., 1997, "Religious Links Between Hadhramaut and the Malay-Indonesian World, c. 1850–c. 1950", in. U. Freitag and W.G. Clarence-Smith (eds), *Hadhrami Traders, Scholars and Statesmen in the Indian Ocean, 1750s–1960s*. Leiden: Brill.

Risso, P., 1995, *Merchants and Faith. Muslim Commerce and Culture in the Indian Ocean*. Boulder, CO: Westview Press.

Scott, A. (ed.), 1997, *The Limits of Globalization. Cases and Arguments*. London: Routledge.

Talhami, G.H., 1979, *Suakin and Massawa under Egyptian Rule, 1865–1885*.

Tibbetts, G.R., 1981, *Arab Navigation in the Indian Ocean before the Coming of the Portuguese*. London: Royal Asiatic Society.

Vikør, K., 1999, "Jihad in West Africa: A Global Theme in a Regional Setting", in L. Manger (ed.), *Muslim Diversity. Local Islam in Global Contexts*. London: Curzon Press.

Voll, J., 1994, *Islam. Continuity and Change in the Modern World*. Syracuse: Syracuse University Press.

My Generation

ᶜUmar b. Aḥmad b. Sumayṭ (1886–1973): Inter-generational network transmission in a trans-oceanic Ḥaḍramī ᶜAlawī family, ca. 1925–1973

Anne K. Bang

Aḥmad b. Abī Bakr b. Sumayṭ (1861–1925) was born in Itsandraa, Grand Comore, in 1861. His father was an ᶜAlawī *sayid* immigrant who had arrived from Ḥaḍramawt in South Yemen. In his life-time, Aḥmad became a long term *qāḍī* (Islamic judge) of the British-Bū Saᶜīdī state of Zanzibar and author of several learned volumes. In the course of his life, Aḥmad also made three journeys to his ancestral homeland Ḥaḍramawt, and he sought learning in the Ḥijāz, Cairo and Istanbul. He soon became a leading figure in the ᶜAlawī Sufi brotherhood and a highly respected scholar both in East Africa and in Arabia. As a consequence he operated wide scholarly networks extending from the Comoro Islands to the Ḥijāz, and (at least at times) even further. Upon his death in 1925, the streets of Zanzibar Stone Town were packed with people following his bier to his funeral in the Friday Mosque in the Malindi Quarter, and verses of condolence poured in from the scholarly centres of Arabia.

Aḥmad's son ᶜUmar (1886–1973) followed very closely in his father's footsteps. So closely, in fact, that in the few pages I awarded ᶜUmar in my biography of his father, I simply put the heading "Tradition Continued."[1] ᶜUmar too, served many years as a *qāḍī* of Zanzibar, and – like his father – he made the repeated return trips to the ancestral homeland. Also like his father, ᶜUmar wrote a book about his experiences in Arabia, and he corresponded widely with fellow members of the ᶜAlawī order in Ḥaḍramawt and elsewhere.

So, it seems by all accounts to be a case of "tradition continued". The question which I did not address in *Sufis and Scholars of the Sea* was how

1. Bang, 2003:194–198.

exactly this tradition was continued? How did the son become immersed in the same networks as his father? Who were his correspondents and how were they related to his father's contacts? Did he directly "inherit" the links of his father or did he form his own? In short: How did inter-generational network transmission take place?

Another question that needs to be addressed is whether tradition continued unchanged or adapted to the upheavals of the 20th century which ᶜUmar lived through (World Wars, the Zanzibar Revolution, the Revolution of South Yemen). In other words: How did altered social and political circumstances affect the transmission and content of an established tradition?

The life of ᶜUmar b. Aḥmad b. Abī Bakr b. Sumayṭ (1886–1973): A circle of a century divided

The life story of ᶜUmar b. Sumayṭ forms a perfect circle. He was born in the Sumayṭ family house in Itsandraa, Grand Comore on 24 September 1886,[2] to a mother from a notable Comorian clan. Eighty-seven years later, he died in the same house and was buried next to his grand-father in the Sumayṭ family grave almost directly on the beach of Itsandraa. However, the years in between are far from circular; they contain all the political and religious developments of the 20th century, while at the same time showing a remarkable continuity in terms of religious tradition.

Being the oldest and most gifted of his father's son, ᶜUmar was destined to carry the Sumayṭ/ᶜAlawī tradition, as was the fashion of the ᶜAlawī *sādā* both in Ḥaḍramawt and in the Indian Ocean lands of the ᶜAlawī *maḥjar* (lands of migration). Viewing themselves as descendants of the Prophet Muḥammad and keepers of deeply rooted mystical secrets incorporated in the ᶜAlawī *ṭarīqa* (mystical path), the ᶜAlawī families were more prone than other Ḥaḍramī migrants to keeping up a close connection with the homeland. In addition, the ᶜAlawīs were in a better financial position to do so, maintaining worldly careers as successful, and often large-scale, traders.[3] Although con-

2. Ibrāhīm and ᶜAbbās, 1989:20. The date is here given in accordance with the date printed in the French passport ᶜUmar was issued towards the end of his life, reproduced by Ibrāhīm and ᶜAbbās. This date corresponds well with the rest of the chronology of the life of ᶜUmar's father. I am grateful to Chanfi Ahmad, Zentrum Moderner Orient in Berlin for providing me with a copy of this paper.

3. For a thorough depiction of the entrepreneurial efforts of Ḥaḍramīs and Ḥaḍramī ᶜAlawīs in the Indian Ocean, see the excellent study of U. Freitag, 2003. Although

crete sources are lacking, we may assume that the Sumayṭ family in Itsandraa were no exception. Amongst other things, they owned several dhows (ocean going lateen rigged boats) with which both the original migrant Abū Bakr and Aḥmad had sailed as traders. However, due to the unfortunate lack of sources, little is known about what exactly their cargos were, nor about who were their trading partners.

ᶜUmar spent most of his childhood in Zanzibar, where his father was working as *qāḍī* from 1888. According to the standard biographies,[4] he learnt the Quran from his father as well as the art of navigation and the world of East African trade winds.

At the age of eight, in 1311/1893–94, ᶜUmar was sent to stay with his father's uncle Ṭāhir b. ᶜAbd Allāh b. Sumayṭ – and his son ᶜAbd Allāh b. Ṭāhir, in turn – in the ancestral home in Shibām, Ḥaḍramawt. His stay lasted for about five years, according to ᶜUmar himself.[5] Chances are that he stayed on until 1898, when his father Aḥmad returned for a visit to Ḥaḍramawt and probably took ᶜUmar back with him to Zanzibar.

Zanzibar around the turn of the century had no lack of teachers to instruct a young man like ᶜUmar – both ᶜAlawīs and non-ᶜAlawīs. Whereas Ḥaḍramawt by that time had seen the emergence of organized religious education (in institutions called *ribāṭ*, pl.: *arbiṭāʾ*), Zanzibar religious education was organized along more traditional lines. One exception was the school run by ᶜAbd Allāh Bā Kathīr al-Kindī (1860/61–1925) – the closest student and disciple of ᶜUmar's father Aḥmad. This institution was spiritually closely connected to developments in Ḥaḍramawt, although not a direct replica.[6] However, the foremost hallmark of scholarship in Zanzibar was the inter-mingling of the various schools of Islam represented on the island – the foremost being the Shāfiᶜī-Sunnis and the ruling class of Omani or Omani-descendant Ibāḍīs.

---

the enterprises in East Africa in general yielded less capital surplus than in Southeast Asia, we can assume that families like the Sumayṭ had enough to move around coastal East Africa relatively freely.

4. Among them al-Mashhūr, Abū Bakr al-ᶜAdanī b. ᶜAlī b. Abī Bakr, 1412/1991–92; and Farsy, 1989.

5. ᶜUmar b. Aḥmad b. Sumayṭ, 1988:28.

6. In contrast to the al-Riyāḍ Mosque College in Lamu run by another ᶜAlawī, Ṣāliḥ b. ᶜAlawī Jamal al-Layl (1853–1936). For a closer discussion of the links between the scholarly institutions of Ḥaḍramawt and their counterparts in East Africa, see Bang, 2003.

Ḥaḍramawt revisited: Visit of ᶜUmar in 1911–1913

Then, around 1911, as a now mature 35-year old, ᶜUmar returned to Ḥaḍramawt, like his father before him in awe of the religious traditions upheld there: "I came to Sayun in 1911 and left it in 1913. It is the most fragrant of flowers and its men full of knowledge and righteousness."[7]

During his two years in Ḥaḍramawt, ᶜUmar performed all the rituals of the ᶜAlawī order (visitations to graves of the pious ancestors, the pilgrimage to the grave of the prophet Hūd, the initiation into the *ṭarīqa* by various representatives of ᶜAlawī families). He also studied diligently, primarily with his great-uncle Ṭāhir who for a long time was *qāḍī* of Shibām. With him, he read – again like his father before him – the works of al-Ghazālī, particularly the *Iḥyāʾ ᶜUlūm al-Dīn*, which was completed around 1100.[8] He was also reading the body of ᶜAlawī Sufi literature, such as the poetry of ᶜAbd Allāh b. ᶜAlawī al-Ḥaddād (1634–1719) and the commentaries by the latter's student, Aḥmad Zayn al-Ḥibshī (d. 1733). Last, but not least, ᶜUmar read some of the works of his father, including the *Manhal al-Wurrād*.[9]

In *al-Nafḥat al-Shadhdhiyya*, ᶜUmar gives a description of how he, at an early age, was literally placed into the network of ᶜAlawī scholars. Revisiting in 1912, he studied with ᶜAydarūs b. ᶜUmar al-Ḥibshī, one of the most central *shaykhs* (if not the most central) of the late 19th century ᶜAlawī *ṭarīqa*,[10] and was reminded of their first meeting:

> My first time in Shibām was in 1311/1893–94 when I was about eight years of age [...] I stayed with my cousin ᶜAbd Allāh b. Ṭāhir b. Sumayṭ and his father Ṭāhir who took me to see the venerable ᶜAydarūs b. ᶜUmar al-Ḥibshī. My uncle explained that I was the son of Aḥmad b. Abī Bakr b. Sumayṭ, Ṣāḥib of Sawāḥil. He (ᶜAydarūs) took me on his lap [bayna yadihi – literally: between his hands] and said that he hoped I would come back and see him later, God willing [...]. I did see him again during my second stay in Shibām in 1331/1912–1913, and under his supervision I read: [list of titles continues].[11]

Significantly, ᶜUmar's narrative is filled not only by the great shaykhs of Ḥaḍramawt, but also by diaspora ᶜAlawīs from other Indian Ocean lands who

7. ᶜUmar b. Sumayṭ, 1988:23.

8. ᶜUmar b. Sumayṭ, 1988:32.

9. Aḥmad b. Abī Bakr b. Sumayṭ, 1315/1897–98.

10. ᶜAydarūs b. ᶜUmar al-Ḥibshī was also one of the most central shaykhs for ᶜUmar's father Aḥmad during the latter's studies in Ḥaḍramawt.

11. ᶜUmar b. Sumayṭ, 1988:28.

converged for shorter or longer stays in Ḥaḍramawt – among them his own relatives. During his stay in Shibām, for example, Muḥammad b. ᶜAbd Allāh b. Ṭāhir b. Sumayṭ from Java arrived, and according to ᶜUmar he was thus put in touch with the Far East branch of the family and with the great *sādā* there.[12]

In December 1912, Ṭāhir died in Shibām. Some time in 1913, ᶜUmar left Ḥaḍramawt, and travelled (possibly by way of the Ḥijāz) to the family home in Itsandraa, where he was to take care of business and possibly also of his mother who seems to have spent most of her life there. ᶜUmar's sister Nuru[13] also lived in Grand Comore, and although it is not known, it is possible that ᶜUmar too had a Comorian wife.

Death of his father, return to the Comoro Islands and onwards to Madagascar: 1925–1936

What we do know is that ᶜUmar returned to Zanzibar around 1923 to "rejoice in the presence of my father and of Shaykh ᶜAbd Allāh Bā Kathīr for a while".[14] At this point, ᶜUmar was approaching 40 years of age, was well educated and travelled and had carried the responsibilities of looking after the family in the Comoros. He was also well immersed in the trans-oceanic network of ᶜAlawī-Ḥaḍramī connections, having spent two prolonged periods in the Ḥaḍramawt. He had fulfilled the ᶜAlawī ideal of "knowing his origins" and, implicitly, the religion of his ancestors. ᶜUmar had, by all accounts, become a traditional ᶜAlawī scholar and trader, a typical representative of the class of his father and grandfather.

This is also evident in the final *ijāza* (certificate) and *waṣiyya* (spiritual will) which ᶜUmar received from his father in 1923. Here, the father hands over to his son the ways of the ᶜAlawīs, their literature and rituals, but also information on more worldly matters.[15] The day after his initiation by his father, ᶜUmar left for Grand Comore. He received the actual text of the *ijāza* by

12. ᶜUmar b. Sumayṭ 1988:58.

13. The presence of Nuru in Itsandraa is known due to her grave near the family house (personal observation, 1998). She does not seem to have accompanied either her father or brother to Zanzibar, a fact which might indicate that she was older than ᶜUmar. Later, however, she came to Zanizbar on at least one occasion, to celebrate the wedding of ᶜUmar's granddaugher in 1952. See ZA-AB26/1.

14. ᶜUmar b. Sumayṭ, 1988:111.

15. On the ceremony where ᶜUmar was initiated by his father, see Bang, 2003:188. For the content of the *ijāza*, see op.cit. throughout.

post. Two years later, by telegraph, he received the message about his father's death on 7 May 1925.

ᶜUmar then returned to Zanzibar to settle affairs there – amongst others the division of the family house in Malindi between himself and his brother Abū Bakr. He did not stay long – about one year, according to family history – but long enough to wreak havoc with his business in the Comoros. For reasons unknown, ᶜUmar returned to Grand Comore to find himself essentially bankrupt.

He then proceeded to find new trade grounds in Diego Suarez in northern Madagascar, probably some time in 1926.[16] It is not quite clear how long he stayed there – two years, possibly more, according to family history.[17] What is certain is that the choice of location was not random. Growing up in Grand Comore and later in Zanzibar, ᶜUmar was familiar with several fellow ᶜAlawīs who had made Madagascar their home. Among these were several members of the Jamal al-Layl clan, including the poet Abū ʾl-Ḥasan b. Aḥmad Jamal al-Layl (1888–1959) who was born in Bukini, Madagascar.[18] He settled on Zanzibar at an early age, where he attached himself to the teaching of ᶜAbd Allāh BāKathīr – the closest disciple of ᶜUmar's father. We can thus safely assume that he was well known to ᶜUmar, even before the latter's departure for Madagascar.

Qāḍī of Zanzibar and Officer of the Colonial State: 1936–1960

ᶜUmar returned to Zanzibar only in 1936, when he was called by the British administration to fill the vacancy of a *qāḍīship* in Pemba. In 1938, he was appointed *qāḍī* of Zanzibar after Shaykh Ṭāhir b. Abī Bakr al-Amawī who had retired. In 1943, he was given the title Chief Qāḍī, which he held until his retirement in 1960. Like his father before him, ᶜUmar heard cases in the Zanzibar High Court, where he would preside with one Ibāḍī *qāḍī* by his side as well as a British judge. Also like his father, it fell to the Chief *Qāḍī* to be part of the Waqf Commission and to advise the British administrators on

16. Ṭāhir Muḥammad ᶜAlawī, p.3.

17. The only known certain date of ᶜUmar's stay in Diego Suarez, can be gathered from two letters from ᶜUmar to Aḥmad b. Ṭāhir Jamal al-Layl (Qāḍī of Itsandraa), dated 23 August and 6 October 1929 – both written in Diego Suarez. Letters reproduced in Ibrāhīm and ᶜAbbās, 1989:64–65.

18. Farsy/Pouwels, 1989:164–166. This Abū ʾl-Ḥasan Jamal al-Layl is not to be confused with the man with the same name in Moroni, known as Mwinyi Bahasani (1801–1883). See following note.

matters relating to *waqf*. In addition, the Chief Qāḍī was expected to advise colonial officers on all kinds of questions that might arise.[19] Finally, as Chief Qāḍī he also led prayer on ceremonial occasions, such as the ᶜĪd and national holidays.

However, there are important differences in the two experiences of Aḥmad and ᶜUmar. While the Zanzibar colonial corps still consisted of a relatively small group of people in the time of Aḥmad b. Sumayṭ, by the time ᶜUmar became Chief *Qāḍī* it had expanded into a proper colonial bureaucracy. This also meant that the work procedures in court were highly formalized, as were the meetings of the Waqf Commission. However, it seems that ᶜUmar, again like his father, managed the balance between being a colonial employee and an esteemed Sufi *shaykh* of the ᶜAlawī (and general) community of Zanzibar.

From 1936 to 1960, ᶜUmar served continuously as *qāḍī* and advisor to the colonial government, with the exception of his leave periods. At least three of these were spent travelling. In 1951–52, he returned for a third period in Ḥaḍramawt.[20] In June 1956, and again in 1958, ᶜUmar went on the Ḥājj to Mecca.[21] While there, he also undertook inquiries on matters pertaining to the Waqf Commission of Zanzibar, especially on the issues of *waqf* transfers from Zanzibar earmarked for the poor of the Ḥaramayn.[22]

The succession of ᶜUmar: The emergence of Abdallah Saleh Farsy

By mid-1959, ᶜUmar was again up for leave. He was also 73 years old and long since due for retirement. The Judicial Department granted him retirement from 1 January 1960 and were subsequently left with the task of finding his

19. An entire file in the Zanzibar Archives is filled with the opinions of ᶜUmar b. Sumayṭ and his Ibāḍī counterpart on questions such as the legality of music at official functions, the possibility for a woman to delay the mourning period to complete exams at nursing school, how long a graveyard must remain untouched before the land can be put to other purposes etc. ZA-HC27/37.

20. Bang, 2003:195.

21. ZA-HD10/5. File relating to *waqf* transfers from Zanzinar to Mecca. On the second occasion, Umar was accompanied by his former student and fellow Comorian-born ᶜAlawī, Sayyid Omar Abdallah (known as Mwinyi Baraka: 1918–1988), then the newly appointed leader of the Muslim Academy of Zanzibar and later distinguished intellectual of both Islamic and Western scholarship. See Muhamad Bakari, 2003. See also Saad Swaleh Yahya (ed.), 1998.

22. ZA-HD10/5.

replacement.[23] Even upon repeated prompting, ᶜUmar did not offer any suggestions as to his successor. Eventually, the position was simply advertised in the newspapers and journals of Zanzibar, Tanganyika and Kenya, with a detailed job description and the salary and extras attached to the position. By January 1960, four applications had been received, the most prominent being that of Abdallah Saleh Farsy, then Headmaster of the Teacher's Training College in Zanzibar and well-known orator in several mosques. Again, ᶜUmar (at least officially and in writing) did not volunteer any preferences, and the *qāḍīship* passed to Farsy as a matter of straightforward colonial appointment procedures.[24]

Revolution: Exile to the ancestral home

Upon the eve of the Zanzibar revolution, ᶜUmar and his family were still living in Zanzibar. The family by that time consisted of his grand-daughter, her husband and their four children. He owned the family house in Malindi as well as a substantial *shamba* in Sharif Musa north of town, and another in Kiungani towards the south.[25]

Upon the revolution, all his *shamba* property was nationalized, but the family was unharmed and kept the stone house in town. According to oral information,[26] ᶜUmar and his retinue did not leave Zanzibar immediately upon the revolution. Reportedly, some weeks after the initial violence, one of the revolutionaries (the anecdote exists in several different versions and names several different individuals) went into the Malindi quarter with a view to humiliating the mainly Arab population there. All males were commanded to strip to their underwear and parade the streets. The post-revolution president Karume himself passed by and recognized ᶜUmar standing there with the others. Upon Karume's astonished outcry as to the state of the

23. ZA-AO1/190

24. Although Farsy took over ᶜUmar's position as a matter of regular employment procedure, this did not mean that he immediately took over ᶜUmar's position in popular esteem. According to oral tradition, on leading his first Friday prayers as Chief Qāḍī, Farsy kneeled on ᶜUmar's prayer carpet in the Malindi Juma Mosque. At this point, the congregation reacted and Farsy had to lead prayer on a regular mat. Oral information, Yunus Sameja, Zanzibar, February 2003.

25. Oral information, Maalim Muhammad Idris Muhammad Saleh, Zanzibar, February 2004.

26. Various informants, Zanzibar, August 2003 and February 2004. As the anecdote exists in several versions I have chosen here to give the least embellished one.

esteemed *shaykh*, ᶜUmar declared himself a loyal citizen of Zanzibar; one who did as commanded by the powers leading it at all times. Karume immediately ordered ᶜUmar to put on his customary ᶜAlawī garb and white headcloth.

About a year after this episode – in 1965 – the Sumayṭs travelled via Mombasa to Aden never to return to Zanzibar. Instead, the family settled in al-Shiḥr, under British protection.

In July 1967, at the age of 81, ᶜUmar returned to Ḥaḍramawt. [27] On this last visit, he was escorted by Sayyid Muḥammad b. ᶜAlawī BūNumay,[28] the husband of his granddaughter, as well as other members of the BūNumay clan. According to the very detailed account of the journey, ᶜUmar arrived in al-Ghurfa on Friday 13 Rabīᶜ II/21 July 1967, just as people were leaving Jumᶜa prayers. For the rest of his journey to Shibām, Sayʾūn and Tarīm, ᶜUmar was escorted by *sāda*, *shaykh*s and scholars, and his week in the *wādī* reads like a series of readings of *fātiḥa*s and Quranic readings in various locations.

Upon leaving Zanzibar ᶜUmar had taken with him the library collected by his father and himself. This collection was now deposited with the al-Kāf Library in Tarīm.[29]

The account of ᶜUmar's last visit to Ḥaḍramawt, although clearly written in retrospect, is filled to the brim with the names that were part of his heritage: the Āl al-Ḥibshī gathered around him, the Āl al-ᶜAṭṭās, Āl al-Saqqāf, the Jamal al-Layls, the Āl Shaykh Abū Bakr b. Sālim as well as the Sumayṭ family itself. Interestingly, in light of family networking, it is noteworthy that ᶜUmar also took the time to visit female members of the Sumayṭ family married off to other *sāda* families.[30]

---

27. Muḥammad Jibrān b. Awaḍ Jibrān, *Riḥla al-Ḥabīb ᶜUmar ilā al-Shiḥr wa-Ḥaḍramawt* 1387, MS, in Sumayṭ family possession. The MS is 18 pages and covers in great detail the 8 days from 21 July-29 July 1967 which ᶜUmar spent touring Wādī Ḥaḍramawt. It accounts for all the people he met, the graves he visited, the prayers said, the fātiḥas read, with whom, where and when.

28. Muḥammad Jibrān b. Awaḍ Jibrān, *Riḥla al-Ḥabīb ᶜUmar*, 1. ᶜUmar had one daughter, Shaykha. She died in childbirth, and her daughter was raised in ᶜUmar's household. In time, she was married to Sayyid Muḥammad b. ᶜAlawī BūNumay (in Kiswahili popularly pronounced Bunumei). Both he and his wife were among those who made the move from Zanzibar to Aden. His son, in turn, escorted the elderly ᶜUmar on the last tour of Ḥaḍramawt, together with another, unidentified member of the BūNumay clan named Aḥmad b. Muḥammad b. ᶜAlawī BūNumay. On the BūNumay family: oral information, Yunus Sameja, Zanzibar, July 2003.

29. Oral information, Maalim Muhammad Idris Muhammad Saleh, Zanzibar, February 2004.

30. Muḥammad Jibrān b. Awaḍ Jibrān, p.7.

Full circle: Grand Comore encore

In the same year, and probably before November 1967 when the People's Republic of Southern Yemen was announced, the Sumayṭ family headed towards the Comoros. This time, they returned to Ngazīja and the family home in Itsandraa. ᶜUmar was offered the chief *Qāḍīship* of Ngazīja, and the family settled again in the same place where ᶜUmar was born some 80 years before. He was also granted a French passport and citizenship.[31] From the people, ᶜUmar was offered a *shamba* on the hillside above Itsandaa, where he recited prayers and where *mawlid*s were held according to the ᶜAlawī tradition.

ᶜUmar b. Aḥmad b. Abī Bakr b. Sumayṭ died in the family house in 1973. He was buried in the family *qubbah*, next to his grandfather, the original Ḥaḍramī migrant Abū Bakr.

After his death, ᶜUmar's image was printed on the 10,000 Franc bill of the new republic of the Comoro Islands.[32] He was remembered there – as in Ḥaḍramawt, and Zanzibar – as a scholar, writer and poet, distinguished *qāḍī* and learned man of the ᶜAlawī *ṭarīqa*.

In the network: Network over generations

The above outline of the life of ᶜUmar again demonstrates the case of "tradition continued". In effect, he followed in his father's footsteps concerning education, employment and travel patterns. Also, like his father, he lived a life very much in a network – a network of like-minded scholars, *qāḍīs* and – not least – traders, although this point is the most difficult to demonstrate with reference to sources. The task here is to look more closely into the network and examine how it was established and how it relates to the network operated by his father.

The family network: Ḥaḍramawt and the Comoros

The most immediate network of ᶜUmar – like his father's – was that of the Sumayṭ family itself. Here, we find that ᶜUmar maintained close contact, first by staying with his father's uncle Ṭāhir in Shibām, and on later occasions with the latter's son ᶜAbd Allāh. Contact with the family in Ḥaḍramawt was kept up throughout ᶜUmar's life, as is evidenced by his final tour of the region

31. Ibrāhīm and ᶜAbbās, 1989:20.

32. Personal observation, Grand Comore, 1998.

in 1967, at which time he – as mentioned above – also made a point of visiting female members of the family.

The continued contact with the family in Grand Comore is also noteworthy, particularly since this side mostly involved the female side of the family: ᶜUmar's mother, his sister and – later – his granddaughter. The tendency of the Comorian female Sumayṭs not to leave Ngazīja, may have to do with the native Comorian emphasis on *inya* – female lineage. We may here speculate that ᶜUmar's mother, being of a notable Comorian family, may have stayed on in Ngazīja as a guarantor for the property deriving from her side of the family.

All in all, the immediate family network was the one that was – naturally – most obviously inherited. The noticeable point is ᶜUmar's life-long upkeep of family contacts, both in the Comoros and in Ḥaḍramawt. In doing so, he kept within the tradition of the ᶜAlawīs, which strongly emphasizes the bloodline, the family and the ancestors.

Sufi Networks: The ṭarīqa ᶜAlawīyya and the Shādhiliyya

As a shaykh of the ᶜAlawī *ṭarīqa*, ᶜUmar – again like his father – sought out the shaykhs and *ᶜulamāʾ* of the order, in Ḥaḍramawt and in East Africa. He was, as is emphatically stated in his biographies, a follower of the *ṭarīqa* of his ancestors, the *sāda* ᶜAlawīyya. However, he also seems to have been very close to the Shādhiliyya order, especially the branch of the order spreading in the Comoro Islands. Given that the ᶜAlawīyya and Shādhiliyya have a common origin,[33] this is neither surprising nor unusual. ᶜUmar's close relations to the Comoro branch of the Shādhiliyya, seem to have been based on personal contacts, especially with the followers of the man who brought the order to the islands, Muḥammad b. ᶜAbd Allāh al-Maᶜrūf (1853–1905). The latter was, like ᶜUmar, a Ḥaḍramī *sayyid* by origin (of the Āl Shaykh Abī Bakr b. Sālim), but in contrast to ᶜUmar, his family presence on the coast stretched several generations back.

During his life, ᶜUmar b. Sumayṭ was an active participant in the Shādhiliyya order of the Comoros and Zanzibar, attending their *dhikr* ses-

33. For a discussion of the common origin of the two orders and the emergence of the ᶜAlawīyya, see Bang, 2003:13–15.

sions on a regular basis.[34] He contributed a number of poems and *awrād* to the rituals of the order, among them a tribute to al-Maᶜrūf.[35]

In this, ᶜUmar differs slightly from his father (or at least, from what is known about his father). Clearly, Aḥmad too, had close relations with the Shādhliyya, but he is not known to have been a participant, nor to have contributed texts. The difference is most likely to be related to personal contacts. ᶜUmar did spend more time than his father in Grand Comore, and his personal network in that relatively small place may have brought him closer to the Shādhliyya than he would have been in, say, Zanzibar.

The scholarly network: Ḥaḍramawt and East Africa

What is available of the correspondence of ᶜUmar, reveals something about the extent and nature of the network he functioned within. Although the correspondence is fragmented, it still demonstrates a lifelong contact with fellow ᶜAlawī scholars in Ḥaḍramawt. One of his correspondents was Sālim b. Ḥafīẓ b. ᶜAbd Allāh b. Shaykh Abī Bakr b. Sālim,[36] resident of Tarīm and also a student of the *Ribāt* (Religious College) of that city. In the surviving letters,[37] Sālim b. Ḥafīẓ reports about news from Tarīm (scholars who had passed away, new arrivals from overseas) and cites poetry and *awrād* to be recited on specific occasions.

We can here only assume that the contacts established during ᶜUmar's visits were kept up throughout his life by means of letters and messages passed on with other travellers. Much of this correspodence is religious or scholarly in content (recitals, poetry, greetings on religious holidays), but there is also an element of simply keeping up with news from the ancestral homeland.

In this, we simply do not know how ᶜUmar's pattern of keeping contact with Ḥaḍramawt differed from that of his father – given that none of Aḥmad's correspondence is to be found. What we can assume is that given the development of mailing systems and – not least – the incorporation of

34. Personal communication, Moroni, Grand Comore, 1997.

35. Nūr al-Dīn b. Ḥusayn b. Maḥmūd (ed.), 1408/1987.

36. Sālim b. Ḥafīẓ b. ᶜAbd Allāh b. Shaykh Abī Bakr b. Sālim d. 1959; see al-Mashhūr, 1984:454–456. Sālim b. Ḥafīẓ was a student of all the shaykhs who had also been the teachers of ᶜUmar's father, including ᶜAlī b. Muḥammad al-Ḥibshī, Aḥmad b. Ḥasan al-ᶜAṭṭās and ᶜAbd al-Raḥmān al-Mashhūr.

37. 3 letters to ᶜUmar b. Sumayṭ from Sālim b. Ḥafīẓ. 1) undated (approx 1940). 2) 4 Muḥarram 1362/11 January 1943. 3) 14 Dhū ʾl-Ḥijja 1360/2 January 1942. Collection of letters to ᶜUmar b. Sumayṭ.

Ḥaḍramawt into the British colony of Aden, contacts in the form of letters and messages were more frequent in the time of ᶜUmar. In other words: the network could be kept up on a more regular basis.

Professional networking: Careers in the colonial system and the traditional network

An example of how the network of Ḥaḍramī ᶜAlawīs functioned in professional terms is demonstrated by a case dating from 1951, whereby the British Colonial Authorities were seeking an appropriate *qāḍī* for the Kenya Northern Territory.[38] The British Judicial representative in Mombasa wrote to his counterpart Mr. Pakenham in Zanzibar and suggested Shaykh Khalifa Muhammad b. Hemed of Kajificheni, Zanzibar as a suitable candidate. He would, however, like Pakenham to confer with chief *qāḍī* of Zanzibar and come up with alternative suggestions.

The matter rested a while as the Chief *Qāḍī*, ᶜUmar b. Sumayṭ was on leave. Upon his return, Pakenham immediately discussed the matter with him, and ᶜUmar responded by suggesting a "more suitable" candidate. The name ᶜUmar suggested was ᶜAlawī b. ᶜAbd al-Wahhāb Jamal al-Layl. A fellow ᶜAlawī of Ḥaḍramī-Comorian origin, ᶜAlawī Jamal al-Layl (1902–1960) was also the grandson of Abū ᵓl-Ḥasan Jamal al-Layl (known as Mwinyi Bahasani: 1801–1833).[39] The latter had taken over the education and care of ᶜUmar's father Aḥmad following the death of the latter's father Abū Bakr in 1874.[40] Having arrived in Zanzibar at a young age with his father, ᶜAlawī was now appointed *qāḍī* on the suggestion of the son of his grandfather's disciple.

In the network in the 20th century: ᶜUmar b. Sumayṭ versus his father

ᶜUmar's father Aḥmad lived through changing times – from the era of BūSaᶜīdī rule to that of the British Protectorate. He also lived in the era when Sufi orders (in East Africa) came to be new vehicles for social organization and true mass movements. However, his son must be said to have lived in

38. ZA-AK1/105.

39. Farsy/Pouwels, 1989:112. See also Maalim Muhammad Idris Muhammad Saleh. On Mwinyi Bahasani, see Farsy/Pouwels, 1989:150.

40. Bang, 2003:51.

an era of even more upheaval, both from the point of view of intellectual thought in the Islamic world and in the political arena.

ᶜUmar b. Sumayṭ as a Muslim intellectual in the colonial era: Tradition and change

The word *muṣliḥ* (reformer) was never used in contemporary descriptions of Aḥmad, although some of his activities clearly would qualify for such a label. His son ᶜUmar, on the other hand, has occasionally been described as a "reformer" – at least in retrospective accounts. Both father and son were most frequently described as "scholars" – learned and pious men and righteous *qāḍīs*. The overall image is that of traditionalism, traditionalism that is linked to the Ḥaḍramī-ᶜAlawī ideals of reform and renewal as instituted by the 17th century scholars of the order.[41]

Clearly, the intellectual position of ᶜUmar was in many ways directly "inherited" from his father, as evidenced by ᶜUmar's own emphasis on the spiritual will left to him by his father. Being sent to Ḥaḍramawt at an early age, he was deliberately (and, as described above, at times even literally) inserted into a scholarly environment for grooming into a particular worldview and a particular attitude towards Islamic scholarship. ᶜUmar was, in short, "placed" into the network that his father before him had sought out on the advice of *his* father.

It is also noticeable that ᶜUmar – like his father – formed a life long career within the British colonial system of Zanzibar, and presumably also personal contacts with fellow British employees, for example at the courts or in the Wakf Commission.

This does not mean, however, that ᶜUmar remained solely within the same colonial framework as his father. One noticeable difference is ᶜUmar's stronger connection to French colonial authorities in the Comoros. While Aḥmad seems to have had little interaction with colonial Grand Comore, ᶜUmar remained closely in touch – as demonstrated by the invitation to become Chief Qāḍī towards the end of his life.

ᶜUmar b. Sumayṭ: Cosmopolitanism in the era of race and ethnicity

On the whole, ᶜUmar's stronger connection with the Comoros is the most noticeable difference. This may have to do with developments in Zanzibar

41. For a discussion of the question of "reform" in the ᶜAlawīyya order, see Bang 2003, Ch. 7.

in the early and mid-20th century, whereby the community tended to be organized along lines of origin. As Laura Fair has demonstrated, much of this emphasis on where people came from (literally, *where people arrived from*) can be traced to the British colonial urge to organize the heterogenous Zanzibari community into comprehensive classification segments.[42] The matter of definition was not only cultural, but implied – as Fair has described – access to political representation as well as to food rations and employment.

The Comorian Association (founded 1911, re-formed 1924) was one result of this development. Immigrants from the Comoros (and their decendants) were now organized along entirely new lines. In other words, ᶜUmar was, to a much stronger degree than his father, living in an environment that encouraged definition according to organizational lines.

Although ᶜUmar – like his father – was termed "Arab" in official British colonial parlance, this did not mean that he was unaware of, or irrelevant to, the Comorian Association. In fact, his prestige – and that of his father – is referred to by Ibuni Saleh[43] in his history of the Comorians in Zanzibar in an effort to raise the status of the Comorians from "African" to "Arab" classification.

The mere presence of a body such as the Comorian Association, as well as the persistent emphasis on origin, may have drawn ᶜUmar more closely to the Comorian community than was the case with his father.

Having said this, there is little evidence that ᶜUmar ever made the step towards self-identification along the "racial" or "ethnic" lines imposed by colonial authorities. Like his father, his primary belonging lay in the bloodline of the Prophet Muḥammad, as brought onwards in time by the ᶜAlawī *ṭarīqa*. Being rooted in the genealogical line, this pattern of self-identification laid little emphasis on place of origin, physical features or even language (except that Arabic remained the preferred one, if not the one regularly spoken). As such, there is every reason to assume ᶜUmar b. Sumayṭ remained an Arabic- and Swahili-speaking cosmopolite in an era that emphasized belonging on entirely different lines.

42. Fair, 2001.

43. Saleh, 1936.

ᶜUmar b. Sumayṭ: ᶜAlawī sayyid and Islamic scholar in the era of the nation state

Contrary to his father, ᶜUmar b. Sumayṭ lived to see the emergence of his homelands (Zanzibar, Ḥaḍramawt and – almost – the Comoro Islands) as independent nations. By all accounts, none were particularly joyful moments for his family and group of followers. Contrary to the Empire (be it British or French), the nation state demanded full identification – a sense of belonging that underpinned the very idea of the concept. This idea must have been – and still is – problematic to the Islamic scholar of ᶜAlawī origin. Firstly, the idea of the division of the lands of Islam into political entities, may have been problematic to a scholar so traditionally inclined as ᶜUmar b. Sumayṭ. There is no evidence that he ever voiced any opinion on the issue of Zanzibari political developments, nor that he maintained any particular contact with organizations such as the Muslim Brotherhood in Egypt or like-minded groups.

Secondly, for a third-generation immigrant – immigrated via two locations – the concept of full identification with one nation state homeland must have been problematic. In this, he was not alone. The process whereby the ᶜAlawī *sāda* – formerly one network of migrants across the Indian Ocean (and the Islamic world in general) – were to be transformed into Comorian *sāda*, Yemeni *sāda* and Tanzanian *sāda*, is still ongoing. ᶜUmar b. Sumayṭ belonged, perhaps, to the last generation who spent a lifetime simply describing themselves as ᶜAlawī *sāda*.

References and Sources

Unprinted sources

Zanzibar National Archives Collection of letters

Letters to ᶜUmar b. Aḥmad b. Sumayṭ. Handwritten, 14 letters dated 1908–1962. In Sumayṭ family possession.

Ḥāj Ḥasan Ibrāhīm and Sayyid ᶜAbd Allāh Sayyid ᶜAbbās, *Al-Ḥabīb ᶜUmar b. Aḥmad b. Sumayṭ. Al-Murabbī wa-l-Muṣliḥ*, paper prepared for diploma at the Ecole Nationale d'Enseignement Superieur, Moroni, Grand Comore, 1989.

Muḥammad Jibrān b. Awaḍ Jibrān, *Riḥla al-Ḥabīb ᶜUmar ilā al-Shiḥr wa-Ḥaḍramawt 1387*, MS, 18 pages, in Sumayṭ family possession.

Nn, *Nubdha min ḥayāt al-Imām al-ᶜĀrif bi-ᵓllāh ᶜUmar b. Aḥmad b. Abī Bakr b. Sumayṭ*, MS, ND.

Ṭāhir Muḥammad ᶜAlawī, *Tarjama ᶜUmar b. Aḥmad b. Sumayṭ*, unpublished TS probably prepared in the 1990s.

Published Arabic material

al-Mashhūr, ᶜAbd al-Raḥmān b. Muḥammad b. Ḥusayn, *Shams al-ẓahīra al-ḍāḥiyya al-munīra fī nasab wa-silsila ahl al-bayt al-nabawī*, 2 vols., 2nd ed., edited by Muḥammad Ḍiyā᾽ Shihāb, Jiddah (ᶜĀlam al-Maᶜrifa), 1984.

al-Mashhūr, Abū Bakr al-ᶜAdanī b. ᶜAlī b. Abī Bakr, *Lawāmiᶜ al-nūr. Nubdha min aᶜlām Ḥaḍramawt*, 2 vols., Ṣanᶜā᾽ (Dār al-Muhājir), 1412/1991–92.

Maalim Muhammad Idris Muhammad Saleh, *Pamphlet on Seyyid Alwy Jamali Leyl*, privately printed.

Nūr al-Dīn b. Ḥusayn b. Maḥmūd (ed.), *al-Safīna al-Shādhiliyya al-Yashruṭiyya*, Dār Iḥyā al-Kutub al-ᶜArabiyya (2nd ed.), 1408/1987.

b. Sumayṭ, ᶜUmar b. Aḥmad, *Al-Nafḥat al-Shadhdhiyya ilā al-Diyār al-Ḥaḍramiyya wa-talbiyyat al-ṣawt min al-Ḥijāz wa-Ḥaḍramawt*, privately printed, Jiddah, 1988. There exists an earlier print of this work, privately printed in Tarīm/Aden, 1955; *Al-Nafḥat al-Shadhdhiyya min al-Diyār al-Ḥaḍramiyya wa-talbiyyat al-ṣawt min al-Ḥijāz wa-Ḥaḍramawt*. Note the change in the title from *min* to *ilā* al-Diyār al-Ḥaḍramiyya.

References

Bakari, Muhamad, 2003, "Sayyid Omar Abdallah (1918–1988): The forgotten Muslim Humanist and Public Intellectual". Paper presented to the conference *The Global Worlds of the Swahili*, Zanzibar, 20–22 February 2003.

Bang, Anne K., 2003, *Sufis and Scholars of the Sea. Family Networks in East Africa, 1860–1925*. London: Routledge Curzon.

Fair, Laura, 2001, *Pastimes and Politics. Culture, community and identity in post-abolition urban Zanzibar 1890–1945*. Oxford: James Currey.

Farsy, A.S., 1989, *Baadhi ya Wanavyoni wa Kishafii wa Mashariki ya Afrika/The Shafiᶜi Ulama of East Africa, ca. 1830–1970. A Hagiographical Account*. Translated, edited and annotated by R.L. Pouwels, University of Wisconsin, African Primary Text Series, III, 1989.

Freitag, Ulrike, 2003, *Indian Ocean Migrants and State Formation in Hadhramaut*. Leiden: Brill.

Saad Swaleh Yahya (ed.), 1998, *Knowledge, Vision and Ecstasy. Selected Works of Seyyid Omar Abdullah (Mwinyi Baraka)*, Majaalis el-Ulaa el-Qadiriyya, Dar-es-Salaam.

Saleh, Ibuni, 1936, *A Short history of the Comorians in Zanzibar*, Dar es Salaam (Tanganyika Standard).

"We Are the Warsay of Eritrea in Diaspora" Contested identities and social division in cyberspace and in real life

Bettina Conrad

Introduction and background

My first two years of research on the Eritrean diaspora in Germany coincided with the so called "border-war" between Eritrea and Ethiopia (1998–2000). While the war dominated almost any private conversation, group meeting and event within Eritrean circles, its coverage by German and international TV and press was by and large woefully inadequate. To bridge the information gap many Eritreans abroad who had the means and know-how turned to the Internet. And so did I. Getting hooked up to the net and checking the news on Eritrea became a sad morning ritual I shared with the people whose community I studied. But the Internet media did not only provide news updates. They also offered a platform to vent anger and frustration, analyse the situation and coordinate activities in support of their home country. For me as a researcher this made information about various groups and events accessible and enabled me to establish and maintain contacts. More importantly even, my "participant webservation" helped to formulate research questions

Without the hospitality and interest of the (past and present) members of *Warsay* e.V. this article could not have been written in its present form. Thank you! I hope this paper does your engagement justice, even though I am aware that my analysis and interpretations will not always overlap with your own. But having controversially discussed so many issues with some of you, I trust that you will still see a value in looking at your organisation from a different – that is, an outsider's – perspective. My thanks also go to friends and colleagues – Tilman Schiel, Mussie Tesfagiorgis, Victoria Bernal, Y., Tom Dassel, Yohannes Fessehaie, Leif Manger, and Munzoul Assal – for their comments, translations and encouragement!

and provided insights I had never bargained for.[1] Thus, with the Internet gradually becoming part of the Eritrean diasporic experience, it also came to be a complementary part of my fieldwork, rather than a mere tool of research.

In 1993, only five years prior to the outbreak of the 1998 war, Eritrea had gained *de jure* independence. The former Italian *Colonia Eritrea* had been federated to Ethiopia after the Second World War, but in 1962 was annexed by its larger partner. Ignored by the international community, this act met with bitter local resistance. In the course of a 30-year guerilla war, almost a third of the Eritrean population were forced to flee abroad. Today between half a million and a million Eritreans live scattered all over North East Africa, the Middle East, North America, Australia and Europe.[2] About 24,000 people of Eritrean origin reside in Germany alone – making it the largest Eritrean community on the continent. Most of them arrived during the 1970s and 1980s as students, refugees and asylum-seekers. Not unusual for exiles, their attention has always been fixed on the developments at home. Before independence, the majority of the refugees were organised with one of the two (major) rivalling liberation movements – the Eritrean Liberation Front (ELF) and the eventually dominating Eritrean People's Liberation Front (EPLF). Especially the latter's exile branches played a central role in shaping individual and col-

1. It is unknown to me who coined the term "participant webservation". A workable definition is provided by a website on cyberethnographical studies: "A research method in which the investigator takes part in the social phenomenon of interest by participating in an Internet-based exchange (such as a blog, bulletin board, or email exchange) with a group and observing the interactions between them". See: <http://moogit.com/fabian/index.php?option=content&task=view&id=28&Itemid=54/>.

   This article is based on both interviews and "classic" participant observation in a real life setting, as well as long-term "webservations" (2001–2004), e.g. as a member of the German-based Yahoo group "warsay-eritrea" (which today has largely fallen into disuse). During this time I also followed the development of two related "German" Eritrean websites: <http://www.warsay.de/> and <http://www.warsay.com/>. Other (though less frequently) "webserved" sites include various "transnational", US-based Eritrean websites, e.g. <http://www.dehai.org/>; <http://asmarino.com/> and <http://www.awate.com/>, as well as the Eritrean government site <http://www.shaebia.org/> and the now defunct <http://www.biddho.com/>.

2. Official estimates (Tekie 2005:176) speak of 4.3 million Eritreans (world-wide); 530,000 of whom reside abroad. Other figures based on host countries' statistics peg the diaspora's size at 600,000 to 750,000 (Schröder 2004:14). In any case diaspora Eritreans make up a considerable proportion of the overall Eritrean population.

lective Eritrean identity, as well as in mobilising moral support and financial resources for the struggle.

After liberation diaspora Eritreans had to make a decision about returning home or settling more permanently abroad. For various reasons the overwhelming majority postponed or even gave up their dreams of return. Nonetheless, they retained close emotional and factual links with their country of origin, which continue to affect their lives. By and large, Eritreans in Germany and elsewhere are still gripped by the legacy of war, haunted by "ghosts and shadows" (Matsuoka and Sorenson 2001) of the past, and spurred into action by the manifold internal and external challenges independent Eritrea is facing today. Especially the unexpected outbreak of the war with Ethiopia stirred Eritreans abroad. But while the crisis itself rekindled national solidarity and cohesion, its aftermaths brought the first serious doubts about the hitherto widely revered Eritrean leadership (made up of EPLF veterans). The cracks that appeared on the surface of Eritrean (trans)national unity showed most clearly in the diaspora. The ensuing debate about the government's legitimacy, its past and present rights and wrongs, and the question of the future course in Eritrean politics have largely been fought out among government supporters and a growing number of opponents in the diaspora. Their preferred battleground was and is the Internet – welcome to "Cyber-Eritrea"!

Some ideas and questions

From the early and mid-1990s onwards, the Internet began to feature prominently in studies on transnational social spaces. Together with better and cheaper means of communication and transportation, authors inevitably listed the Internet among the facilitators of transnational existence and catalysts in the gradual process of de-nationalisation (Basch et al. 1994; Pries 1996). It was thought that by overcoming national boundaries and real life distances migrants and others might eventually subvert the monopolistic powers of the nation state. This "globalisation from below", optimists suggested, would also lead to more participation and democracy, and foster the spread of civil societies world-wide. In the first (and for a long time the only) study on Eritrean cyberspace activities, John Rude (1996) finds no tendency to subvert and do away with the newly created Eritrean state. Yet he asserts that the popular US-based Eritrean mailing list *dehai* not only provided exiles with "a home away from home", but also served as a "laboratory" for the Eritrean state-in-making. On *dehai*, Rude argues, democratic participation was put into practice and exiles found a direct channel to influence the course of events at home.

In the light of the 1998–2000 Ethio-Eritrean war, the limits of such optimistic and romanticizing notions about the possibilities of cyberspace began to show. Looking at the Eritrean state as a global actor, Victoria Bernal elaborates the thesis that Internet media (and other transnational mechanisms) are indeed perfectly suited to serve nationalist purposes (Bernal 2001, 2004). Rather than being curtailed or diminshed by transnational activities, the Eritrean state, too, was able to use them in order to push its influence beyond the nation's geographical borders. The thus "de-territorialized" and "transnationalized" state not only has the means to include citizens living abroad, but also to control them, enforce their loyalty and even curtail their freedom of opinion. In their comparative study on Bosnian and Eritrean refugees, Al-Ali et al. (2001) even speak of "forced transnationalism", a phenomenon that could also be described as the state's attempt to subvert transnationalism by nationalism.

Today, we find Cyber-Eritrea has become a highly contested and fragmented space. While various competing actors use Internet media to influence or oppose the state/the regime, the regime itself uses them to counteract such attacks. The questions remain if and how these activities in Eritrean Cyberspace actually influence social and political patterns at home and in the diaspora? Or whether they merely reflect real life developments but are themselves inconsequential? Like the invention of the printing press, the Internet media certainly have some impact on our societies, the way we relate to each other and how we look at ourselves. Yet, I hold that whatever changes might be triggered they cannot simply be ascribed to the mysterious qualities of the medium. The Internet is, after all, a neutral tool to be used for any cause, as the Eritrean case demonstrates. While it makes information and ideas accessible to a potentially larger audience and in a shorter period of time, it does not generate them independently of real life contexts. Here I find myself in accordance with a recent anthropological approach to the Internet by Daniel Miller and Don Slater who suggest that:

> We need to treat the Internet media as continuous with and embedded in other social spaces, that they happen within mundane social structures and relations that they may transform but that they cannot escape into a self-enclosed cyberian apartness. ... new mediations indeed, but not a new reality... . That is to say, these spaces are important as part of everyday life, not apart from it (Miller and Slater 2000:5–7; emphasis as in original text).

Similarly I try to open up a perspective from "below" and show how people in the Eritrean diaspora make use of the Internet media and how their ways of doing so are shaped by real life locations and conditions. How do diasporic people living in one particular location place themselves within the transnational field of cyberspace? Or do they at all? Who can be reached using the Internet media and who is excluded from these technologies? Who exactly are the actors on this local level? What impact does the Internet have on people's daily lives and organisations, on their image of themselves? And finally: how are developments in real life, local community(ies) and in cyberspace influencing one another?

Before looking more closely at the case of an Eritrean youth group in Germany and its various uses of Internet media, however, it seems useful to cast at least a brief look at the development and present day extension of "Virtual Eritrea".

Mapping out the virtual field

Today, more than a decade after the emergence of the user group *Dehai* as the first Eritrean representation on the World-wide Web, the number of Eritrean Web sites, chat rooms, mailing lists and e-groups is growing on an almost daily basis. Among the popular Yahoo e-groups you found more than 60 groups devoted to discussing Eritrean topics in late 2004. At the same time *Dehai*'s link list alone – making no claims to completeness – featured 276 Eritrea-related Web sites, ranging from business sites and semi-professional news sites to privately owned Web space. Their purposes and topics are quite diverse, as are the background and locations of those who created them.[3] You find US-Eritrean Evangelicals wanting to spread the gospel, a Canadian youth group campaigning against the practice of unlimited National Service in Eritrea, a Germany-based Eritrean band promoting their CDs, or an Eritrean amateur photographer from Italy displaying his gallery of shots taken in Asmara. Other sites offer services such as online purchase of goats to be paid for by credit card and delivered to your loved ones' doorstep in Eritrea. Yet another category of site provides online Tigrinya lessons for Eritrean chil-

3. Internet use is, for example, likely to differ in Germany and the US. The host countries' infrastructure, language, composition of the respective diaspora in terms of education and gender, patterns of settlement etc. all play a role.

dren growing up in the diaspora.[4] Self-declared representatives of the Bilen or Jeberti ethnic groups introduce their cultures on the web. And, of course, you can also try to find your "Eritrean sweetheart" via a dating site and later share your online wedding pictures with your scattered friends and family.

The various Eritrean sites differ in quality, popularity and outreach. While many are very specialised and attract limited interest, others have become household names in Eritrean (diaspora) society. Some sites – which I will label "transnational" sites – are accessed by Eritreans all around the globe. Other "national" sites draw their main readership from the narrower circle of Eritreans living in a particular host country. Finally, you will even find "local" sites that are only of interest to Eritreans based in a region/city or belonging to the same community or association. Another distinction concerns not so much the location of potential users, but rather their political, ethnic or religious affiliations. Most sites of the "transnational" category are devoted to disseminating news and discussing Eritrean politics: *Asmarino.com*, *Dehai.org*, *Awate.com*, and *Shaebia.org* feature prominently among them. Their news and comments sections are dominated by an growing but countable number of regular contributors, or even by a team of (semi-)professional Web masters and bloggers. But chats, discussion forums and guest books also offer space for the participation of a wider group of visitors. Eritrean radio programmes can also be accessed from some of those sites and extended link lists connect scattered "islands of Eritreanness" making them "nodes" in the decentralised realm of the Web. A few sites also advertise Eritrean businesses or promote Eritrean artists. A commonality of all "big sites" is that they use English (but increasingly also Tigrinya and Arabic) as language of communication. The majority of these sites are owned and maintained by US-Eritreans, who also seem to dominate the discussion (especially in the early years). This is not to say that Eritreans residing elsewhere in the diaspora are absent from discourses taking place here. But very often they have created additional sites on which they use their respective host country's vernacular. "Eritrean" Web sites, hosted in actual Eritrea or created by Eritreans still living within the country, did not emerge before late 2000, when Eritrea – as the last African country – became connected to the Internet.[5]

4. One of the major languages spoken in Eritrea and the mother tongue of most Eritreans living in the West. Written in the ancient *Ge'ez* script, Tigrinya could only be used on the Web once special software was available.

5. From 1997 it has been possible to receive email via private email service providers, but access to this technology was rather limited. See: <http://www.reliefweb.int/IRIN/

A short history of Eritrea-online

In the following brief historical overview of Eritrean online activities, I will leave aside Cyber Eritrea's business and entertainment sections, and focus on the development of Web usage in a political context. Three fairly distinctive phases can be made out here. The first is more or less congruent with the Eritrean post-independence "honeymoon" from 1993–1997. The beginning of the second "fiercly nationalist" phase was clearly marked by the outbreak of the border war in May 1998. Its transition to the (ongoing) third phase of dissent and fragmentation of was less clear-cut. It took place over a continuum stretching from the end of the war in late 2000 to the clampdown on the private press and the arrest of political dissidents in September 2001.

The "honeymoon" phase was dominated by the mailing list (and later website) *Dehai* – the pioneer of Eritrean cyberspace (cf. Rude 1996, Bernal 2001). *Dehai* is a Tigrinya word, commonly translated as "news" or "voice [from home]". Founded in California in 1994 for and by diaspora Eritreans, *Dehai* soon became the home of the world-wide "hidden intelligentsia" among exile Eritreans.[6] The *Dehaiers*, as they called themselves, were a literally exclusive club of mostly college and university educated Eritreans living in North America or Europe. To join you were required to find a member who would vouch for you. This exclusivity seems to contradict common ideas about the Internet's assumed borderless, inclusive nature and globalising force. Yet, it was very much in line with developments in Eritrea and its diaspora, and in a way reflected the creation of an independent Eritrean nation state – also a seemingly anachronistic event at a time when the nation as such began to be looked at as a moribund concept.

Dehai emerged at a time when the demise of the EPLF's exile branches had left a temporary organisational vacuum. Many Eritreans where still pondering about return. Others felt oddly stranded as the cause they had lived for was accomplished and the home they had found in the mass organisations no longer existed. Both a more general re-definition of the diaspora-homeland relationship, and a re-structuring of diaspora networks seemed necessary. So far the EPLF had employed a rather rigorous top-down approach towards

cea/countrystories/eritrea/20001116.phtml>, 25 November 2002.

6. See Pnina Werbner (as cited in Bernal 2005). And though it is harder to conclude from written sources the gender of an author than his/her education, *Dehaiers* and analysers alike seem to agree that the majority of *Dehai* members (particularly active ones) were in fact male.

its supporters abroad, that emphazised vertical, rather than horizontal links. *Dehai* also sought to strengthen contacts within the diaspora and also to establish a more equal relationship with the newly installed EPLF government.[7] Like the members of real life organisations (that some of them were also members of), *Dehaiers* tried walking the plank between the wish to lead a more open and critical dialogue, both within the diaspora and with home, and the equally strong wish to remain an integral part of the EPLF nationalist project.

When the war started in May 1998 *Dehai* was soon almost entirely given over to conflict-related postings. *Dehai* membership figures and the number of postings rocketed. Apart from providing a forum where people could share their grief and outrage, *Dehai* also took over the mobilising and lobbying functions once held by the EPLF's real life exile organisations, such as coordinating the logistics for protest marches or monitoring western media coverage of the war. A special subsection with war-related background information and essays was added to the Web site. Perhaps most importantly, *Dehai* eventually came to serve as an outlet through which the Eritrean government and its representatives abroad issued official statements (cf. Smidt 2000:235). But also beyond *Dehai* there was an enormous upsurge of both real life and cyberspace activities. New Eritrean Web sites sprang up and competed for an ever growing diaspora audience that was no longer limited to a few hundred intellectuals.

Unsurprisingly the war brought a general rush of nationalism into cyberspace (and into real life organisations), that helped to rally all Eritreans behind a common cause again and led them to contribute huge sums for their homeland's defence (cf. Tekie 2005). Once again it is difficult to assess to what degree the medium Internet was involved in mobilising Eritreans, and whether the utilization of the Web made this conflict different from the independence war that had taken place prior to the Internet era. Wolbert Smidt finds that the Internet indeed did a lot to "democratise" the availability of information that could be accessed both faster and more directly by a larger number people.[8] Nonetheless, he comes to the conclusion that the increase of freely available information did not lead to a more sober analysis

7. In 1994 the EPLF was officially renamed People's Front for Democracy and Justice (PFDJ).

8. Only Eritrea itself was still largely excluded from the blessings of IT technology. Only a few individuals had access to email facilities and were in touch with exile Eritreans that e-mailed, posted or faxed them information available on the web. These

of the events. Rather, facts and accusations were interwoven in such a way as to denounce the opposing side rather than to evaluate where "the truth" lay: "... debates hardly led to a discussion with the other, but all the more against the other side". (Smidt 2001:32, translation B.C.). By and large the war rather reinforced self-censorship and the notion that dissent was a sign of treason, thus falling way behind the earlier efforts of *dehai* to make constructive criticism politically acceptable.

However, one side effect of the war certainly was that the Internet had finally become a medium to be reckoned with as it made a large group of Eritreans in diaspora directly accessible. This at least partly broke the EPLF's/ the government's monopoly in passing on information and also put potential dissenters out of the immediate reach of negative repercussions (though we will see in the case study, that engagement on the Web does not always remain inconsequential for real life).[9] If the Eritrean cyberspace until 2000 had mainly served to reinforce an all-embracing transnational Eritreanism, it now began to be seen as a platform for challenging official notions and government politics. During late 2000 and 2001, criticism of the regime's handling of the war, as well as its previous omissions such as the failure to implement the new constitution came under scrutiny. And not surprisingly, the EPLF's old adversaries, splinter groups of the ELF, also discovered cyberspace as a means to escape their political marginalisation and find new audiences. The potential influence of the Internet also came to be acknowledged by the government itself. In 2001, the government/ruling party eventually launched its own website, a measure which clearly aimed at counterbalancing the otherwise hard to control criticism found on the web.[10]

When a group of diaspora intellectuals, commonly referred to as the G13, wrote an open letter to the Eritrean president urging him to embark on democratic reforms, Eritrean cyberspace was buzzing with outrage. The ensuing discussion in some ways paved a direct road from "cyber war" against Ethiopia to "cyber civil war" between the supporters and critics of the Eritrean

texts were often clandestinely copied and distributed in friendship circles (cf. Smidt 2001).

9. In *Dehai* most people had still signed contributions with their real names, after the war the use of nicknames increased.

10. The website is called *Shaebia*, which is the popular Arabic short form for EPLF. Another government Web site named *Shabait.com*, went online in 2003 and is explicitly designed to cater for the diaspora Its motto "Serving the truth" is a frequent subject of ridicule among government opponents.

government that polarized both cyber and real life communities. Before long the two factions did not even share the same virtual space anymore. Eritrean Internet users of different political hues sorted themselves into neat containers arranged along an invisible frontline, each creating and maintaining their own version of Eritreanness.[11] Only a few websites continued to display diverging political opinions as had been the case on early *Dehai* (which itself became a largely "pro-government" forum). With an increasing number of political dissidents, representatives of sub-national groups and government supporters all using the Internet as a screen for their own projections of Eritreanness, Cyber-Eritrea has become increasingly segmentary, both reflecting and reinforcing real life divisions in the diaspora and Eritrea proper. As during the war, the mere flood of new (dis)information and plurality of opinions has not led to constructive discussions, let alone has it had any positive effect on the more and more repressive situation in Eritrea. Thus, for many in the diaspora the vast array of websites that each claim to have found "the truth", seems confusing and frustrating:

> Today I had a bit of time to browse through many Eritrean sites. The more you read, the more confused you get, I think. biddho/alenalki [pro-government] versus hadishtesfai/n-d-p [dissidents, claiming the current Eritrean government is in fact Tigrayan] versus nharnet/meskerem [ELF opposition]. It is absolutely sad and in parts even mad to see that the Internet has become a melting pot for communists, fascists, Islamists, indeed racists etc. For some ****** [President Issayas Afeworki] is the bad guy, for others the Jeberti [Muslim Tigrinya speakers, not officially acknowledged as a separate "nationality" i.e. an ethnic group often found in opposition to the government], the highland Christians … the Agame [derisory term for the Tigrayans of Ethiopia], the Tedla Bairus, the Mesfuns, the Melekins … [names of opposition politicians], the Doctors, the Professors and, and, and… .[12]

It might be claimed that the Internet's segmentary structure has greatly facilitated the fragmentation of Eritrean diaspora communities along those vari-

11. Indeed, this "process of spatial division" has been described by Peter Waldmann as one of the first stages of civil strife in real life: "… often there is an eclat at the beginning [G15 – B.C.] … tensions that before had been present in everybody's mind but had not determined everyday life now suddenly become visible and turn into the dominant principle which subjects all other spheres of life. A profound restructuring and reordering of society takes place as much in a mental as in a military geographical respect" (Waldmann 1999:66).

12. On: <http://www.warsay.com/> Guest book entry, 30 March 2004 (translated from German and explanations B.C.).

ous fault lines. Indeed, the Internet has generally proven to be a "natural" ally of segmentary forms of organisation (Zurawski 2000:223), both real and virtual. Nonetheless it would be ridiculous to claim that it was the Internet which brought about these divisions in the first place. When Zurawski (2000:228) finds that "... 'virtual' ethnicity in cyberspace cannot take any imaginable form, but is always historically connected to earlier forms of ethnicity which are rooted locally (in a cultural as well in a geographical sense)", this is, as I have tried to show, also true for the (re-)emergence of particularist identities in the Eritrean context. What the Internet does, is that it seems to make visible, manifest, accelerate and possibly transform real life divisions for instance by spreading (mis)information and discontent and making critical opinions more tangible and eventually also more socially acceptable. While often denied, ignored, minimised or made taboo in real life, Eritrean political oppsosition and dissent have materialised in the virtual realm (e.g. in the shape of home pages) and thus have become a reality that provokes further reactions within real life settings (such as the increasing pressure to choose sides).

Case study

"Nomen est omen": Warsay – The real and the virtual

Having thus tried to sketch out some general historical developments I now want to take you along to my field and give you an example of how the virtual and the real overlap and intersect on a local level. The case of the Eritrean Youth group *Warsay* in Frankfurt I present here illustrates local expressions and limits of Internet usage in the Eritrean diaspora in Germany.[13] In the summer of 2000 I joined a new German-Eritrean e-group, called *Warsay*. *Warsay* means "heir" or more precisely "my heritage" in Tigrinya. But it is also the term for the young Eritrean soldiers who fought in the recent war against Ethiopia.[14] Like many other youth groups and websites *Warsay* e-

13. With about 5,000 Eritreans living in the city and its vicinity, Frankfurt can be seen as the Eritrean capital in Germany.

14. According to an Eritrean colleague, the term *Warsay* (pl *Warsot*) only came into use in 1998 after the outbreak of the Ethio-Eritrean border war. It was used to distinguish the young generation of soldiers drafted into the Eritrean Defence Forces (EDF) after independence from the EPLF veteran fighters many of whom had become regular EDF soldiers (called *Yeke'alo* – "those who have made [independence] possible"). As *Warsay* means heir or inheritor, my colleague explained, there is the question what

group, too, was a child of this war. To join you had to register with your full name, but unlike *Dehai*, you needed no member to vouch for you. The majority of the subscribers I came to know more about were Eritrean men between 20 and 40 years of age. Most had completed at least 12th grade (A-Levels) in Eritrea or Ethiopia or had completed a comparable grade in exile. Many of them had come to Germany as unaccompanied youths or young men in the mid- and late 1980s. By contrast most of the fewer female members were Eritrean students that had been brought up in Germany. There was, however, also a number of interested Germans – journalists, researchers, members of solidarity movements. Interestingly, many e-group members were again members of other transnational (for example *Dehai*) and German-Eritrean virtual and/or real life groups. This linking up was to some extent the doing of one very engaged individual who had helped to set up the group and for a long time functioned as one of its administrators.

For more than two years the group that had been started in May 1999 worked well. It provided both information on Eritrea and the diaspora and also offered a platform for open discussion. Texts posted by its up to 78 subscribers came from various sources such as English-language Web sites, German and international newspapers, UN publications etc.[15] Easily the most popular topic was Eritrean politics. There were lengthy discussions about the G13, the issue of democratisation, or the best way to criticise German media for incorrect footage of the war. A critical stance on Eritrean government politics was tolerated, but usually provoked some defiant replies (not unlike *Dehai*). Other postings covered various issues from German development policies to the advertising of political, cultural and sports events as well as parties organised by various Eritrean groups in Germany.

It was some time after I had joined the e-group that I realized there was also a real life youth group in Frankfurt that was called *Warsay*, and at first

they inherited and from whom. His answer, which he says is also the official meaning of *Warsay* (given to him by Tekie Beyene, former EPLF fighter and now the Director of the Bank of Eritrea), is that the *Warsot* have inherited not only independence from the Yeke'alo, but also certain traits that are thought to characterise the liberation fighters (*Tegadelti*/*Yeke'alo*), notably, courage, nationalism and the readiness to make the ultimate sacrifice. Accepting their heritage thus also makes the *Warsot* custodians of a national tradition that started with the struggle for independence.

15. A message by e-group administrators from 17/03/02 claims 78 subscribers – but that was after some had already left. As with any e-group, the number of passive "consumers" outnumbered the activists, but over time at least half, if not more, of the users also contributed to the discussions.

I failed to understand the connection between both of them. The *Warsay* members I eventually met in late 2000, however, were only the "remnants" of the much larger 1999 *Warsay* movement which had been started as a reaction to the war, but whose momentum had since petered out. While it has mostly been described as a grassroots movement I later learned that the first impulse for the foundation of the *Warsay* movement had, in fact, come from the Eritrean Consulate General and the Eritrean community association in Frankfurt, and could be seen as part of a concerted campaign to mobilise the world-wide Eritrean diaspora youth. According to one of the founders, the later arrested Consul General Besrat Yemane had called a meeting in Frankfurt and asked the youth to do something to help their home country. A group of about a dozen young Eritreans spontaneously organised themselves. One of the founders describes their motivation:

> There was a seminar informing about the situation in Eritrea organised especially for the youth in Frankfurt and vicinity by... the Eritrean Consul Ato Besrat Yemane ... "MENESEI TERAKA ENTAI EYU?; TERAKA FLET, GUBUEKA GBER, TELEAL!!" [You (Young man), what is your role? You have to know your role, do your duty, Stand up!!]. These were about Ato Besrat's words ... about 10–12 young people (including myself) decided to think about this ... as founders of the movement we had taken on the task of mobilising youth in Frankfurt as quickly as possible in order to contribute to improving the situation in Eritrea. ... First, we wanted to make Eritrea's problems public and second, we wanted to show our unconditional solidarity with our people... .[16]

Though the first impulse had come from "above" – the quote shows that the *Warsay* movement's involvement in the struggle was rooted in the deep-felt wish to do something for Eritrea and not to remain mere on-lookers of the unfolding drama in the Horn of Africa. Despite the sombre background of their engagement, former members get nostalgic when they talk about the impressive number of youth that came together for long nights of discussion. In its heyday this mostly local group of youngsters amounted to about 500 members of diverse social and educational backgrounds and included ages from 14 to 30 plus. This time of crisis had them cooperate in a very engaged and disciplined manner, invoking memories about the sense of solidarity of the days prior to independence. Amongst other things *Warsay* marched in protest against the war, invited experts to speak about the current situation

16. E-group message 12/04/02, emphasis as in original, translated from German/Tigrinya text B.C.

and organised parties to raise funds that were sent to Eritrea. They also became active on the web. Apart from a "financial" and "social task force", an "info task force" was established within the *Warsay* movement.[17] This latter group – with the help of the above-mentioned "networking specialist" – set up both the *Warsay* e-group and a Web site called *Warsay.de.* Attracting members from all over Germany the e-group came to exist more or less independently from the actual *Warsay* movement which, even though widely known, remained largely local regarding its membership.

Not surprisingly, the real life movement lost its initial momentum after the war. Some *Warsot,*[18] however, realized the necessity to do something for the younger generation to keep them interested in Eritrea and also to help them integrate in Germany. The idea was to continue their work but shift the focus onto youth in the diaspora rather than merely rallying support for Eritrea. But this transformation from a spontaneous movement to a regularly working association was not smooth. It seems that the growing criticism of the Eritrean government that was to be observed in Eritrean cyberspace (including the *Warsay* e-group and *Warsay.de*'s guest book) did not leave the *Warsay* movement and its members unaffected. Moreover, personal quarrels and diverging interests led further members to drop out while new ones joined. It is clear that a much smaller *Warsay* registered as a non-profit youth association later in 2001. As *Warsay* e.V. (e.V. means registered association) they continued their mixture of organising parties, seminars and other events. In 2002 they joined the *Stadtjugendring,* the umbrella organisation of Frankfurt's youth groups, providing them with a solid financial background and the possibility to extend their networks beyond Eritrean circles.[19] *Warsay* e.V. now meet once a week and – until recently – had an office in the Guild of Students building at Frankfurt's Johann Wolfgang Goethe University. Seminars and parties also often take place there, though most of the *Warsot* are not students.

From January 2002 until December 2003 I joined Warsay on various occasions, sometimes invited, but also once or twice just "popping in" as I was nearby. The meetings were usually attended by about eight to 20 people.[20]

17. The setting up of committees shows that real life organisations and networks are still modelled on the organisational structures of the independence movements.

18. *Warsot* is the plural form of *Warsay.*

19. Which so far is happening only to a very limited extent.

20. According to a guest book posting from 3 August 2002 by the *Warsay.com* webmaster, *Warsay* e.V. has about 40 active and 300 passive members.

Most of the core group are men between 20 and 40 years of age. Topics vary, but very often concern the planning of up-coming events, for which a far larger number of members and sympathisers who do not attend the meetings regularly can be mobilised to help out. The beginning as well as the end of each meeting is marked by a one-minute silence for the Eritrean "martyrs" that is ended with a slogan of the liberation war: *Awet nHafash.*[21] The language of communication is Tigrinya interspersed with German. While some members clearly are not too comfortable with speaking German, most of the younger participants are more fluent in German than in Tigrinya, making it sometimes difficult for them to contribute to the debate.[22] Asked to translate a list with planned events written in Tigrinya two young members said somewhat embarrassed that they found it laborious to decipher the *Ge'ez* script. Yet, the protocol that is written for each session is in Tigrinya, and I sometimes got the impression that using Tigrinya also has a ritual aspect along with the silence for the war heroes and, indeed, the group's name. After the meetings that usually take between two and three hours, the group often go out together. Whenever I joined them we went to one of the numerous Eritrean restaurants in Frankfurt. Just as with any other association it seems that the informal part of the evening is for some participants the main reason for coming. The debates are often continued in a more lively and inclusive manner, with everyone speaking the tongue he or she prefers.

Some *Warsay* members are also active in other Eritrean associations, such as the *MahbereKom* (community association), the Football Club and another youth group called JEF.[23] Others are actively involved with the Eritrean Orthodox *Medhane Alem* congregation. *Warsay* e.V. has also joined an umbrella organisation of Eritrea associations in Frankfurt, including the *MahbereKom.* Yet, the group's standing in the community remains difficult. Like *Dehai* in its first phase *Warsay* is accused of being too much "pro-government" by some people, while others count them among the government opponents. *Warsay* without doubt and openly has contacts with the Eritrean Consulate General

21. "Martyrs" is the official term for the Eritrean war dead of both the independence and the recent war. The slogan *Awet n'Hafash* translates as "victory to the masses" and is also a popular sign-off in Internet communication (see Bernal 2005).

22. Some younger people that are organised with another youth group even said that language was one of the reasons for their not joining *Warsay* e.V. as they felt uncomfortable with speaking Tigrinya.

23. JEF is an abbreviation for *Junge Eritreer in Frankfurt und Umgebung* – Young Eritreans in Frankfurt and Vicinity.

in Frankfurt and with the National Union of Eritrean Youth and Students (NUEYS) in Asmara, though these relationships have – for various reasons – not always been free of tensions. And while *Warsay* do not refuse cooperation either with NUEYS or the Consulate on a project to project basis, they strongly emphasise their autonomy. Therefore, one recurring problem – seen from the perspective of Eritrean authorities – has been the integration of *Warsay* into the structures of a transnational or extended Eritrean nationalism. In other words, there have been repeated efforts to get *Warsay* to join NUEYS as a branch, something they have so far avoided. In this context, registering as a non-profit association within the framework of German legal structures, and also joining the umbrella organisation for Frankfurt's youth, may be seen as measures to safeguard *Warsay*'s autonomy vis-à-vis Eritrean national demands.[24]

Warsay.de: Whose 'Warsa'? – Claiming a virtual heritage

Warsay e.V., though differently composed in terms of membership, felt they had more or less inherited the *Warsay* movement's Web site *Warsay.de*. In 2001 at least two former members of the "info task force" that had left *Warsay* earlier founded a new Web site called *Biddho.com*. To launch it they installed an eye-catching link on *Warsay.de*, and some time later simply incorporated the older site into *Biddho*. Then *Biddho.com* suddenly turned professional and it is widely rumoured by friends and foes alike that they are funded by the

24. Independently from one another two long-term observers (both until recently supporters of the EPLF/PFDJ) from within the Eritrean community interpreted the consulate's efforts in terms of control and interference. Pointing at the EPLF/PFDJ's long history of either incorporating or destroying potential rival organisations they found (I paraphrase): "The EPLF will never allow independent organisations to grow" (see also Hepner 2004 and 2005). Quite obviously there are competing versions of *Warsay*'s origin. A member of the now defunct youth group *DA'ARO* claimed that "the warsay movement was founded by the then active youth and students of the Union of Eritrean Youth and Students of Frankfurt (NUEYS-F), better known as *DA'ARO*, and the Consulate of the State of Eritrea in Frankfurt." (*Warsay* e-group, 11/04/02.) There are other *Warsay* groups, e.g. in Washington DC or San Diego (USA) that are in fact branches of the NUEYS. However, when I interviewed the official youth coordinator of NUEYS in Germany in his office at the Consulate, he mentioned *DA'ARO* as one of many youth groups that came into being in the mid- to late 1990s, but made no reference to the fact that *DA'ARO*, or for that matter *Warsay*, had ever been a NUEYS branch. Nonetheless, a contact list of Eritrean groups in Frankfurt (compiled by the Consulate) that I came across in 2003, names *Warsay* as a NUEYS branch.

Eritrean government.[25] Indeed, coinciding with the closure of independent newspapers and the arrest of opposition politicians in Eritrea in autumn 2001, a professionalised *Biddho.com* adopted an increasingly fierce pro-government stance. When *Warsay* e.V., wanted to use the *Warsay* section of *biddho.com* the *Biddho* makers first offered their help, but later asked to be paid for these services, something *Warsay* e.V. was both unable and unwilling to do.

Meanwhile, the *Warsay* e-group had become completely independent of the real life developments in Frankfurt, despite overlapping membership. Nonetheless, the e-group was apparently a thorn in the side of *Biddho*'s webmasters, who – as mentioned earlier – had set it up when still members of the *Warsay* movement. Trouble started when early in 2002 one of the administrators (now also *Biddho* webmaster) began to criticise certain postings and attack members for forwarding "anti-Eritrean" newspaper articles. A heated debate ensued about his patronising behaviour before moving to the question of the group's origin and actual "ownership". Eventually, the e-group administration decided that all members ought to renew their membership, giving more information about who they were and accept that the group was "pro-Eritrean". As the debates got increasingly harsh in tune, including insults and attempts at character assassination, some of the more liberal-minded members left in protest. Others followed silently. And though it was never officially declared, this was the beginning of the end. With both *Warsay.de* and *Warsay* e-group more or less defunct, *Warsay* e.V. found themselves disowned by the *Warsay* movement's web-heritage and thus decided to start a new Web site. Its launch in April 2002 was announced to the ailing e-group, saying: "We have news for all who want to enjoy a free discussion without preconditions. Warsay e.V. … has a new Web site: … <www.warsay.com>."[26]

The new website, *Warsay.com* tried to be both a platform for debates among Eritreans in Germany, as well as an online extension and media organ of real life *Warsay* e.V. Since 2002 it has once or twice changed its design but

25. *Biddho* means challenge in Tigrinya – initially there had also been plans to start a German-Eritrean Magazine with that name. As with Warsay, *Biddho*'s original members largely dropped out, and while retaining the name, the aims were changed in the process. In the early days the main language was German, later *Biddho* used mostly English and Tigrinya.

26. E-group posting from 20 April 2002, translated from German B.C. The e-group still exists and is occasionally used to announce an event etc. A few discussions have flared up over the past three years, but the overall number of postings and active members has sharply dropped and there are often no messages for a couple of weeks or even months now.

otherwise retained most of its features. There are two young webmasters who run the show, but several other members can also access the site to load up files or make changes. The Web site's logo shows a "coat of arms" crowned by the skyline of Frankfurt. Below you see the outlines of Germany and with a sketch of Eritrea drawn within its borders. Above and below the sketch it says in Latin and *Ge'ez* script: "Warsay Germany" and "Warsay Ertra". But not only the symbol refers to the (trans)local. The language of communication is German with occasional use of English and Tigrinya transliterations. *Warsay.com* is a typically "local" site in the sense that it mainly caters for German Eritrean, or even Frankfurt-Eritrean visitors. Unlike the "transnational" sites or the *Warsay* e-group, it is less of a place to get information about and exchange thoughts on the developments in the world-wide diaspora and Eritrea proper. On the whole it is geared towards younger, more local visitors that are encouraged to join the real life *Warsay* youth group or at least come to their parties and seminars. The events calendar has recently been somewhat neglected, but used to announce planned events on a fairly regular basis. A huge link list with various sub-categories refers the net surfer to hundreds of Eritrean sites, including sites and businesses owned by *Warsay* members.[27] Another interesting feature is the photo album with pictures taken at *Warsay* parties, seminars, demonstrations, outings and holidays.

However, the most interesting and also the most popular feature is the *Warsay.com* guest book which has become transformed into a discussion forum by its users: "Finally a chat room for Habesha living in Germany" enthuses one of the guests in July 2002.[28] Though debates here partly lack the intellectual depth of the *Warsay* e-group discussions, it is interesting to note

27. Aimed at providing an overview of Eritrean sites, *Warsay*'s link list can be read as yet another attempt to avoid political classification via their chosen links. That links are indeed seen as an indicator of political opinion might be illustrated by the following sarcastic comment made by one the (pro-regime) *biddho/warsay* e-group administrators in reply to the launch of *Warsay.com:* "... of course I visited the Web site to experience the new freedom. There is a guest book, the dates of some cool and interesting events, as well as a few links. What I rather liked was that I find my favourite sites *Awate.com* and *Asmarino.com* [seen as anti-government and critical respectively] straight away now. Wow beautiful free world." (*Warsay* e-group, 16 May 2002, translated from German B.C.)

28. "Chat room" is here used synonymously with "guest book". "Habesha" is a term for highland Eritreans and Ethiopians. Eritreans in Germany and elsewhere in the diaspora, however, also use it as a self-description. One reason for preferring the guest book to the discussion forum might be that making an entry in the guest book does not require registration.

how the "guests" have made themselves at home and that it is mainly Eritrea and local Eritrean matters that are touched upon in this forum. Broadly the guest book is used on two levels and by two groups of users: The first group are younger Eritreans that have presumably been born or brought up in Frankfurt. The second group are *Warsay* members, and other older Eritreans most of whom grew up in Eritrea or Ethiopia. They can be identified not only by the contents of their messages, but are also distinguishable by their orthography, syntax, style of writing, greetings, nicknames and the use of abbreviations commonly used in sms messages or chat rooms. For the youngsters the guest book is a message board, chat room, gossip exchange and flirt line rolled into one – a virtual meeting place. Topics such as parties, concerts and other events, exchanges about music, but also questions concerning *Warsay* figure most prominently among their postings. Their background knowledge about Eritrea varies greatly. From some of the entries, however, it is quite obvious, that the topics debated on the transnational Eritrean Web sites, be they independent, pro- or anti-government, are more or less by-passing younger visitors to *Warsay.com*.

But the younger users dominated only the first few months of *Warsay.com*'s existence. In the course of 2002 the entries became increasingly political. It seemed the guest book had been discovered as a forum for political debate by another group of visitors. From the contents of their postings it can be concluded that most of them are at least in their twenties and thirties; that is the very age group of the real life *Warsay* members. Some of the guests appear to have been involved with the *Warsay* movement, or others Eritrean youth groups.[29] Thus even I could identify rather easily, and not infrequently, that their heated exchanges seemed to be the continuation of some older real life disputes. Discussions tended to be dominated by two or three individuals, sometimes seconded by others. Apart from various more or less sober debates revolving around the criticism or support of the current government and the role of diaspora Eritreans, there were also a few discussions about Eritrean culture and history, showing clearly the guest book users' uneven knowledge in these fields. An exception in any respect were two very lively and open exchanges about male/female relationships in the diaspora. Not only were these

29. Though one can never tell for sure who hides behind a nickname, it seems that online discussions (especially about politics) are still a male-dominated field. This impression is substantiated by my real life observations where many women not only tended to abstain from making political utterances, but often also professed a dislike of politics in general.

discussions some of the rare non-political ones but apparently also involved a greater number contributors – including both men and women as well as different age groups. Recurring topics of discussion have also been the role and positioning of *Warsay* itself (as a Web site and as a real life organisation). The name "Warsay", the group's aims and activities (or the lack thereof), its political standing and its practice of censoring or not censoring guest book entries, have repeatedly been praised and criticised by "guests" of different political hues. In the following I will analyse some of their entries (and *Warsay*'s reactions) more closely as they illustrate how the real and the virtual interact and how local conditions are reflected and reinforced, but possibly also re-configured on the web.

Squaring the circle: Legacy, loyalty and liberty

In the summer of 1999, in the midst of the Ethio-Eritrean border war, a war ultimately costing the lives, health and sanity of thousands of Eritrean *Warsot* and their Ethiopian peers, a Swedish Eritrean youth group posted a both very emotional and uncanny message on *Dehai* (crossposted on the *Warsay* e-group) inviting young Eritreans to join them to celebrate the millennium shift in Eritrea:

> This is not just about partying … *We are the warsai of Eritrea in Diaspora*, at this special occasion we want to join the warsais [sic!] which are defending and building our home country and show our belongingness with them! *This is about making a new oath to our martyrs and our people, a new dedication* that we Eritrean youth where ever [sic!] we are shall strive for Eritreas [sic!] prosperity and always will be ready to defend her whenever threatened! The new millennium is ours![30]

It is not unreasonable to assume that the *Warsay* movement in Frankfurt was spurred into action by similar sentiments. The adoption of the name "Warsay" alone is, as outlined above, highly symbolic, signifying both continuity with the past and integration into the Eritrean nation at present. It provides a sense of pride, belongingness and identity. It is very much emotionally charged and has an almost semi-religious quality in as much as almost everyone in Eritrea and its diaspora had to mourn "martyred" relatives and friends killed during the independence struggle and also in the 1998–2000 war. Thus to say "We are the warsai of Eritrea in Diaspora" is more than rhetoric. Claiming your "*warsa*" or heritage also means to take on a twofold "sacred" duty, once

30. *Dehai.org* posting from 19 August 1999, emphasis B.C.

towards the bestowers of this heritage (including the war dead or "martyrs") and twice to the "real" *warsot* (peers still living in Eritrea and bearing the brunt of defending the nation). This duty or obligation includes coming to the defence of what earlier generations have achieved and continuing their struggle for a free, peaceful and prosperous Eritrea. The legacy of the independence struggle, the solidarity with the *warsot* at home and the fight for a better future are, however, inextricably interwoven with loyalty to the present Eritrean government (the former EPLF) as the winner, guardian and embodiment of Eritrean independence. In this version of history Eritreanness and loyalty to the Eritrean government have become the two inseparable sides of one coin. Especially the *sedetegnatat*, Eritreans in diaspora, who lived "comfortably" abroad while others sacrificed their health and lives, grew up with a feeling of indebtedness to the EPLF and its "martyrs". Hence when Consul General Besrat said: "... You ... have to know your role, do your duty. Stand up!!", he was appealing to this twin sense of guilt and duty to incite the young diaspora Eritreans to provide at least material and moral support while, yet again, Eritreans at home had to risk their lives.

During the war there was no apparent contradiction between unconditional loyalty to the Eritrean government and the vision of a prosperous and democratic Eritrea. One government supporter in the *Warsay* e-group came up with the formula "government + people = Eritrea". Unfortunately, with the increasingly repressive post-war politics of the Eritrean government this became a demand rather than a promise or a fact. And with growing criticism of the Eritrean leadership and the above-described polarisation of political opinion at home and abroad, there was also pressure on the *Warsay* movement to choose sides. A compromise was hard to find as the general tune was one of "who isn't for us, is against us". More than that – who is against the government is against Eritrea and the Eritrean people, and indeed can no longer be regarded as a "true" Eritrean. It appears that a similar polarisation took place within the dissolving *Warsay* movement. The majority, neither wanting to openly challenge the government nor join the ranks of a yet undefined and often dubious opposition, chose the "exit" option. Others, like the founders of *Biddho.com* finally decided for reasons of their own to link their fate unconditionally to that of the Eritrean government.[31]

31. Financial aspects are said to have played a role as well as the acquisition of "power" and status. The *Biddho* "kids" as well as other "pro-government" groups have meanwhile split up and seem to quarrel mainly about money. In some instances people were allegedly also promised remuneration for their cooperation or services. And as

The remaining *Warsay*, i.e. *Warsay* e.V., find themselves in an unadmitted dilemma – trying to be true to their "legacy" as *Warsay* they cannot condemn the Eritrean government. Yet, influenced by Western ideas such as pluralism and democratic principles (which they practise within their own organisation while the Eritrean state is becoming increasingly repressive) they also refuse to succumb to the government's totalitarian demands on their loyalty that allow neither criticism nor autonomy. *Warsay*'s way out of this predicament is showing themselves to be loyal to the Eritrean state, whilst acknowledging the general right to freely utter diverging opinion (again something the government does not allow). In practice that might for instance mean advertising government events on *Warsay.com*, but also offering a space like the guest book where it is possible to voice dissent. The same goes for the decision to become a registered association and join Frankfurt's union of youth groups while continuing to cooperate with Eritrean government agencies. In other words, *Warsay* tries to square the circle by showing "loyalty" to the Eritrea government (thus staying true to their legacy as *Warsay*), and also demonstrating dedication to "liberal" principles. Both elements are part of their image of themselves.

Yet, while the group itself seems to find no contradiction in advocating both democracy *and* supporting a government that is anything but democratic, some of the guests take a different view. Numerous guest book entries demand that *Warsay* show their "true colours" or else accept being seen as traitors either to the government or to their vision of a democratic Eritrea. Often it is the name *Warsay* that is regarded with suspicion. A critic writes: "… call yourselves differently. When I hear Warsay I always think about war. It's too nationalist, reminds me of isejas [President Issayas Afewerki]. Consider it, brothers… ." (24 February 2003). Another, almost dadaist version reads: "warsay=say war!!!!!! war say!!!! say bush!! bush say: war say!!! afewerki=bush=war… ." (24 February 2003). One entry hints that the "real" warsay are no longer partisans but conscripts, many of whom nowadays seek to escape from unlimited national service (symbolized by Sawa, the main military training camp) and a life controlled by the state and overshadowed by the threat of war: "Warsay e.V. who are you? … What is your identity? Warsay flee from Sawa and you are on the side of the government … hypo-

everywhere personal sympathies or animosities play a crucial role and are often inseparable from political conflicts that also tend to be highly personalised.

crites… ." (27 May 2003).[32] But also government supporters who think *Warsay* e.V. unworthy of carrying its name, have their say:

> Why can warsay not longer demonstrate that it stands by the Eritrean population and the government? So-called Warsay e.V. should first earn the right to call themselves warsay…

A leading *Warsay* member replies:

> Warsay e.V. is the youth movement that stood demonstratively at the Eritrean government's side during the war. It is anti-imperialist, against neo-colonialism and racism. Warsay fights for a tolerant and democratic society. Warsay is against narrow-minded nationalism … [33]

Warsay's insistence on being both loyal to an undemocratic and highly nationalist regime and devoted to creating a "tolerant and democratic" society, must also be understood as an attempt to carve out some space within the community that gives them a wider scope of action in order to influence developments from within. At the same time, however, it makes them vulnerable to attacks from all sides. *Warsay*'s equivocal standing within the wider community is aggravated by the fact that the group has a heterogeneous and not always clearly defined membership. Someone who is now either an opposition or staunch government supporter might say "I'm Warsay", referring to his or her participation in the original movement. But also *Warsay*'s tactical shifting and turning both on the Web and in real life has contributed to the confusion. In a climate of mutual distrust, fear and polarisation of political opinion their efforts to reconcile "loyalty" and "liberty" resemble a tightrope walk and are often understood either as mere opportunism or badly concealed support of either the pro- or the anti-government side. Accordingly they have been labelled "traitors", "*weyane*", "*adgi*" or "donkeys" (derogatory term for Ethiopian soldiers), "anti-Eritrean" and "regionalist" by the

32. All quotes on *Warsay* are from the warsay.com guest book. Translation from German B.C.

33. Both quotes from warsay.com guest book 10 September 2002, translated from German B.C. On another occasion *Warsay* e.V. defined itself referring to its adopted role as custodian of Eritrean tradition: "Warsay means = heritage. The heir/heiress should continue, cherish and develop his/her traditions and customs … that is Warsay e.V." (2 April 2003).

pro-government faction, as well as "hypocrites", "opportunists", "government agents", "spies" and again "traitors" by those who count themselves among the opposition. On the other hand *Warsay* are also praised by both admitted government supporters and opponents. But on the whole, rather than helping to extend their scope of action, their ambiguity makes both *Warsay*.com and *Warsay* e.V. easy prey to manipulation, instrumentalisation and or "collective character assassination". [34]

As we have already seen infiltration or, alternatively, the destruction of politically unwanted forums also works on the web. Below an example of such an "attack" on *Warsay.com*, allegedly carried out by the same person who destroyed the *Warsay* e-group. After someone nicknamed "Ezewedehankum" (meaning "this is all [I have to say] to you") had posted several comments criticising the Eritrean government, the self-declared "Halawi Ertra" (meaning "the guard of Eritrea") emerges on the scene to complain about *Warsay*'s lack of intervention.[35]

> Why does Warsay e.V. look on? Do they still think what "Ezewedehankum" does is all right? The silence and the looking on may be an answer. But maybe "Ezewedehankum" and Warsay e.V., too, have really become Ethiopia fans?

A *Warsay* e.V. member warns him:

> Everyone can voice his opinion freely as long as Eritrean sovereignty is respected. You are trying to play Warsay e.V. off against the Eritrean government. You'll never succeed because Warsay e.V. is the government itself. [this is but another version of the EPLF's "one people, one heart" motto meaning that the Eritrean people and the Eritrean government have one common goal].

34. All quotes in this section from Warsay.com guest book (2002 and 2003), translated from German (where needed) B.C.

35. Without wanting to overstretch my interpretation, let me point out that the choice of the nickname *Helawi Ertra* might not have been coincidental. During the liberation war the EPLF had a secret internal security called *Halewa Sawra* (Guardians of the Revolution). Its main task was to prevent infiltration and fight internal political dissent and/or collaboration with the enemy. As Adam Hadera claims the *Halewa Sawra* were particularly feared because once you were singled out as a culprit, there was no way to appeal. They were also in charge of arresting returning exile Eritreans who had behaved illoyally abroad. Adam reckons that the general knowledge about their existence and ruthless methods as well as their undercover operations inspired general mistrust, thus effectively preventing political dissent within the front (Hughes 2004:13).

But "Halawi" does not give up:

> As I conclude from your comment you think it is ok when someone here in this guest book openly talks about a coup d'état in Eritrea? Don't you ask yourself why Warsay e.V. looks on when such entries and opinions are made? Don't you think Warsay e.V. should say something about this?[36]

After several similar entries "Halawi" finally announces he is leaving the guest book, yet not without denouncing Warsay e.V. as "pro-Ethiopia", among one of the worst insults for an Eritrean:

> Had I known right from the beginning that Warsay e.V. guest book represents the Ethiopian side I would not have stayed here. Now I understand why all these anti-Eritrean comments have been tolerated. Long live the Eritrean people!

Whoever "Halawi" is, he used the guest book very cleverly to alternately provoke anti-government posters to make radical comments and then accuse the webmasters of conspiring with the critics. For if they did not conspire with them, why should they allow such postings? This tactic was clearly used to put *Warsay* in a Catch 22 situation. If they censored the critical voices they could no longer claim to be an open forum. If they did not, they would be ousted as traitors. Both would cause considerable problems for their real life work and their attempts to cultivate an image of critical but devout patriots. According to a *Warsay* member, the confusion become total when some individual(s) pretended to be *Warsay* members and made radically pro-government statements contradicting earlier postings by the real *Warsay* that they wanted to create an open forum. Similar attempts to discredit *Warsay* also happened in real life, for instance when another, formerly befriended group wrote a letter to the Eritrean Consulate and the local *MahbereKom* accusing them of being anti-government.

Not surprisingly, *Warsay* e.V., have become eager to keep criticism at bay, either by a cautiously practised censorship (which again infuriates the users concerned and also casts the shadow of doubt on *Warsay*'s devotion to pluralistic principles), or by the contributions of individual members that try to counterbalance critical postings or tell the "guests" to remain civil and rea-

36. In fact *Ezewedehankum* had never called for a coup d'état but had predicted that if politics in Eritrea continued as it was there would be an uprising which the current government would not survive (see warsay.com guest book, 19 September 2002). The quotes from *Halawi* and the Warsay member ("EMES") are from the debate ensuing after *Ezewedehankum*'s initial posting, and ended with *Halawi*'s exit on 4 October 2004. Translation from German B.C.

sonable.[37] A more radical form of "de-escalating" certain "hot" debates seems to be resetting the guest book so that older messages can no longer be read and current exchanges are discontinued. One time the guest book was closed for more than two weeks after a discussion about the youth festival held at the Sawa military training camp in west Eritrea. The event had also been advertised on Warsay.com by the Eritrean embassy which was criticised by some "guests". When the guest book was re-opened its closure was explained by technical difficulties. But *honni soit qui mal y pense*, as one non-*Warsay* Eritrean remarked in a private conversation. Apart from the government supporters, various opposition groups also attempt to exert some influence on *Warsay*, or at least to use the *Warsay.com* guest book to raise awareness for their issues (e.g. by posting their links or calling for a boycott on certain events). And as with the pro-government side it is hard to distinguish if this involvement is "directed" from above, or simply is the unsolicited work of some individual zealots.

In spite of these shortcomings and difficulties, *Warsay.com* has nonetheless something to offer that neither real life organisations nor "transnational" Web sites can provide. It has become a link between "local" and "transnational" Eritrean cyberspace and between various local groups that are difficult to bring together in a real life context where circuits of opposition and pro-government groups hardly overlap. Interestingly the advantages of virtual versus face-to-face meetings have become a topic of discussion on *Warsay.com*. When *Warsay* members challenged on-line critics to attend their real life meetings, some guest book writers then pointed out the benefits of online discussion – reaching a wider audience, more freedom for everyone to really say what s/he thinks without risking verbal attacks, ostracisation or getting even mugged by "HiGidefs' street rambos".[38]

37. The censoring I observed was partly justified because of "flaming" (insults and foul language), but sometimes it was also used to remove "too" critical entries, e.g. a link to an unfavourable *Amnesty Iinternational* report on Eritrea.

38. Warsay.com, 14 April 2004. *HiGidef* is the Tigrinya acronym for the Eritrean ruling party (PFDJ). Asked to come along to a seminar organised by *Warsay*, an Eritrean government critic voiced similar reservations: "At the moment I see no chance of getting together. I wouldn't feel good there either. Haven't you heard of the incident in Sweden?" The incident in Sweden had taken place at a seminar organised by group of recent Eritrean refugees and an opposition group. Government supporters severely disrupted the meeting, shouting and throwing chairs at panellists and audience. The case was also debated on some of the "transnational" Eritrean Web sites, and mentioned on *warsay.com*.

The advantages described above of cyber debates over "real" ones have given rise to hypotheses that the Internet might indeed provide a space for an incipient Eritrean "transnational" or "cyber civil society" (cf. Hepner 2003; Bernal 2004). Yet, while I am not generally adverse to the idea, I have my reservations when looking at the concept from a local perspective (and where, if not locally, can "civil society" take place?). The creation of a "civil society", real or virtual, is about participation. This is also the crucial problem when we talk about cyber-diasporas and their impact on real life communities including their home society. Who are the participants or "citoyens" on the net? In the previous two sub-sections I have tried to roughly portray one such group of local actors. However, the question is not merely who becomes active on the web, but also who can be reached at all by the activists?

Locality reveals:Limits and opportunities of Web use among Eritreans in the diaspora

As pointed out above Eritrean cyberspace used to be an elite thing, and in some ways it still is. Apart from the costs involved and the necessity of having at least some basic technical know-how, there is the language problem. Those sites that are thought to have an impact on Eritrean politics and/or dominate the political debate tend to use English as medium of communication. This inhibits for instance a fair number of Eritreans living in Frankfurt from using these sources as they lack the necessary language competence (either completely, or to a degree that allows only for a biased picture of what is going on). Even the considerable increase of online publishing in Tigrinya or Arabic does not mean that at least those sources are now accessible to anyone with access to the Internet. One group that is excluded from this information too is the relatively large number of illiterate or semi-illiterate rural refugees who came to Germany via Sudan in the mid-1980s.[39] The same goes for parts of the so-called second generation who are in a particular predicament. Many Eritrean children growing up in Germany attend types of schools that do not provide them with enough proficiency in English to read Web sites such as

39. Also Eritrean diaspora women seem to be under-represented on the web, both as consumers and as activists.There is no "hard evidence" of this, yet it mirrors both studies on the world-wide use of the Internet by women as well as my fieldwork observations. Eritrean women also tend to be less formally educated than men (cf. Schröder 1992) and constitute a minority among those of my informants showing interest in cyber-Eritrea's favourite topic: politics.

Asmarino.com.[40] The same goes for their knowledge of Tigrinya which tends to be limited to oral communication skills on a family level. Speaking their mother tongue in varying degrees of fluency, most youngsters find it very hard (or they are unable) to decipher the *Ge'ez* script which they might or might not learn at a Sunday school. For those whose mother tongue is not Tigrinya the situation is presumably even worse. Unless they have a higher education, the only written language German-born Eritreans can communicate in is German, thus making Eritrean Web sites using German their first choice on the Web.

But the choice of one language over another is not always an innocent act that leads *nolens volens* to the (partial) exclusion of groups such as the less educated or diaspora-raised children. Language can also be a political statement or became part of a policy aimed at including or excluding certain groups of people. At least three such forms of "language policy" can be distinguished – firstly, there is the general preference for one or two languages by certain Web sites, thus appealing *per se* to a certain constituency and excluding another. An example of this is the extensive use of Arabic on some Eritrean (opposition) Web sites. Choosing to write in Arabic (the widely used *lingua franca* among lowland/Muslim Eritreans speaking different mother tongues) some of the opposition Web sites exclude most highland Tigrinya speakers that are less likely to read and write Arabic than their lowland compatriots.[41] A positive effect of this discrimination is that it again *in*cludes non-Tigrinya and non-English speakers that have so far been *ex*cluded from most other online discourses. Generally the growing choice between various languages on the Web might therefore be seen as a step towards creating equal opportunities and a wider platform for participation that would include Eritreans of all backgrounds into cyber-debates. Yet, as the use of a particular language

40. As a part-time English language tutor I also earn my keep thanks to the shortcomings of foreign language teaching in German schools that do not prepare for higher education. Graduates have great difficulties reading e.g. an English newspaper article. Not surprisingly children whose mother tongue is not German tend to have even more problems. On *Warsay.com* some visitors have recently asked for help with the translation of articles from English Web sites.

41. The majority of diaspora Eritreans are Christian, highland Tigrinya. And though it is officially denied, there is a nexus between being a Muslim lowlander and being close to opposition or dissident movements in the diaspora. Many Muslims feel marginalised by the Christian highlanders, who in turn eye them with suspicion. It is also in this context that the issue of language policy has become highly politicised in Eritrea proper.

on the Web often goes hand in hand with a certain political, ethnic or sectarian bias, it can hardly be denied that it also serves to reinforce ideologies, fragmentation and polarisation.

A second instance of language being used in a sometimes deliberately discriminatory fashion is the preference of Tigrinya and/or Arabic (as opposed to English or the host countries' vernacular) for particular announcements, comments and publications on the Internet. An example is the web-coverage of the *hizbawi mekete* (roughly: "in defence of the people/nation") seminars conducted throughout the diaspora. The campaign started in the autumn of 2002 and was meant to raise money for Eritreans suffering from drought as well as demonstrating support for the Eritrean government's efforts to protect the country from internal and external "enemies". Pro-government sites such as *Biddho.com* almost exclusively announced these events in Tigrinya. On the one hand, this ensured reaching a greater number of Eritrean non-English readers (often the announcements were pdf-documents that could easily be forwarded, printed, copied and distributed). On the other hand, it prevented too much publicity outside Eritrean circles at a time when Eritrea's deteriorating human rights situation came under international scrutiny. By contrast, opposition sites soon reported about the seminars in English.

A third, mostly individually employed method, is the occasional switching from e.g. English or German to transliterations of Tigrinya that is found in "local" discussion forums, e-groups or guest books.[42] This too seems an acknowledgment of the fact that the Internet, despite Eritreans using it exclusively for "national" purposes, is still a public sphere, that can also be accessed by interested or "nosy" *ferenjis* (foreigners). Here transliterations of Tigrinya may be used as a mechanism to "close" certain debates even within a formally open forum. This goes particularly for the discussion of controversial issues belying the myth of unity and therefore feared as they can weaken Eritrea vis-à-vis malevolent external forces. Other, more worrisome ways of using language as a means of avoiding attention among outsiders allegedly include

42. Of course, one should be careful not to overstress such phenomena: mostly the use of Tigrinya in such forums is pragmatic, e.g. when it is difficult to translate a phrase, term or proverb into German or English, or when emphasis is made. Moreover, interspersing one's postings with Tigrinya phrases is also a means of demonstrating competence in one's mother tongue and showing a deeper knowledge of Eritrean traditions, history and culture.

threats to opposition members in Tigrinya.[43] In contradiction to what "The Internet" stands for, such considerations and strategies illustrate how the "culture of secrecy" and "self-reliance" stemming from the days of the liberation war continue to have an impact on the way Eritreans use the Web.

Another point must be made concerning not so much the issue of language itself as the general attitude towards the written word. It is a fact that vernacular literacy is not a strong feature of Eritrean culture, neither at home nor abroad. Even in diaspora, oral information transmitted in a face to face context is still considered more "trustworthy" than written sources,[44] especially when their origin seems doubtful (as it is the case with the Internet). This lack of trust in information found on the Internet is also related to the high degree of assumed or actual manipulation described above and the difficulties to establish which website is owned or used or (secretly) financed by whom (e.g. by the government, the opposition, the Ethiopians or even the CIA). Hence many Eritreans will rely more on the *bado seleste* (an Eritrean synonym for rumour mill) passed on by a trusted friend than on news gathered on an Eritrean Web site which is often little more than online *bado seleste*, passed on by someone hiding behind a pen name. But also "hard facts" and documents about widely debated events that are published on the Web seem to reach directly a far smaller number of people than one might expect.

Two incidents made me aware of the gap between those who actually *read* news on the Internet, and those who talk about the topics featured on the net. The first incident was the above-mentioned open letter written by a group of Eritrean intellectuals ("G 13") criticising President Issayas Afewerki. Despite the considerable stir up caused by this document and its fateful publication on an Ethiopian Web site, I found that hardly any of my informants had actually read the *corpus delicti*, even though it was later to be found on numerous Eritrean Web sites too. They had *heard* that the letter said this or that, they had *heard* rumours about the leakage and had *heard* that X, Y and Z were

43. These are very sensitive and complex issues, and I assume that the aspect of "inclusion" might indeed be the more important one. After all, the events were eventually controversially debated on Web sites of all political hues, both in English and in Tigrinya and Arabic. Yet an amazing fact is that despite the most fierce political infighting Eritreans have a strong tendency to keep problems "within the family". And in spite of frequent cases of libel and character assassination on the web, one rarely hears about anyone taking legal action.

44. Nor is this notion particular to Eritrea or other developing countries. The German phrase "Lügen wie gedruckt" (meaning literally "Lying like print"), for example, hints at a similar reserve towards the written and (especially) the printed word.

among the signatories. Even in online debates, some participants admitted to not knowing the contents of the letter they either praised or condemned.

The second incident involved another open letter published in a German newspaper and (some time later) on Eritrean Web sites. It included a petition to release presumed Eritrean prisoners of conscience and had been signed by German journalists, politicians, activists and researchers, including myself. On my next arrival in Frankfurt I was promptly reproached by an Eritrean acquaintance: "I *heard* you signed *that* letter. Is that true? I cannot believe you did something like that!". Like him, most *Warsay* members and others were convinced that the letter demanded stopping humanitarian aid to Eritrea and this at a time of severe food shortage. It turned out that the letter had been posted together with a second one that neither myself nor the other signatories knew about. This second letter appealed to the European Union to keep development (not humanitarian!) aid frozen unless the Eritrean government committed itself to democratic reforms. Someone had read and misinterpreted the admittedly confusing postings, and then the news was spread by word of mouth. I sent an explanatory e-mail with an official clarification to several people in the community, yet, I suspect that again it was not the written word, but personal communication with some individuals that led to my "reputation" being at least partially restored.

Both incidents show that Internet has indeed become an important source of information (no one reacted to the letter's publication in a German print medium), but only when combined with local *bado seleste*. One could also say, that in the Eritrean context Internet media transport themes and topics rather than facts or detailed news. Topics flow from the transnational level to the local level and from the realm of the Internet to real life settings. This also becomes obvious when we look at the late *Warsay* e-group or the *Warsay.com* guest book, where issues discussed on "transnational websites" were debated again in a local context using the German language. But with language skills – as well as gender, education and material means – inhibiting unlimited access to the net for a sizable group of Eritreans in Frankfurt, the transport of Internet discussions into real life does not work without intermediaries. This role, I argue, is taken on by *Warsay*, as well as other groups and individuals with "full" access to both the local and the transnational level of Eritrean cyberspace. In Frankfurt, these groups mainly include three identifiable "types" of Internet users and actors with "full" access to Cyber-Eritrea on both a "local" and "transnational" level: (1) younger German-raised Eritreans with higher education, (2) relatively well-educated younger men in their late twenties to early forties who came in the 1980s and 1990s directly from Asmara or Addis, and (3) finally an even smaller group of now middle-aged and elderly men that arrived in Germany in the 1970s and early 1980s – either as students or political activists.

These three groups clearly serve as mediators, interpreters and disseminators, passing on news from the Internet to those who lack access to the Web or parts thereof. This can for instance happen by printing texts and taking them along to the local Eritrean bar, like some of my interviewees do. More commonly, you discuss what you have read in family and friendship circles, add your own ideas and perhaps return to your computer to post a comment that reverberates the opinions of your real life discussion partner or group, thus also bringing the local back into the transnational or global space of the Web. It seems to me that much could be learned about how and to what extent Internet contents are transported into local communities (and *vice versa*) by doing further research into the role such intermediaries play. Being not only mediators but also interpreters in both the literal and figurative sense of the word, they certainly have considerable influence, e.g. via the selection and assessment of the news they pass on in either direction. In the words of a US-Eritrean this makes the Internet a place where:

> ... the literate and the young technologically savvy become in some sense responsible for the communication and creation of an "Eritrean" culture. The elders in the community, who have hitherto been responsible for transmitting knowledge of Eritrean history, politics, religion and culture are largely excluded from this form of diasporic communication, although they are often informed about the discussion which takes place here... . Young Eritreans who have had limited direct contact with the actual history of Eritrea are engaged in redefining community and identity in the global and largely impersonal arena of cyberspace, a space which largely excludes both elders in the diaspora and Eritreans in the homeland.[45] (E-mail correspondence, March 2005)

This also rings true in the case of *Warsay*, whose engagement on the Web and in real life also shows a component that can merely be mentioned here – a "power struggle" between established local community leaders and those who challenge them, between different flight vintages and generations, veteran cadres and newcomers. This process abounds with political overtones, but it also reverberates regionalist, ethnic, religious, gender, vintage and genera-

45. According to the 2003 report of the US State Department, about 75 per cent of the Eritrean population are illiterate.

tion struggles in the diaspora, and judging from *Warsay*'s continued political tightrope walk, this is only the beginning.

Summary

I have analysed the often contradictory impacts of Eritrean Internet use in a local diaspora community. The case study clearly shows that the Internet has not created a kind of "third space" that will radically change a diasporic society and the way people connect. Rather, the opposite rings true – it seems that real life exigencies, traditions, norms and forms of organisation have played a dominant role in mapping out the limits and possibilities of virtual Eritrea. In addition, while the Internet connects local Eritreans in Frankfurt with those scattered across Germany and the rest of the world, the grassroots perspective also reveals that large sections of the local (and global) community are – either by default or by design – excluded from direct access to Cyber-Eritrea or parts thereof. Internet media help new and marginalised groups to create their own platforms, thus fostering more diversity and participation, but again, at the same time reinforce fragmentation within the community. As the example of *Warsay* shows, anyone who becomes active on the Web is under close scrutiny by various local and/or transnational interest groups, making it hard to establish an open and tolerant discourse without facing real life repercussions. Partly this is due to personal conflicts and power struggles on the local level, but it also reflects the current regime's totalitarian demands that do not stop at Eritrea's physical borders but extend into the real and virtual diaspora.

This setting is also what gives me little hope about the Internet's role in creating an Eritrean civil society in the near future – be it in Eritrea proper, in a however virtual realm of cyberspace or in a concrete diaspora community. It is certain that the medium itself cannot work miracles. Discourses need to be transferred from cyberspace into real life in order to evoke changes. This means developing a more open and transparent culture of communication in real life, too, as well as structures and channels to voice opinions that are accepted by a majority as legitimate and trustworthy (cf. Conrad 2005b). So far the impact of using the Web in a locality such as Frankfurt has been contradictory and whether it will serve rather to widen and cement rifts and fissures remains to be seen. There are however, positive and hopeful signs, too, that ways might be found to reconcile the various factions or at least to foster a dialogue. At the time being this may not be possible across the main polarisation of pro- and anti-government sides, but only within these factions. It is partly the merit of Internet forums that diverging opinions within these two circles can no longer be completely suppressed or ignored, but have actually become topics in real life discussions too.

In contrast to other studies on the Internet's powers to overcome this-worldly obstacles for diasporic people (cf. Levine 2003), the picture I have drawn here seems largely pessimistic or ambivalent at best. But a picture, or rather a snapshot of a moment in time is all that it can be. Even while I am writing this, some younger members of *Warsay* have started a new and different attempt at conquering the World-wide Web. Even though the group seems to be standing more firmly on the side of the Eritrean regime these days than some years ago, they see the limitations that an all too clear political stand would bring for their private and business ambitions. The new website (showing no relation to *Warsay*) avoids blatant political statements and sidesteps political pitfalls by focussing on "international" Eritrean festivals, parties and concerts as well as providing a growing database of Eritrean businesses. Their political orientation shows merely insofar as the site omits links to critical websites, ignores opposition events, but advertises "official" ones. The site's guest book and chatroom have become a popular meeting place for the mostly apolitical local second generation. Here too occasional attempts are made to spread propaganda, but regime opponents are not immediately censored. Nor does politics seem to rouse much interest amongst the wider audience. They use the Internet in a much more matter-of-fact and liberal manner than the older generation. If and when they stray into a political topic, they seem to worry less about the "behavioural templates" the older generation remains straightjacketed into even when moving in an anonymous virtual realm. This rift between the differently socialized generations is perhaps the most convincing evidence that the Internet does not simply shape our reality but is indeed a part of it.

References

Al-Ali, Nadje, Richard Black,and Khalid Koser, 2001, "The Limits to 'Transnationalism': Bosnian and Eritrean Refugees in Europe as Emerging Transnational Communities", *Ethnic and Racial Studies* 24(4):578–600.

Barth, Fredrik, 1969, *Ethnic Groups and Boundaries: The Social Organisation of Culture Difference.* Bergen/Oslo: The Norwegian University Press.

Basch, Linda, Nina Glick-Schiller and Cristina Szanton Blanc, 1994, *Nations Unbound: Transnational Projects, Postcolonial Predicaments, and Deterritorialized Nation-States.* Belgium: Gordon and Breach.

Bernal, Victoria, 2001, "Nationalisierung des Transnationalismus. Transnationalism, Diaspora, and the World-wide Web of Eritrean Nationalism", *epd-Entwicklungs-politik* 23/24/2001, 26–29.

—, 2004, "Eritrea Goes Global: Reflections on Nationalism in Transnational Era", *Cultural Anthropology* 19(1):3–25.

—, 2005, "Digital Diaspora: Conflict, Community and, Celebrity in Virtual Eritrea", in Hepner, Tricia Redeker and Bettina Conrad (eds), *Eritrea Abroad. Special Issue of the Eritrean Studies Review* 4(2):185–209.

Conrad, Bettina, 2003, "Eritreans in Germany: Heading from Exile to Diaspora?" in Bruchhaus, Eva-Maria (ed.), *Hot Spot Horn of Africa. Between Integration and Disintegration*, 175–184. Münster; Hamburg; London: LIT-Verlag.

—, 2005a, "From Revolution to Religion: The Politics of Religion in the Eritrean Diaspora in Germany", in Adogame, Afe and Cordula Weissköppel (ed.), *Religion in the Context of African Migration Studies*, Bayreuther African Studies Series, 217–241. Bayreuth: Breitinger.

—, 2005b. "We Are the Prisoners of our Dreams: Exit, Voice and Loyalty in the Eritrean Diaspora in Germany", in Hepner, Tricia Redeker and Bettina Conrad (eds), *Eritrea Abroad. Special Issue of the Eritrean Studies Review* 4(2): 211–261.

Hepner, Tricia Redeker, 2003, "Religion, Nationalism, and Transnational Civil Society in the Eritrean Diaspora", *Identities: Global Studies in Culture and Power.* 10(3): 269–293.

—, 2004, *Eritrea and Exile: Trans/Nationalism in the Horn of Africa and the United States.* Ph.D. Dissertation, Michigan State University.

—, 2005, "Transnational *Tegadelti*: Eritreans for Liberation in North America and the Eritrean People's Liberation Front", in Hepner, Tricia Redeker and Bettina Conrad (eds), *Eritrea Abroad. Special Issue of the Eritrean Studies Review* 4(2):37–83.

Hughes, Howard, 2004, "Eine Volksarmee der besonderen Art - Der Militärkomplex in Eritrea". <http://www.connection-ev.de/Afrika/eri_militaer.pdf> 05/05/06.

Levine, Donald N., 2003, *Reconfiguring the Ethiopian Nation in a Global Era.* From: <http://www.ethiomedia.com/press/reconfiguring_ethiopia.html>.

Matsuoka, Atsuko and John Sorenson, 2001, *Ghosts and Shadows. Construction of Identity and Community in an African Diaspora.* Toronto: University of Toronto Press.

Miller, Daniel and Don Slater, 2000, *The Internet. An Ethnographic Approach.* Oxford, New York: Berg.

Pries, Ludger, 1996, "Transnationale Soziale Räume. Theoretisch-empirische Skizze am Beispiel der Arbeiterwanderungen Mexico–USA", *Zeitschrift für Soziologie*, Jg. 25, Heft 6, 456–472.

Rude, John C., 1996, "Birth of a Nation in Cyberspace", *Humanist* 56(2):17–22.

Schröder, Günter, 1992, *Eritreer in der Bundesrepublik Deutschland. Materialien zur Soziographie.* Arbeitsheft, Berliner Institut für Vergleichende Sozialforschung. Berlin: Edition Parabolis.

—, 2004, *Eritreer in der Bundesrepublik Deutschland. Materialien zur Soziographie.* Unpublished update of the author's 1992 publication.

Smidt, Wolbert, 2000, Äthiopisch-eritreische Kriegsführung in den Medien", *S+F Vierteljahresschrift für Sicherheit und Frieden* 2/2000.

—, 2001, "Kriegsführung und Demokratisierung im Internet. Wie sich die Diaspora am Äthiopien-Eritrea-Krieg beteiligt hat", *epd-Entwicklungspolitik* 23/24/2001, 30–33.

Tekie Fessehatzion, 2005, "Eritrea's Remittance-Based Economy: Conjectures and Musings", in Hepner, Tricia Redeker and Bettina Conrad (eds), *Eritrea Abroad. Special Issue of the Eritrean Studies Review* 4(2):165–183.

Waldmann, Peter, 1999, "Societies in civil war", *Sociologus, Beiheft 1: Dynamics of Violence*, Georg Elwert u.a. (hgs), Berlin 1999:61–84.

Zurawski, Nils, 2000, "Virtuelle Ethnizität. Identität und Informationstechnologie", in Best, Günther und Reinhart Kößler (eds), *Subjekte und Systeme. Soziologische und anthropologische Annäherungen*, 222–231. Festschrift für Christian Sigrist zum 65. Geburtstag, Frankfurt: IKO.

Southern Sudanese – A community in exile

Roqaia Abusharaf

For a long time, I believed that the men of Africa would not fight each other. Alas, black blood is being spilled, black men are spilling it, and it will be spilled for a long time to come.
Franz Fanon, in conversation with Jean-Paul Sartre

The horrific media images of the war-ravaged, ailing, starving people of the southern Sudanese provinces of Bahr El Ghazal, Equatoria, and Upper Nile bear witness to the longest ongoing civil war in the world. They also conceal the nobility and pride of a people whose rich culture, means of livelihood, and cosmology have seized the imagination of generations of travelers, artists, and photographers from all over the world. Anthropologists too have supplied well-wrought descriptions of the peoples and cultures of the southern Sudan. Classic ethnographic works by Sir Edward Evans-Pritchard, Godfrey Lienhardt, Charles Seligman, Simon Simonse, Pierre de Schilippe, and Francis Deng offer a convincing affirmation of the cultural complexity of the region. The scene, however, has been shattered by a civil war between the north and the south that has raged since 1955. Today, in the words of Roger Winter of the United States Committee for Refugees, "the people of Sudan, particularly in the south, whom I know best, are vibrant, with lots of pride, fond of jokes and smiling, hauntingly beautiful in their singing. But in the 15 years of this phase of Sudan's war, they have known more suffering, terror, and death than any other population on earth" (Winter 1999). According to the US Committee for Refugees' Sudan Fact Sheet (1999), more than 1.9 million people in south and central Sudan died between 1955 and 1999 as a result of war. The massive loss of life surpasses the civilian death toll in any war since World War II. Over four million southerners have been compelled to flee their homes and have become displaced internally and internationally.

This conflict, which figures prominently as a determinant in the current migratory streams to the United States and Canada, reflects a quandary that the majority of postcolonial African states have had to grapple with since independence from European rule (Abusharaf 1998). The current borders of the Sudan were drawn by the British in 1899 when the Condominium Agreement was signed. Yet for the duration of British colonialism in the Sudan, the north-south division was administratively enforced. Fearful of the spread of northern cultural practices (such as female circumcision), the Arabic language, and Islam, the British governed the two regions as separate political units. This was accomplished by way of the Closed Doors Ordinance, which diminished interaction between the two regions (Abdel Rahim 1969). In so doing, British colonial policies planted the seeds of disunion in a country with such remarkable ethnic diversity, pitting northerners versus southerners and "Arabs" versus "Africans". Indifferent to the long history dividing and connecting the two regions (as well as the internal diversity of each), and failing to allow contact to develop between their peoples, the British combined both portions into a united Sudan at independence in 1956. So, like other modern African states, the Sudan may claim that the British colonial regime was responsible for blending disparate ethnic groups into one country.

The question of north-south relations became widely seen as an "ethnic" conflict between "Arabs" and "Africans" at the time of independence. However, just as there is no monolithic "Arab" north, the south also is a land of extraordinary ethnic variety. Ethnographers of southern populations depict marked differences in kinship structures, ethnolinguistic groups, social organization, and modes of subsistenee (Wai 1973). According to Mohamed Omer Beshir (1968), southern Sudanese could be distinguished into three groups; the Niolitics, comprising the Dinka, Nuer, Shiluk, and Anuak; the Nilo-Hamitics, including the Murle, Didinga, Boya, Toposa, and Latuka; and the Sudanic peoples, including the Azande among other smaller social formations. In light of the heterogeneity of both south and north, it can be argued that the civil war has been prompted mainly by political objectives, and that ethnicity is but one component. More widely, as Talal Asad argues: "In any attempt to treat political domination as a central problem, it is necessary to inquire into such questions as the institutional sources of power deriving from the overall social and economic structure" (Asad 1970:8). For southerners, "ethnic" or "racial" differences became exacerbated in the large scheme of power relations in Sudanese society. As Manning Marable explains: "Race only becomes real as a social force when individuals or groups behave towards each other in ways that either reflect or perpetuate the hegemonic ideology of subordination" (Marable 1995:364).

Following independence, the new national leadership was not successful at mobilizing the Sudanese peoples, southerners and northerners alike, behind a political and economic program that could fulfill basic needs and ensure stability. Political authority was then seized by military governments after short-lived interludes of democratic rule. This reality has perpetuated a political arrangement that has encouraged the continuation of the war and subjected the Sudan in general and the southern region in particular to widespread instability, destruction of the economy, disruption of social cohesion, and death and displacement on a large scale (Abusharaf 1998; Bechtold 1992; Deng 1995; Holt and Daly 1988; Khalid 1989). Bona Malwal is right to argue that the causes of the war "stem from a lack of basic democracy. This has led to a situation in which those who exercise power abuse the right of those who are excluded from state power; the exclusion of the vast majority of the people of the regions from state power has led to a perpetual state of tension, civil war and conflict" (Malwal 1993:3).

The Sudan is a perfect illustration of an African country unable to achieve nationhood despite a successful struggle for independence. In Nations and Nationalism since 1780, Eric Hobsbawm points to the impact of the colonial legacy on the question of postcolonial nationalism:

> Decolonization meant that, by and large, independent states were created out of existing areas of colonial administration, within their colonial frontiers. These had, obviously, been drawn without any reference to, or sometimes even without the knowledge of, their inhabitants and therefore had no national or even proto-national significance for their populations; except for colonial-educated and westernized native minorities of varying, but generally exiguous size. Alternatively, where such territories were too small and scattered, as in many colonized archipelagos, they were combined or broken up according to convenience or local politics. Hence the constant, and eventually often vain, calls of the leaders of such new states to surmount "tribalism", "communalism", or whatever forces were made responsible for the failure of the new inhabitants of the Republic of X to feel themselves to be primarily patriotic citizens of X rather than members of some other collectivity (1990:170).

Extensive border crossings have been a consequence of the Sudan's civil war. For example, an estimated 71,500 refugees had fled the Sudan to neighboring Ethiopia by 1970. In addition, there were unknown, yet enormous, numbers of refugees in Chad and Kenya (Holborn 1975). Policies toward the south continued to swing between warfare and short-lived peaceful resolutions. One resolution toward peace was the Addis Ababa Agreement in 1972, which provided for the unification of the southern provinces into a single region with full administrative and political autonomy. This agreement put a temporary end to years of internecine strife and granted recognition to the pluralistic nature of Sudanese society (Warburg 1992:92).

The peace agreement encouraged refugees to return home. The recognition of the south as an autonomous administrative and political unit was a positive step toward ensuring the right of self-rule for southerners. According to Philister Baya, her own family, which had lived in exile in Uganda since 1966, decided to repatriate along with thousands of refugees. "We enjoyed a relative peace for eleven years. After a decade the peace collapsed and the armed hostilities resumed" (Baya 1999:61). The resumption of the war can be attributed to President Gaafar Nemeiri's decision in 1983 to revoke the Addis Ababa Agreement. By fragmenting the south again, Nemeiri prompted another war, made worse this time around by his espousal of the hegemonic policy of Islamization. Since then, the adoption and firm application of *sharia* law have developed further, irrespective of the complex nature of the multiethnic, multireligious Sudan. In his 1998 book *Politics and Islam in Contemporary Sudan*, Abdel Salam Sidahmed explains that Islamization incorporates legal, political, and ideological aspects to legitimize central power. The legal component addresses offenses such as theft, consumption of alcohol, apostasy, and rebellion against the state. The firm application of sharia under the current regime since 1989 has been accompanied by the imposition of jihad (holy war) and the official imposition of the Arabic language, creating a situation best described as "a tyranny of the majority" (see Guinier 1994). Consequently, these impositions have inflamed the strife. As Deng puts it: "The conflict has increasingly been viewed in religious terms. Although this has the effect of oversimplifying the situation, it makes religion symbolic of all that is contested, a critical factor in the definition of the national identity and in the shaping and sharing of unity of the country that is becoming increasingly accepted while religion, paradoxically is becoming a highly divisive factor" (Deng 1991:25–26).

Since the recurrence of war under the current military regime, the mass departure of refugees has begun all over again. Large movements have taken place internally as well as across the national border. According to Sudanese geographer M.E. Abu Sin, human dislocation due to the war reached its peak during 1989–90, when a million southerners took refuge in northern Sudan. Statistics published in the United States Committee for Refugees News (1999) show that, with four million southerners now living in the north, the Sudan leads the world in internally displaced persons. Furthermore, many of them have been displaced more than once, and often repeatedly, since 1989.

As can be expected during a time of war, human distress multiplies and takes on different forms. The displacement of southerners is not the sole outcome of the war. Another adverse consequence that southerners talk about has manifested itself in the resuscitation of slavery. In 2000, slave raids were reported to have been taking place routinely in some parts of the south. Several news programs in the United States addressed the efforts of one group of American school children who donated their lunch money to redeem the freedom of slaves in the Sudan. About 25,000 slaves have been freed – redeemed for about fifty dollars each – with the help of Christian Solidarity Intemational in Switzerland (Sudanet, 7 September 2000). Although this organization has been criticized, many southern Sudanese confirm its views.

Slavery is intimately linked to a war economy (Bales 1999, 2000). War-slavery has been documented as a disturbing effect of the government's military operations. Bhatia Shyam describes a pattern in which Arab militias from the northern part of the country, including officers in the army, have engaged in kidnapping children and women from villages in the south and forced them to work as field laborers, domestic servants, or sexual concubines (US Committee for Refugees 1999). As many as 100,000 Sudanese are enslaved, according to Charles Jacob, president of the Anti-Slavery Group in Boston (Sudanet, 7 September 2000). Some are also sold to countries in north Africa or the Persian Gulf. War-induced interethnic conflict among southerners was also reported as a cause of slave raids.

The most obvious example of interethnic conflict is that between the Nuer and Dinka. Hiram Ruiz (1998) provides a helpful analysis of the displacement of Sudanese and points out that in East Equatoria Province the overwhelming majority of the displaced are Dinka from the Bor region, all of whom have been displaced two or three times by Nuer raids. But as Kevin Bales points out, tribes that have been victims of slave raiding have sometimes themselves raided other tribes (Bales 2000:18).

Rebecca, a Dinka woman, last saw her home seven years ago. She says combatants from neighboring ethnic Nuer attacked her town in the Jongli region and killed and raided Dinka (US Committee for Refugees 1999). However, in October of 1999 the leaders of both the Nuer and the Dinka met to discuss the return of women, children, and cattle captured in raids or abducted during the years of hostility. These talks were facilitated through the People to People Peace East Bank Nilotics Reconciliation Conference that was launched on 8 May 1999. The October conference was the second and called to end hostilities, halt further displacement, and reconcile the Nuer and Dinka (Sudanet, 2 May 2000).

Before 1955 southern communities perceived migration efforts as threatening to the well-being of both the individual and the collectivity, and outmigration from the southern region of the Sudan was extremely uncommon. "To a Dinka, his country with all its deprivations and troubles is the best in the world. Until very recently going to foreign lands was not only a rarity, but a shame. For a Dinka to threaten his relatives with leaving Dinkaland was seen as little short of suicide. What a lot to give up, and for what?" (Deng 1972:6). Ator Ayiik, a Dinka, confirmed this view when she said, "It is difficult for someone like me to depart my own land. Although we have difficulties here, it is my own land. If I die, I will die here. In another country you are not free. My land is better" (US Committee for Refugees 1999, 52).

This view has changed only with great unwillingness as millions of people were forced to flee their region. The southern Sudanese experience is different from other Sudanese migrations, then, in that these are refugees under direct coercion of war. As Kunz has noted, "It is this reluctance to uproot oneself and the absence of positive original motivations to settle elsewhere, which characterize all refugee decisions and distinguish refugees from voluntary migrants" (cited in Bariagaber 1995:209). As a result, southern migration has become a solution of last resort.

This spatial dislodging has had profound social ramifications. Devastation of the social cohesiveness of entire communities occurred as a result of population dispersal (see Bascom 1995). The most severe impact of war on southerners manifested itself in the eroding of lineage and family structures, destruction of traditions such as initiation and other rites of passage, homelessness, and abject poverty within the receiving communities. Southerner Christina Dudu, herself displaced in Khartoum, argues that the majority of the refugees were originally "agriculturists or agro-pastoralists whose rural skills do not provide them with opportunities to make a living in their new urban surroundings" (Dudu 1999:51). In the words of Salah El Din El Shazali, the powerlessness of southerners is linked to lack of access to "objects and symbols that are central to the maintenance and propagation of socio-cultural identity, value systems and practices" (1995:42). Added to these problems are intensified intercommunity conflicts, personal bafflement, and social confusion.

Although displacement is typically hurtful for everyone involved, it is far worse for women (Baya 1999; Eastmond 1993; Hackett 1996; Indra 1999). Dudu's (1999) study on southern displaced women delineates gendered forms of exploitation that have accompanied the displacement. She has cast light on sexual abuse, prostitution, harassment, and other practices that were hitherto virtually absent among these societies.

I discovered this abuse during my own fieldwork in the Sudan, where I was informed by a social worker at a Sudanese non-governmental organization that one of the most distressing aspects of the experiences of the internally displaced is that they begin to adopt cultural practices previously unknown to them, including female circumcision. With no money to pay for a traditional wedding dowry, women are barred from marriage and become outcasts in the eyes of their fellow countrymen (Adam 2001). Mary, a nurse, explains: "These people lost everything back home. Practicing circumcision is a way to imitate their neighbors, to be like them; and to become more marriageable."

These newly transmitted customs of the "north" to southerners is a source of concern to southern Sudanese scholars. The cultural borrowing underway is seen, for instance, by Pressla Joseph, professor at Bahr El Ghazal University, in this way: "The cultures of Southern Sudanese suffer from the borrowing of Northern Sudanese practices. For example, marriage practices are changing. Now the bride asks for *shaila* (a dowry which consists of money, jewelry and other goods). Also in funeral services, Southerners started to mimic Northerners. The Dinka language is also under the threat of extinction as Southerners now speak Arabic among themselves. I am fearful that this will entail loss of identity" (Adam 2001).

When southern Sudanese cross the border to neighboring African countries, their problems transcend those of cultural borrowing. Southerners who go to Cairo, for instance, embark on a journey that promises trouble as much as it offers hope and optimism. The journey by train lasts for several days in crammed conditions, and is fraught with hardship and suffering. Once in Ramsis Station in Cairo, they head for the Catholic church in Zamalik, Abbassia, and to various Anglican churches. The Catholic church on Ahmed Said Avenue in Cairo is the official residence of southerners. The church oversees their affairs in Egypt and helps in their resettlement applications to the United Nations High Commissioner for Refugees. The arrival rate is 500 per month, and by 1989 over forty thousand had come.

Needless to say, they meet a life that is proportionately filled with strain and anxiety. Unemployment, homelessness, and overcrowding while waiting to be resettled are some of the many challenges they face (Daughtry 2001). Twenty people share an apartment with little to do but work as servants or peddle herbs and small items in the market. A resident in the Abbassia neighborhood where large numbers of southerners live maintained that almost seventy men and women who were kicked out of their apartments in summer 2000 for not paying rent became homeless (Rose Al Youssif 2000). A southern Sudanese refugee woman described the situation eloquently when she remarked that Sudanese here face another war. A recent article published in Rose Al Youssif (2000), a prestigious Egyptian magazine, was titled "Migration to Egypt: Are Refugees Guests or Criminals?" The incident that precipitated the article involved a fight in Cairo between southern Sudanese refugees and Egyptians. Some accused the refugees of dealing in drugs. A Catholic priest from the church came to their defense. "I was in the church when people came in to tell me about the fight. When I arrived at the gas station (*benzina*), I saw Sudanese and Egyptians there. I tried to talk the Sudanese into going back to the church. In the meantime Egyptians picked up wood logs and tried to beat them up. People must know that the Sudanese who where arrested because of this did not instigate the fight. They were not drunk either, as people reported to the police. The injury done to these people was extensive. At the time of the fight, we already had 400 people in the church. Everything was just chaotic."

This incident depicts a bleak picture, one in which tension is building in areas where refugees are concentrated. The criminalization of these refugees also points to strong sentiments of exasperation and resentment on the part of the Egyptian hosts. The southerners' reaction to the incident also reflects strong refugee emotionality – produced and sustained by an unfriendly atmosphere. In spite of this, what gives southern Sudanese some hope and optimism is the knowledge that Cairo is only a transit station from which they move to the United States, Australia, New Zealand, or Canada. By summer 2000, 3,230 claims for resettlement had been processed (Rose Al Youssif 2000). The happy news that their application has been accepted invites celebration and delight for those waiting their turn to relocate.

Arrival in the United States and Canada

Probably one of the most highly acclaimed fashion models in the United States and Europe today is Alek Wek, a Dinka woman who lived with her family as a refugee in England. Alek Wek, who has graced the covers of magazines and made appearances on several talk shows in the United States, now resides in Manhattan – "a model life", as Constance White (2000), a magazine writer, describes her current existence of elegance and affluence. Alek Wek's trajectory does not mirror that of the majority of southerners, even though she herself is a refugee. One cannot belittle her experience, but the grief that thousands of southern Sudanese have endured remains unspeakable, and almost inarticulable.

The following account of Philister Baya communicates the more typical traumas that southern Sudanese, especially women, are forced to withstand. She writes:

> I came to live in Khartoum in 1987 and worked in the Council for the South until it was dissolved in January 1991. Soon, in March 1991, the Sudan People's Liberation Army (SPLA) occupied the town of Maridi. As Mundri, my home place, is just few miles from Maridi, the government army decided to evacuate Mundri, walking away on foot and accompanied by the civilian population, including my family. Upon their arrival at Rokon, fighting took place between the army and the Sudan People's Liberation Army. Many civilians were killed in crossfire. My dear father, sister and cousin were amongst those killed in that incident on Good Friday (1999, 62).

Baya's story is by no means an anomaly – it echoes those of thousands of men and women. No wonder that the southern Sudanese see the current Islamic government as an extremely aggressive regime in relation to defenseless civilian populations. For southerners, the problem is aggravated by racial, political, and economic exclusion via the twin processes of Arabization and Islamization. All of this has converged in what they perceive as nothing less than a total annihilation of their indigenous cultures and beliefs.

To learn more about southern Sudanese migration to the United States and Canada, I interviewed southerners in New York City, Washington DC, Michigan, and Toronto. Others who resided in Texas, Arizona, California, and New Jersey responded to my survey (see also Holtzman 2000). Although these interviewees were of different ages, occupations, ethnicity, gender, and class backgrounds, they all considered migration as a means to sidestep war, Islamization, and militarism.

The arduous processes of transformation for southerners are reflected in their stories of their experiences in exile. These southern Sudanese were mainly young or middle-aged individuals who began arriving in the United States and Canada in the 1980s and have continued to arrive (up to the time of this writing in early 2002) as a result of the civil war. Civil war refugees are mostly Christians, and those I encountered were generally highly educated, having either completed college or at least secondary education at the time of arrival (but compare to Holtzman 2000). The majority have high levels of proficiency in English. Most of the respondents indicated that they received substantial help from refugee resettlement organizations like the US Catholic Conference, Christian Outreach, and the World Council of Churches. Although one interviewee maintained that the resettlement process is a highly selective procedure that automatically rejects illiterate displaced people, current reality refutes this view.

Civil war migrants who make it to North America can be grouped into three migratory streams according to individual histories. The first consists of a number of migrants who resided in Kenya, Ethiopia, Zaire, Uganda, Egypt, and Central African Republic before their move abroad, which was facilitated by refugee resettlement programs. (Most civil war migrants reported that their last place of residence prior to coming to North America was another African country.) Leaving the Sudan to enter these countries was only the first step in their migration journey; most had to wait months, sometimes years, before placement and resettlement in a new country. A second stream consists of university scholars and government employees who had already been in North America for training programs and who, like their northern counterparts, preferred to remain. These, who arrived directly from the Sudan, were commonly government employees, some of whom resided and worked in the north prior to migration. Third was a small number of Sudanese who migrated to North America from Europe. The majority of these civil war migrants received refugee resettlement services. Of paramount importance in all these cases was the role of political and religious factors, with the government's policies of Islamization adding to a pre-existing sense of subordination and relegation to second-class citizenry. The polemics of identity – and its manipulation for political purposes thus plays a significant role in both the civil war and the resulting migratory phenomena. (This is highlighted in the experiences of northern Sudanese, Christians as well.)

One of the first people I interviewed in 1993 was Peter. He was thirty-three years old and was born in Ngusuluku, in the western part of Bahr El

Ghazal Province. Peter arrived in Washington, DC, in 1987, four years after the revival of the civil war. Peter voiced the motives behind migration of the majority of southerners I interviewed: "Education, political unrest, and persecution of Christians are the reasons why I came." He explained that the church helped him to settle by providing financial aid. He also related a personal revelation that became a recurring theme in my research: "The best thing about living here is discovering myself as an African. In the US I continue to suffer, namely in the form of arbitrary police arrest and questioning. I see no possibility of assimilation, and I very much keep my relations with other Sudanese. This experience forces me to never lose sight of where I came from and of going back if the conditions that pushed me here in the first place end."

Peter went on to say that the subordination of the south is a concern for every southern Sudanese here in the United States and Canada, as well as in the Sudan. The exclusion of the region from socioeconomic development, the unequal distribution of resources, and the under-representation of southerners in the political sphere are seen by Peter as significant factors in the underdevelopment of the south and in the war.

The survey and interviews also identified the particular "pull factors" important in the experience of these southern Sudanese. Factors such as political and religious freedom in North America, assistance provided by churches and refugee resettlement organizations, and encouragement by family members and friends who were already here. As Joseph, a thirty-six-year-old refugee living in Connecticut, put it: "Almost everybody knows what is happening in the Sudan. The reasons for my leaving are religious persecution, disrespect for human lives, political oppression, and the war in the Sudan. I had no home in the Sudan. I was just living as a refugee in another African country, in Kenya. The reason why I am here is because of the freedom of worship and the respect of human rights." Joseph's viewpoint was reflected in the survey: although only 21 per cent of Muslim northerners indicated they had migrated for political reasons, 82 per cent of Christian southerners specified this as the main reason. Here are some representative stories.

John

Like many other Sudanese professionals, John describes his migrant experience like someone who is unexpectedly stranded away from home. As he spoke, I could see he was reliving the trauma of discovering the impossibility of returning there. Normally a quiet gentleman, he became animated, and spoke passionately as he told his story, his voice often rising with anger, as if feeling it for the first time.

> I am forty-one years old. I was born in Equatoria Province. I am a Latuka. I am Christian. I arrived in the US in 1981. I completed my education up, to my Ph.D. in the United States. Before joining the University of Khartoum, I used to live in Uganda and then Zaire. I left for Khartoum to go to college. I was a teaching assistant at the University of Khartoum. So I came as an exchange student with the sponsorship of a church organization. When I came here I worked like everybody else very hard to make ends meet. I worked odd jobs here and there till I finished. But still I don't have a full-time job. I am not really satisfied with the job situation, because I have to send remittances to family members back home. The main reasons for staying on after my degree was finished are war and persecution. I would like to go back to the Sudan once peace [and] racial, religious, and cultural equality is established. Because life here is not problem-free. Loneliness, stress, and racism are the most common problems. But I try to overcome this feeling by socializing with Sudanese and by joining the Sudanese Pax Sudani Network with other southerners. I feel these things help me keep my Sudanese culture, which, consciously, I feel not too strongly about, but unconsciously I do feel strongly about keeping.

William

Most of the southerners I interviewed understandably perceived Islamic law as a mechanism of northerner-forced Islamization and Arabization in the southern region. Among these was William, a fifty-year-old Presbyterian minister born in Akobo. His wife, also a southern Sudanese, from Rumbek, and children moved with him to Chicago in October 1984, a year after the imposition of Islamic law in the Sudan.

> In the Sudan, I was chairman and managing director of a pastoral organization. Now I work on an international development project and my interest in it emphasizes development at the grassroots level. I also worked for two years in Addis Ababa (Ethiopia) as host for Radio Voice of Gospel Liberation. I left that job to take up a ministerial appointment in the Sudan. I left the Sudan as protest against the Islamization and Arabization of southern Sudan, which continues to be a marginal region. Once we arrived, we received a lot of support. Church groups, friends, and non-governmental organizations spared no effort in helping us. My friends here also helped us tremendously – not only did they provide us with a place to live when we first came but assisted in the process of settlement itself. They offered us accommodations and showed us where to find shops and the best deals for clothing. Life here is a lot easier in terms of access to material goods. But overall there is something about the Sudan that makes your life

> easier there, it is home. Sure you struggle to obtain basic necessities like milk, sugar, and gas, but you know it is easier, because life in America has its problems such as the exaggerated individualism with all its implications and consequences, and the inability of citizens to try to understand people who are different. But my relations with Americans are good, although generally business is humanly superficial. My thoughts of my culture are very frequent and deeply ingrained inside of me. I am unequivocal about going back home when the (government's) pursuit of Islamic and Arabic policies changes. I hope that the Sudanese people will work and struggle to influence the return to a secular constitution. Believe me, life is much easier there.

Like the majority of interviewees, William maintained that permitting the continuation of the war is tantamount to the disintegration in civil society of the Sudan as he knew it. Southerners recognized that a de-politicization of religion and an acknowledgment of the multicultural character of the Sudan are critical to any peaceful resolution. Putting an end to the war is an important precondition for refugees to reclaim their lands and their lives. Nevertheless, they do not hold any conviction that this goal is within range under current political circumstances.

Morris

Morris, forty-six years old, was born in Yei. He is Catholic and married to a woman from Kajo-Keji. Morris was resettled in the United States in 1991 with the sponsorship of the D.S. Catholic Conference; until then, he was living in Kenya. Morris first worked in a government job in the United States. After a period on welfare, he now works as a supervisor in a different field and reports feeling underemployed. Morris is attending school in New Jersey.

> My problems in the Sudan are religious and political. I will only go back if the south becomes independent. The United States refugee and asylum seekers admission enabled me to be resettled here. The United Nations High Commissioner for Refugees and the World Council of Churches are the main organizations that provide resettlement services in refugee camps. I encountered many problems here: loneliness, racial discrimination, and cultural shock are only some. Subjection in the cultural sphere stems primarily from the current Sudan government's attempts to create a "unicultural" Islamic society.

For Morris, as for a considerable number of respondents, total secession of the south is the only condition under which they will be ready to return. According to Lado, another refugee, "The time to let our people go is long overdue.

We cannot continue to be a nation of masters and slaves; pursuing peace in the context of a unified Sudan sustains Arab hegemony over Africans in Sudan. Partitioning the country would deliver African Sudanese from centuries of bondage at the hands of the Arabs" (Lado 1994:10).

David and Lisa

David and Lisa were both born in the town of Rumbek, he in 1953 and she in 1959. David held an administrative position at Juba University until 1987, when he left the Sudan with Lisa and their three children. They lived in Kenya for two years until the US Catholic Conference was able to resettle them in Virginia. Eventually David brought his family to New Jersey, where he attended graduate school with outside financial assistance. David sees their migration as a temporary situation – "Home is home, and when the war is over I will go back. Right now at home people are barely surviving bullets. They should run for their lives." Lisa told me that she was a housewife in the Sudan but, with the help of her friends, currently works at a daycare center in her neighborhood. "Before I was attending to my family; in the USA I have to leave my own children to a baby-sitter and leave early for work outside my house. I was well-off in the Sudan. Here our salary can't afford a thing. Bringing our children was also very expensive. I can't wait for the war to end and go home."

Michael

Michael, thirty-four, was born in Juba. He owned a business in the Sudan but currently has a part-time job and attends school, working toward a bachelor's degree in business. As a refugee, Michael was resettled in Connecticut with the assistance of Church World Service. When he arrived, says Michael, he met with a "Good Samaritan" who helped him.

> I was given the basic necessities for life: food and accommodation and winter clothing. I found life here a lot easier because of religious freedom and my physical well-being. I was driven from the Sudan by war, resulting from our resistance to northerners' forced Islamization and the marginalization of the south in social, economic, and political spheres. Life became intolerable as a result of the northern Sudanese government policies. It torments me to see my other fellow southerners on TV, and I think about the harrowing conditions they live under. I wish there were something that could be done fast to save them. People have to realize that they are entitled to live as humans. It is obvious that I am here because of the war. The relentless attempts by the Islamic government to isolate

the South and policies limiting our participation in areas of power and influence make me believe that secession is the answer to the southern predicament. It is the only legitimate solution, and southerners should fight until this goal is reached.

Frank

Frank now lives in Toronto, Canada. Originally from Equatoria Province, Frank is Bari and a Christian. He provided a detailed account that offers insight into the inner life of a southern migrant.

I moved to Toronto with my wife and children in 1992 after living as refugees in Kampala,. Uganda. I graduated from college in Sudan and currently attend school part-time in Canada, hoping eventually to obtain a graduate degree in Divinity Studies. Before my departure to Uganda, I was working as a civil engineer and the principal of a vocational training center in Juba. Currently, I do not have a job and in fact I have not been able to get any since I landed in Canada. Depending on government assistance, I volunteer as a community worker. I really worked so hard to find a job, tried to network, mailed in my applications, and physically went from one place to the next, stopping by, asking for a job, but to no use.

Coming to Canada was a blessing because I prayed for safety, but it was hard because coming as a refugee makes you feel that as a human being you can't have choices, you are forced to leave and stay abroad indefinitely. Before I came I was corresponding with church groups and other people I knew from home. The Canadian government was responsible for my resettlement and really helped me a lot to get a visa, arrange travel plans, and provide airfare and a lot of things. They were very helpful to our families.

I came from a country where people's lives are worthless, people die every day. But coming here with that knowledge makes one very emotional, it is very upsetting when people die like that. The good part of living in Toronto, however, is the presence of so many Sudanese northerners and southerners. We get along very well with everyone. We celebrate national events, play cards on weekends and keep in contact. That is what is lifting the pressure off our shoulders, the fact that we were forced into leaving. As far as thousands of southerners in Canada are concerned, let me say that the war and the Islamic religious oppression are the reasons why they are here.

No one seems to understand the pain of leaving your home, your relatives, friends, just everything. You can never recover from that. But you try your best to adjust the best you can. The moral support and other kinds of help that we provide each other here are essential. Maybe if I manage to get a job, that will also help alleviate the pressure.

> Now, my family and I have Sudanese roommates, and we live in government-subsidized housing. We cannot afford anything else. This neighborhood is infested with drugs and problems. As a visible minority, a Black, I encounter racist attitudes here as well. This is a problem, when you find yourself confronted with so many differences, especially cultural differences. But again we go back and forth, we have lived through a lot and we just feel lucky to be alive. For that we feel very grateful. But we are still anxious and worried about family members and relatives who did not get out. This is a nagging worry that never goes away, no matter what you do to occupy your mind. I feel like I want to help, but I have no means.
>
> I do hope that more Sudanese will be able to come to Canada until the situation gets better. For them, coming here will be an eye-opener. Different people have different experiences, but it will be educational for our Sudanese folk who have only heard about modern life but have not seen it. I want to stress that regardless of what I do here, I want to return if or when the southern question is resolved. If that happens today, I will go home.

A recurring theme in these statements is that being able to flee subjection, war, and marginalization is only one step toward freedom. This perspective underpins southern Sudanese patterns of adjustment and adaptation in North American society. It makes for a lingering discontent, whereas the greater number of northern migrants expressed complacency and satisfaction with their move. However, like northerners, southerners do join activities and associations like the political Pax Sudani Organization that not only help them maintain ties with fellow southerners but also help raise awareness in the international community about conditions in the Sudan. Like the rest of Sudanese migrants, southerners yearn to go home should political conditions change, either through the return of democracy or, for some, after their region secedes.

Naya

It is mid-moming on 18 July, 2000, when I receive a telephone call. A social worker from a hospital in New Britain, Connecticut, is trying desperately to locate a Nuer interpreter who can translate for twenty-two-year-old Naya. She had been brought to the hospital by her sixteen-year-old brother-in-law, who himself speaks very little English. Naya had fled with her family to a refugee camp in Ethiopia after the renewal of the war in 1983, as had her future husband with his two brothers. In spite of the hardship and uncertainty associated with life there, it was the only home that Naya had known since she was a child. Then, early in 2000, she and her husband – along with her husband's two younger brothers, both born in the camp – were finally resettled with the help of Catholic Charities and the Archdiocese of Hartford. It took me two days to locate a Nuer interpreter in Wisconsin, and he proved extremely helpful and cooperative with the hospital staff. Through a series of conference phone calls, Naya and her family were able to communicate their innermost thoughts and concerns about their loneliness and their homesickness in this new place. An invitation was extended to me to join a meeting with hospital staff, a representative of Catholic Charities, and the two social workers who were in charge of her case. Along with a fellow Sudanese in Connecticut, we attended the meeting, which turned out to be extremely informative about the predicaments of exile and uprootedness. The nurse practitioner began by identifying Naya's problem.

> Her brothers-in-law, who are sixteen and twelve years old, brought Naya here. Her husband never came with her before. We were so concerned and frustrated because no one could communicate with them. I have the phone number of a northern Sudanese who kindly came to help, but since she did not speak their language she was not able to communicate either. The hospital staff then managed to contact a southern Sudanese family in Hartford, but they apologized because they are not Nuer-speaking. The person you helped us get in touch with is really helpful. Naya's brother-in-law was talking to him the whole time about how lonely and bored they are, and that they don't want to stay here. But what concerned me was that in the beginning of our conference call with him, Naya was reluctant and embarrassed to tell him about her symptoms. She is four months pregnant and her symptoms indicated the possibility of serious problems with her pregnancy. We ran a series of tests. Our resident obstetrician felt that the interpreter should explain to Naya that there are problems with her pregnancy and with the fetus. We wanted to make sure that she understands why she was undergoing these laborious procedures and why the doctor is very anxious to know how she feels about the next stage, which might entail termination of the pregnancy. That, too, proved to be difficult because we have to make absolutely certain that is what she and her husband want. I am not sure how they would feel about it. Is this something done or acceptable in their culture? This is the most emotionally draining case for us. We are so worried about Naya but we are not able to inform her with the details and the medical information. We are going to call the interpreter today to share with him the latest diagnosis.

Listening to the most intimate problems of Naya's encounters in the hospital was at the same time fatiguing and difficult. The discussion then moved from Naya's health to the subject of their life in New Britain. A social-worker started to tell us about her experience with them.

> I have been very busy with this family since they came because of the fact that they don't speak English, and they don't speak the language of other people from their country who live here in New Britain. I take them to the store for grocery shopping. I also take them to the bank, and I taught Shol, the sixteen-year-old, how to use the ATM machine. This was very hard. It took a while to explain to him that the money they get is enough for the rent, utilities, and phone bill. I also showed them how to use the stove and told them to make sure that the burners are turned off if they are not in use. Almost every little thing that seems obvious turns out to be very difficult because of their particular situation. Also, with the use of electricity, I try to explain to them that the bill can be very high. I told them to be careful with that too. Also about the monthly rent – that they have to pay it every month so that the landlord should not throw them out.
>
> I think that Shol is very smart and he pays attention to everything, but still, he is a teen-ager who is in charge of the family now. His brother, Naya's husband, is very quiet and he did not take any English lessons at the camp. So for the most part, he is home day and night and doesn't leave except when he comes with us to the store. This is the other problem. I tell Shol that I am very busy and I can't come more than once a week to drive them to the store. I told them to buy enough groceries, but every time I take them, oh, they buy so little all the time. They buy milk, bread, and meat. I don't know how four people can survive for the whole week on so little.

At this point the other social worker added,

> I worry about this family so much. They are very nice people and my heart goes out to them. But I don't want them to get in trouble. The other day the little boy was riding a brand new bike. When I asked him where he got it, he pointed at the sky. I did not know what he meant by that, whether it belongs to someone in the building who lives upstairs, or whether it fell from the sky (she added jokingly). We have to mention to the interpreter to tell them that if they find things sitting around in front of the building they should not touch them, so that they will not be accused of theft. See, there is a lot of work to be done.

When I told the representative of the Archdiocese of Hartford that there is a Nuer community in Minnesota (see Holtzman 2000) and that there might be a possibility of relocating Naya's family in a community in which they can belong, she explained that the logistics are quite involved, and that their resettlement here was only possible because they had a sponsor in Connecticut. However, after our meeting, things did change dramatically for Naya and her family. The twelve-year-old started school and joined the school's track and field and soccer teams. I was told that he was "absorbing English like a sponge," while sixteen-year-old Shol now insisted he wanted a job. The three brothers all enrolled in English as a second language (ESL) classes. Naya, however, lost her baby two months later. The hospital social-worker told me, "Naya sobbed and cried bitterly. She did not want to see the baby or hold him. She was in shock. We were so sad. She is a very sweet girl. She knew that we cared for her so deeply."

In January 2001, the two Nuer families in New Britain boarded a bus to New York City and then traveled to Minnesota. I learned they were soon in touch with other Nuer families, probably introduced to them by the Wisconsin interpreter. They left ready and anxious for their reunification with other Nuer in the Twin Cities. The social worker added:

> We were very worried about what they were going to do once they got to Port Authority and all these bus connections. But obviously they got concrete directions and in fact the tickets were sent to them by the people there in Minnesota. I am convinced that these people are survivors. If they survived the camp, I am sure they will survive here. When we got a call from Shol to thank us for everything, one forgets that Shol is just a teenager. He is so mature, so responsible. I think they will make it.

Naya's experience is very similar to those described by Jon Holtzman (2000) who studied the Nuer community in Minnesota. He identified problems in dealing with the new environment, from landlords to housekeeping. Holtzman found similar patterns in the resettlement process, the development of community ties, and relations to American hosts. Yet the great ingenuity and resourcefulness of a community that has suffered life's worst blows to human dignity and imagination was also apparent as Nuer migrants carry on in yet another challenging habitat.

The southern Sudanese refugees' ties to their American and Canadian hosts are increasingly mobilized to increase public awareness about the continuing tribulation of their kith and kin in the Sudan. For example, the southern Sudanese community in Alexandria, Virginia, called upon Sudanese and non-Sudanese to join them on 29 July, 1998, for a morning protest march on Pennsylvania Avenue in front of the White House. This event was an effort to bring the displacement, starvation, and death of millions of southerners to the attention of the American government. Professional athlete Manut Bol has initiated dozens of similar events; the seven foot, seven-inch retired center in the National Basketball Association has used his physical stature and popular notoriety to raise the awareness of the international community to the political impasse in the southern Sudan. Although Bol later reconciled with the Sudanese government and was appointed by President Omer El-

Bashir as a cabinet member in the Ministry of Youth and Sports, his earlier efforts registered widely.

Another large protest took place in September 2000 when the United Nations in New York City celebrated its Millennium Summit. The assembled diplomats faced waves of Sudanese migrants, exiles, and their supporters who were protesting the presence of President El-Bashir. Their protest centered on the claim that El-Bashir's military regime had perpetuated atrocities and was responsible for the conditions that propelled them to leave their homeland. This demonstration was not the first; Sudanese migrants and refugees had protested numerous times in front of the Sudanese Mission to the United Nations. Protesters have expressed their concern about a wide range of issues, including slavery and human rights abuses in their homeland.

One account in particular stands out: the story of Bak, who comes from a Catholic Dinka village in southern Sudan. Bak was one of the protesters demanding the arrest of President El-Bashir for directing his military forces to make slaves of civilian captives. In an article entitled "Outside the Summit, a Former Slave Speaks Out," Bak described her ordeal. When she was twelve years old, Muslim horsemen galloped into her Catholic village. According to her, they "burned our houses, and killed many people, including my grandfather, right there in front of my eyes. The attacking Muslim militiamen sold the women and children into slavery as domestics and shepherds. I was like an animal. I escaped one night after my nomadic master tried to rape me. I resisted, and he cut my leg with a knife. I slipped away, got on a truck and hid among the animals." Bak eventually ended up in Khartoum, where she met a fellow Dinka named Majak. In 1998 she married his brother, and six months later was resettled by the United Nations. Bak concluded by stating: "I am dismayed to learn that El-Bashir is walking the streets of New York City, a great city of freedom" (Sudanet, 7 September 2000).

The "lost boys and girls of the Sudan"

On a sunny Khartoum morning in December 1998, I left for Takamul Camp along with two Sudanese social workers whose job often took them to various locations where the internally displaced are concentrated. We traveled for about an hour in congested traffic until we reached the outskirts of the city, a distance of about fifteen to twenty miles. Quite suddenly, the noise and traffic thinned, and for the next mile or two as we drove into Takamul Camp past the densely packed buildings, we were acutely aware of the extent of poverty and hardship everywhere. Stopping at the clinic, we found ourselves in a relatively quiet sector where a group of dwellings made with *gana* (a bamboo-like plant) had been erected by the displaced themselves. The two social workers noted that even for housing these people are more often than not left to their own devices. And indeed, the absence of any substantial building materials or personal possessions in and around these huts was as glaring as the stark sun. In a nearby stall, some refugees were selling salt, peanut butter, and bread, which they had walked several miles to purchase at the market. Although it was very sunny, the weather was cold by Khartoum standards. Still, a group of thirty little boys who might have been in school had they been home were outside barefoot, playing *dafori*, a soccer game using a ball made of socks and old clothes, and wearing only thin handmade cotton pants and shirts tattered from years of wear. During that winter, I visited many similar settlements where displaced southerners live in Sudan – Jebel Awaliaa, Salarna, Wad El-bashir, Soba, Mayo, and Magzoob. All reminded me of Takamul, with similar living conditions and surrounded by disease and suffering.

At Takamul I talked to Mary, a nurse who worked in a nearby clinic which provided limited assistance to the migrants with supplies from the government. She told me the residents of the camps were mostly mothers and children. There are few men, a situation typical of other refugee camps, since most of the men are either killed, join militias, or try to cross the border alone. Many camp girls are employed as maids nearby, and some employers even send the girls to school when they are not working. There is a reluctance to hire southern boys, however, who are less docile and often feared. They are stigmatized, called *shamasa* (thugs), and are largely left alone.

Beyond our conversation, the camp was quiet, except for the sound of younger boys playing. Mary and I decided to talk with them. As soon as they saw us approaching, they stopped their game and ran to us, speaking fluent Arabic. Several of them wanted to hold my camera; one lifted it to his face, pretending to take pictures. When I asked them if I could take their picture their faces shone as they quickly lined up for their photo to be taken. In their adversity, I thought, these young boys had not lost their purity of heart or their charm. These, and tens of thousands of boys like them, are biding their time uselessly in refugee camps. They are unlikely to be resettled while they remain within the Sudan. Their lives are being wasted by a relentless war and by neglect. Thousands of Sudan's youth, driven from their homes, are hoping against hope that the United States will give them a chance at a new life (Corbett 2001; Simmons 2000).

Unlike the refugee boys within Sudan, the experience of those in neighboring Kenya and Ethiopia – now recognized as "the lost boys of the Sudan" – has received considerable media attention in the United States as they leave life in refugee camps to resettle in American cities. Many of these refugees have been living in Kenya for nearly ten years after being orphaned in southern Sudan and fleeing in the late 1980s. Their original number was estimated at 30,000, but it is believed that only 12,000 made it to Kakuma, Kenya, avoiding the wild animals, combat, hunger, and disease that killed others. They have forged their own self-created society in the chaotic world of a northern Kenya refugee camp. Of these, some 3,800 "lost boys" have been cleared for resettlement in the United States.

Numerous reports in the *Los Angeles Times*, the *Atlanta Constitution Journal*, *USA Today*, the *New York Times Magazine*, and the *Lincoln Journal Star* have addressed the subject of resettlement of the "lost boys" in the United States. The move was recommended by the United Nations High Commissioner for Refugees and is overseen by the US Department of State. It is the first time the UNHCR has approved the overseas resettlement of such a large number of unaccompanied minors. The UNHCR has said the move was approved after fruitless efforts by the Red Cross to locate relatives of the boys still in the Sudan (Sudanet, 13 November 2000).

In November 2000, fifty of the boys arrived in the United States and settled in Omaha and Lincoln, Nebraska, with assistance from Lutheran Family Services, Catholic Charities, and other church groups. The plan is to place them together because, as one social worker put it, "We're very conscious of the kin relationship they have established. We will put people who have grown up together as family in the same apartment or apartments in the same building." About 300 more teens are being resettled via charitable agencies in Lansing, Fargo, Phoenix, Boston, Grand Rapids, Philadelphia, Seattle, and Washington, DC They will live with foster families, some of whom are Sudanese. Other cities being considered in this resettlement effort include Richmond, Virginia, and Jackson, Mississippi, as well as sites where substantial Sudanese communities already exist in Minnesota, North and South Dakota, and Texas. The difficulties that resettlement services have identified are numerous. According to the executive director of Church World Service in Nebraska: "It is going to be a challenge… . The world to them is what is in this camp. They have no sense of money. No sense of cooking, shopping, driving, social interaction with adults. The only constant they have is each other" (see Lange-Kubick 2000).

Experienced charity organizations are key to the transition of these Sudanese boys into American life. Already the Roman Catholic Archdiocese of Atlanta has relocated refugees to safe houses in parishes where volunteers sponsor them (Teegardin 2000). Aowe, a refugee in Atlanta, for instance, has an entire parish dedicated to helping him make it in the United States; volunteers from All Saints Catholic Church help him pay his rent and provide childcare while he and his wife attend ESL classes. Like most refugees, the skills he brings from rural Africa are not easily transferable to the American job market, the same problem the "lost boys of the Sudan" will face.

Many southerners in the United States maintain that this longest civil war in history has not achieved any of the goals of either warring party. On the contrary, they maintain, allowing the war to continue only results in the wearing down of Sudanese society. Despite good intentions of charitable organizations helping to resettle refugees, as long as the war continues, the depletion of the southern Sudan's human capital will also persist – at escalating cost. The only certainty is that the "lost boys" will be joined by more lost boys and girls who remain trapped within the Sudan.

References

Abdel Rahim, Mudathir, 1969, *Imperialism and Nationalism in the Sudan: A study in constitutional and political development, 1899–1956.* Oxford: Clarendon.

Abusharaf, Roqaia, 1998, "War, Politics, and Religion. An exploration of the determinants of southern Sudanese migrations to the United States and Canada", *Northeast African Studies* 5(1):31–47.

Adam, Sabah, 2001, "Northern Sudanese Customs Adopted by Southerners in Khartoum", Interviews with Pressla Joseph, Rose Paulino, and Veronica Lewis (in Arabic), *Alayam Newspaper* 6834 (21 August), Khartoum.

Asad, Talal, 1970, *The Kababish Arabs: Power, authority and consent in a nomadic tribe.* London: Hurst.

Bales, Kevin, 1999, *Disposable People: New slavery in the global economy.* Berkeley: University of California Press.

—, 2000, "The Expendable People: Slavery in the age of globalisation". Paper presented at the University of Connecticut Distinguished Human Rights Lecture Series.

Bariagaber, Assefaw, 1995, "Linking Political Violence and Refugee Situation in the Horn of Africa: An empirical approach", *International Migration* 33(2):209–29.

Bascom, Jonathan, 1995, "The New Nomads", in Baker, Jonathan and Tade Akin Aina (eds), *The Migration Experience in Africa*. Uppsala: Nordic Africa Institute.

Baya, Philister, 1999, "Seeking a Refuge or Being Displaced?" in el Sanosi, Magda (ed.), *The Tragedy of Reality: Southern Sudanese women appeal for peace*. Khartoum: Sudan Open Learning Organisation.

Bechtold, Peter, 1992, "More Turbulence in Sudan: A new politics this time", in Voll, John (ed.), *Sudan: State and society in crisis*. Washington DC: Middle East Institute.

Beshir, Mohamed Omer, 1968, *The Southern Sudan: Background to conflict*. New York: Fredrick Praeger Pulishers.

Corbett, Sara, 2001, "From Hell to Fargo: The Lost Boys of Sudan Land in America", *New York Times Magazine* (April 1/section 6):28–56.

Daughtry, Carla, 2001, "Ethnographic Notes on a Dinka Language Institute in Cairo". Paper presented at the twentieth anniversary of the *Sudan Studies Association: The Sudan and Its Community of Scholars*. East Lansing: Michigan State University.

Deng, Francis, 1972, *The Dinka of Sudan*. Prospects Heights, IL: Waveland Press.

—, 1991, "War of Vision for the Nation", Voll, John (ed.), *Sudan: State and society in crisis*. Washington DC: Middle East Institute.

—, 1995, *War of Visions in the Sudan*. Washington DC: Brookings Institutions Press.

De Schlippe, Pierre, 1956, *Shifting cultivation in Africa: The Zande system of agriculture*. London: Routledge and Kegan Paul.

Dudu, Christina, 1999, "Southern Sudanese Displaced Women: Losses and gains", in el Sanosi, Magda (ed.), *The Tragedy of Reality: Southern Sudanese women appeal for peace*. Khartoum: Sudan Open Learning Organisation.

Eastmond, Maria, 1993, "Reconstructing Life: Chilean refugee women and the dilemma of exile", in Buijs, Gina (ed.), *Migrant Women*. Oxford: Berg.

Evans-Prichard, Edvard, 1940, *The Nuer*. Oxford: Oxford University Press.

Guinier, Lani, 1994, *The Tyranny of the Majority: Fundamental fairness in representative democracy*. New York: The Free Press.

Hackett, Beatrice, 1996, *Pray God and Keep Walking: Stories of women refugees*. London: McFarland.

Hobsbawm, Eric, 1990, *Nations and Nationalisms since 1780*. Cambridge: Cambridge University Press.

Holborn, Louise, 1975, *Refugees: A problem of our time. The work of the United Nations High Commission for Refugees, 1951–1971*. Metuchen, NJ: Scarecrow Press.

Holt, Peter and Martin Daly, 1988, *A history of the Sudan: From the coming of Islam to the present day*. London and New York: Longman.

Holtzman, Jon, 2000, *Nuer Journeys, Nuer Lives: Sudanese refugees in Minnesota*. Boston: Allyn and Bacon.

Indra, Doreen (ed.), 1999, *Engendering Forced Migration: Theory and practice*. Oxford: Berghahn Books.

Khalid, Mansour, 1989, *The Government They Deserve: The role of the elite in Sudan's political evolution*. London and New York: Kegan Paul International.

Lado, Augustino, 1994, *Arab Slavery in Southern Sudan*. London: Pax Sudani Organization.

Lange-Kubick, Cindy, 2000, "Lincoln Offers New Life for Boys from Sudan", *Lincoln Journal Star*, December 16.

Lienhardt, Godfrey, 1961, *Divinity and Experience. The Religion of the Dinka*. Oxford: Clarendon.

Malwal, Bona, 1993, "Sources of Conflict in Sudan". Paper presented at a symposium on the situation in Sudan. Washington DC: United States Institute of Peace.

Marable, Manning, 1995, "Beyond Racian Identity: Towards a liberation theory for multicultural democracy", in Collins P. and M. Anderson (eds), *Race, Class and Gender: An anthology*. Belmot, CA: Wadsworth.

Rose Al Youssif, 2000, "Migration to Egypt: Are refugees guests or criminals?" *Rose Al Youssif*, no. 3764, p.25–31.

Ruiz, Hiram, 1998, "The Sudan: Cradle of displacement", in Cohen, Roberta and Francis Deng (eds), *The Foresaken People*. Washington DC: Brookings Institution Press.

Seligman, C.G., 1932, *Pagan Tribes of Niolitic Sudan*. London: Routledge.

Shazali, Salah, 1995, "War displacement: The socio-cultural dimension", in Eltigani, E. (ed.), *War and drought in Sudan: Essays in population displacement*. Tallahassee: University Press Florida.

Sidahmed, Abdel Salam, 1998, *Politics and Islam in Contemporary Sudan*. Richmond: Curzon Press.

Simmons, Ann, 2000, "Sudanese Teens Begin Journey to New Life: Resettlement in US poses challenge for "Lost Boys" of country's civil war", *Hartford Courant*, 5 November 2000, A12. (Reprinted from *Los Angeles Times*).

Simone, Abdou Maliqlalim, 1994, *In Whose Image? Political Islam and Urban Practices in Sudan*. Chicago: Chicago University Press.

Sudanet, Website for discussions of Sudan's affairs. <http://www.sudanet.net> (2 May, 7 September, 13 November, 2000).

Teegardin, Carrie, 2000, "Life Better for Refugees, but Some Still Live in Squalor", *Atlanta Journal Constitution*, November 26.

US Committee for Refugees, 1999, *Sudan Fact Sheet*. Washington DC: US Committee for Refugees.

Wai, Dunstan, 1973, "The Southern Sudan: The country and the people", in Wai, D. (ed.), *The Southern Sudan: The problem of national integration*. London: Frank Cass.

Warburg, Gabriel, 1992, "The Sharia in Sudan: Implementations and repercussions", in Voll, John (ed.), *Sudan: State and society in crisis*. Washington DC: Middle East Institute.

White, Constance, 2000, "Alek Wek: Living a model life", *Essence* 31(5) 160–224.

Winter, Roger, 1999, Afterword to *Sudan: Personal Stories of Sudan's Uprooted People*. Washington DC: US Committee for Refugees.

Somalis and Sudanese in Norway – Religion, ethnicity/clan and politics in the diaspora

Munzoul A.M. Assal

Coming together is a beginning
Staying together is a progress
Working together is a success
A dictum in the Somali Welfare Union's office, Oslo

Intoduction

This chapter is a critical addition to the growing literature on diaspora and transnational subjectivities. It is based on field research on Sudanese and Somali migrants to Norway.[1] I argue that *diaspora* as a concept is useful with respect to opening up new directions in migration research, which may result in better theorising about identity. But, inasmuch as diaspora is used to theorise about a lineal relationship between people (immigrants, refugees, exiles, etc.), and their homeland, it tends to err with respect to two issues that will eventually be discussed at length in the chapter: a) it homogenises immigrants or generally those peoples who are characterised as diasporic, by overlooking divisions along ethnic, religious, and political lines, or other aspects that corroborate heterogeneity; and b) the longing of diasporic people for a homeland to which they will eventually return is, at worse, a myth and, at best, an argument that must be empirically based and substantiated. This second issue is a bit tricky as it comprises what people think, wish, and what

1. The fieldwork on which this chapter is based was done in Bergen and Oslo at different points in time during the period June 2000–December 2002. For more details see Assal (2004). I use the term 'migrants' here as a general concept that includes both immigrants and refugees. Throughout this chapter, I use the terms 'refugees' and 'immigrants' together and sometimes interchangeably. I believe a clear-cut distinction between the two, in my case, is dubious (see Hein 1993).

165

they actually do when it comes to their relationship with their homeland, which they left behind and to which they will *eventually* return. My starting point will be providing a context within which my subsequent analysis will be pursued. Then I will present some empirical material that is meant to shed light on issues of religion, ethnicity and politics. My thrust in the chapter will be an endeavour to show that these newly established communities face challenges of adaptation in the new setting, characterised by divisions along ethnic, political and religious lines, as well as a problematic relationship with their respective homelands; Somalia and the Sudan. To understand the dynamics of these two communities, the chapter shall give some space to the discussion of aspects of categorisation in Somalia and the Sudan, and how this affects the ways people interact and adapt to their new realities. Since diasporic subjectivities relate to both nodes, it is imperative to problematise both nodes, something which I intend to do in this chapter. Somali and Sudanese organisations in Oslo are taken as an arena where issues of politics, ethnicity and religion can be intelligible. The final part of the chapter will be devoted to discussing the concept of diaspora, in light of the empirical material presented in the chapter.

The context: Somalis and Sudanese as migrants

Somalis

From a few hundred in the 1980s, the number of Somalis in Norway increased to over eleven thousand in the year 2002. The flood of Somali refugees to the West in general started in 1988 with the Barre government's bombardment of Somalia's northern towns and the persecution of the Isaaq clan, which was suspected of having connections with the underground opposition, the Somali Nationalist Movement (SNM). The stream of Somali refugees started first from the north, where the Isaaq dominate, and then, after the ousting of Barre in 1991 and the subsequent civil war, from Mogadishu and the south (Lewis 1994; McGown 1999; Samatar 1991; Deng 1993).[2] The movement of Somali refugees has never been a uniform process and inasmuch as many Somalis lost their loved ones, tortured, raped and subjected to different kinds of

2. In addition to these, there are many books, articles and reports on the breakdown of the state in Somalia and its consequences on the civil order. See for example, Adam and Ford 1997; Brons 2001; Samatar 1994; Salih and Markakis 1998; Farah 2000; Adam 1995; Africa Watch 1993; Africa Watch 1990; Wohlgemuth and Salih 1994; Deng 1993 etc.

trauma before their flight, the fission that followed the breakdown continues to plague the Somalis, even after leaving their country. The events that led to the collapse of Somalia also led to the separation of families, and consequently resulted in having members of one family being scattered in many countries, sometimes as many as five (Farah 2000). The arrival of Somalis in their present refuges, those who left after the collapse, was not a uniform process either. Many had to spend years in convoluted journeys or stop in what are known as *first asylum countries* (Kenya, Ethiopia and Yemen) before proceeding to Europe, the United States and Canada.[3] For many Somalis, Kenya is a notorious station. In Kenya, "the Somalis are described by government officials and in the lingo of ordinary folks as *shifta*-bandits, as poachers, as people engaged in fraudulence" (Farah 2000:31).[4] The dire conditions of Somalis in Kenya and Yemen led to the appearance of "*Carriers*" and resulted in human trafficking, where refugees paid huge sums of money to obtain documents that would enable them to travel to Europe.[5] The process of carrying illegal persons is a risky venture for both the carrier and the carried. But for the Somalis, the risk they take in being carried is the least of their worries.

With the exception of those who come through the UNHCR quota programmes, or through the process of family reunification, the majority of Somalis who are in Norway neither came directly from Somalia, nor from a first asylum country. They came to Norway, mostly, through Russia, Finland, Sweden and Denmark. It is impossible or extremely difficult to get information about the intrigues involved in coming to Norway, and the greater part of the stories told about such intrigues are anecdotes and hearsay. A refugee would tell that he came to Norway through Germany for example, but he would not tell about what type of transport he used, who helps him to get to Norway, how much money he paid for the journey, etc. The tough screening and questioning by immigration authorities refugees go through affects the way people react to research questions, and the responses are mostly anecdotal. According to these anecdotal stories, some Somalis come to Norway after they get refugee status in Denmark or Sweden, for example, others

3. In these countries of first asylum, refugees suffer the most. They are often abused, denied the right to basic services and insulted. Even those who are in UNHCR camps are not immune to abuse. See African Rights 1993.

4. *Shifta* (Arabic) is a derogatory word used to describe merciless robbers or thugs.

5. See Farah, ibid., p. 77–81. Refugees stationed in these first asylum countries receive money from family members or relatives who have already made it to Europe or the United States, or from expatriates in the Gulf.

keep moving between the Nordic countries, and yet others leave for the US and Canada on their own, or join other family members who are already there.[6] The implications of these movements of Somalis within the West are of far-reaching consequences for the Somalis themselves, and for theorising on identity and diaspora, as well as for research on refugees and immigrants in general.

The total number of Somalis in Norway was 11,269 individuals in 2002, out of which 65.2 per cent are officially categorised as refugees (see the annexes). All the major clans are represented because when Somalia collapsed as a state in 1991 the impact was devastating and felt by all clan-families in different part of the country. Unlike in the UK where the status of asylum was initially given to the members of particular clans (McGown 1999; Griffiths 1997, 2000; Farah 2000), in Norway, especially during the 1990s, the stream of refugees consisted of a mosaic of clans, reflecting the extent of the Somali predicament after the ousting of Barre's regime. Consequently, it is very difficult to get information about which clan is dominant in Norway, although some informants argue that the Hawiye and Isaaq are the dominant clans, in terms of numerical preponderance in Norway.[7] On the level of interpersonal relationships, membership in a particular clan determines to a greater extent with whom somebody is supposed to mingle and be friendly. Suspicion and mistrust are rampant in inter-clan relationships, although community organisations' slogans are geared toward countering the negative impact of clanism and fostering a sense of unity, and providing help to the needy regardless of their clan affiliation.

Immediately after arrival in Norway and establishing themselves as a refugee community, the Somalis had to face a set of complex worries. Having passed tough questions and screening by immigration authorities and established themselves as refugees, they started to ponder on their fate in the new society. They did not have the luxury of relaxing for a while before thinking over issues of maintaining their Muslim identity, guaranteeing a safe upbringing of their children, and how they would maintain their relationship with the homeland. Sixteen Somali organisations were established in Oslo to confront such issues and, paradoxically, to advance the integration of Somalis in the Norwegian society. Among the particular issues that Somalis

---

6. One of my first informants in Oslo whom I met in July 2000 left for the United States. He left Norway after twelve years of residence.

7. Interviews with Abdi Aden (Bergen, 1 May 2000) and Dohrre Rasheed (Bergen, 13 January 2001). Both claimed they are Hawiye.

had to confront and deal with is the difference in parenting between Somalia and Norway.

Respecting the elderly is unquestionable and is sometimes enforced, if needed, by corporal punishment (McGown 1999), something which is totally unacceptable in Norway. The laws that bar corporal punishment of children, routine in Somalia, can distress parents who do not realise that local authorities can claim the right to take away children who they believe to be at risk. The result is that Somalis feel their traditions are threatened and that they cannot enforce certain behaviours on their own children the way they used to. Added to this is that the male position of authority has been challenged, both because gender relations are perceived differently in Norway, and because men have not necessarily continued to be breadwinners for their families:

> The situation in Norway changed for both men and women. The father is no longer the one who works and earns income to cater for his family. In Norway he is often a welfare-client or student. It is no longer that he is the boss. The role of the woman also changed. She has bigger possibilities to have a say in important decisions. She is no longer dependent on the man to get food and shelter, and will no longer accept that he is the undisputed decision-maker.[8]

For many reasons, chief among which are non-transferable qualifications (Griffiths 2000) and discrimination, unemployment within the Somali community in Norway is very high (Djuve and Hagen 1995). This is of course not to say that the Somali familial systems have crumbled or collapsed under the stresses of the new situation, but such stresses feature in significant ways in interviews with Somalis. Even those who are not yet married raise concerns about the threats facing family and kinship systems. A man who takes a significant part of his identity and pride from his ability to be the breadwinner of his family is bound to find the situation overwhelming if or when he cannot provide material support for his family. This is further compounded by the feeling of marginality in the Norwegian society, where many Somali men are not sure what role they are going to play and in what way they are going to play it, in a society they can barely understand. It is in these circumstances that people tend to invent their traditions. For the Somalis, one such tradition is the institution of clan.

8. Interview with Jama Ali, Oslo, 24 July 2001.

Clans

The centrality and dominance of clan politics is hotly debated by Somalis in the diaspora (Farah 2000; Griffiths 2000). For the Somalis in Norway it is a sensitive issue also, even though there are variations among Somalis when it comes to the actual effect of clan on their lives in their new home.[9] Many Somalis I talked with agree that they would not be in their current state of affairs were it not for the exploitation of clan loyalties by both Barre's regime and ambitious clan leaders in Somalia. Government bodies in Norway that are concerned with the integration of refugees and immigrants in the Norwegian society are aware of the centrality of clan for the Somalis. But they encourage Somali organisations to transcend narrow clan objectives in the programmes they design, in their respective organisations.[10]

The effect of the clan and the feeling of the strong sense of belonging to it are so much essentialised in the Somali scholarship, as well as in the narratives relayed by Somali informants. According to a satirical Somali creation myth, "God first created the family of the prophet Muhammad and he was very pleased with the nobility of his handiwork, then he created the rest of the mankind and was modestly pleased; then he created the Somalis and he laughed" (Samatar 1991:12). This tale manifests the cheerful self-mockery the Somalis have (also see Farah 2000). It also signifies the Somalis' consciousness of corporate unity; by viewing themselves as created separately and distinct from others, even though they may remain a laughable sort of creation. The sense of belonging to a distinct national community with a common destiny is rooted in a belief that all Somalis descend from a common founding father, the mythical Samaale to whom the overwhelming majority of Somalis trace their genealogical origin (Lewis 1982).

There are six major clan-families in Somalia: the Darood and the Hawiye which control Mogadishu, the Isaaq which dominates in northern Somalia, the Dir which is divided into two branches, and finally there are the two

9. In her study of Somalis in London and Toronto McGown (1999:20) illustrated the importance of clan for the Somalis and observed that "the refugee communities are thus divided over whether and how to overcome clan divisions, both in the diaspora and with respect to their relations with kinsfolk back home. Older Somalis who are determined to return home as soon as it is safe to do so may be more concerned with ensuring that their clan is well-positioned, but there are others who are convinced that so long as Somalis care about the relative positions of their clans, there will be no safe Somalia to which they can return".

10. Interview with the Executive Officer, *Flyktning og innvandreretaten* (the Municipal Service for Refugees and Immigrants, Oslo), 17 August 2000.

agricultural clans of Digil and Rahanwayn in the riverine lands of southern Somalia. Dir, Darood, Isaaq and Hawiye practise the pastoral mode of economy. They raise camels and cattle and flocks of sheep and goats, and they undertake annual seasonal migration. The Somalis trace descent through the male line and young people are taught to memorise the entire genealogy of their descent from immediate father to founding one. A person's full name is composed of his/her given name, and the father's and paternal grandfather's name. Although matrilineal relationships play a significant role in political networking (Lewis 1982, Samatar 1990), the male line determines a man's or a woman's identity. Unlike the practice in most Western societies, a Somali woman does not change her family name upon marriage to her new husband's name. She retains both her father's name and his clan identity. Should a woman be a victim of homicide, her paternal kin, not her husband's, receive the blood money compensation (*diyya*).The pastoral clan organisation is an unstable, fragile system, characterised at all levels by *shifting* allegiances. Power and politics are exercised through temporary coalitions and ephemeral alliances of lineages. The political organisation of the Somalis is similar to what Evans-Pritchard (1940) depicted among the Nuer of southern Sudan, that of a segmentary opposition between clans and sub-clans.

There is *no* permanent alliance between clans or lineages. An alliance fragments into competitive units once the situation that necessitated it in the first place ceases to exist. The race for alliances accelerates or dwindles with self-perpetuating momentum. Alliances expand and contract according to the character of the conflict. In urban areas, like Mogadishu for example, where large scale economic and political stakes are contested, the whole nation may be segmented into opposing camps as happened in 1990 (the Darood clan on the one hand, and an alliance of the Hawiye and Isaaq on the other). This segmentation goes down right to the household level. For example the children of a man's two wives may fall on each other to contend an external threat. But the segmentation system in general is not stable and it is particularly vulnerable to external factors. According to Said Samatar (1991:13), the system has its weaknesses which effectively contribute to the plight of the Somalis.[11]

11. S. Samatar (1991) summarised his argument in the following way: "First, the system lacks individual culpability. When a man commits a homicide, for example, the guilt does not remain with him as an individual murderer as is the practice in most societies; the crime is instantaneously transmitted to the members of the murderer's kin who become guilty in the eyes of the aggrieved party, by reason of their blood connection with the perpetrator. Members of the aggrieved kin would then seek out for

Samatar's perspective on the Somali crisis is one that blames the segmentary lineage system. He sees instability, anarchy and the murderous shifting in the Somali scene as inherently endemic, deeply embedded as they are in the very warp and weft of the Somali world, both as individuals and as corporate socio-political units. In their personal autonomy, Somalis are extremely individualistic, in their attribution of privilege and obligation they are inflexibly collective-oriented. Samatar claims that instead of bringing development and progress to Somalia, independence only revealed the true predicament of Somalia. The institution of the military forces as a coercive power by the colonial powers brought to the fore persons who do not have any sort of respect other than their command of the coercive military power.

Although Somalia is generally portrayed as a homogeneous society, linguistically and religiously there are serious divisions along geographical and clan lines.[12] Clans that are primarily engaged in pastoralism (Hawiye, Dir, Issaq, Darood) consider their members noble, and consequently different from the southern clan-families (Digil, and Rahanwyin), which are traditionally engaged in agriculture, or combined it with pastoralism, and which were seen as mixed with the African Bantu (Lewis 1994:95). But Lewis argues that all the six major clans are originally of Arab heritage, even though the strength of connection is strongest among the four northern pastoral clans. The northern clan-families are politically dominant. Governance, from the time of independence, was in the hands of the northerners and this may

revenge not just the perpetrator but any member(s) of his lineage they might chance upon. In the Somali system one literally gets away with murder, because the actual murderer may escape and never see punishment, while an innocent kinsperson of his may fall to a flying spear of vendetta ... Second, it should be obvious how vulnerable the system is to an external manipulation by, say, an unethical head of state such as Siyaad Barre, who used the scarce resources of the state to reward and punish entire clans collectively."

12. Ahmed I. Samatar (1994:17–18) notes that there is heterogeneity in Somalia but in the final analysis he argues that homogeneity dominates: "... there are areas of Somali society that diverge from the mainstream in the forms in which certain social practices and rituals are administered. Moreover, even in the category of Somali language, it is important to note that some of the Somali people of the riverine area (Juba and Shabelle) speak *Maai* – a regional and distinctive dialect – whereas those of some of the old urban centres of Mogadishu, Merca, and Brava speak a dialect called *Banaadri*. In view of this, critics of the homogeneity thesis... have a point... In the final analysis, however, I insist that Somali homogeneity, construed in the Wittgensteinian sense of "family resemblance", is more than defensible, for beyond these differences in dialect and ritual administration, Somalis hold on to a common ancestral origin, a broad tradition of rights and obligations (*heer*), and the principles of Islam."

explain why the pastoral myths, not those of the southern minorities, have often been described as those common to Somali culture as a whole. The protagonists of the Somali state and power wielders propagate the nomadic identity as the national identity, and state policies have historically marginalised the sedentary Somali, both economically and politically (Brons 2001:89; also see Kapteijns 1994:214–218). Islam is yet another source of identification for the Somalis. A brief historical note on the relevance of Islam for Somalis is in order here.

I have dealt with Islam and Muslims in the diaspora, in relation to Somalis and Sudanese in Norway elsewhere (Assal 2004:156–185), and there is no need for detailed discussion here. But there are certain points, which relate to the penetration of Islam in Somalia, that deserve noting. It is safe to say that all Somalis are Muslims and actually they identify themselves as such. While the presence of Islam in Somalia is dated to the first century after the *hijra* (622 A.D.), the actual penetration of Islam into the Somali society took place in the tenth century when Islamic city states developed along the Somali coast, as Arab and Persian settlers brought commercial links to the larger Muslim world. These trading centres facilitated the islamisation of the country and eventually developed sophisticated administrative and legal systems based on Islamic law (see Laitin and Samatar 1987; Hersi 1977; Mukhtar 1996; Ahmed 1996). Clan-families became organised around various patriarchal Muslim saints. But there are competing and conflicting accounts about the penetration of Islam into the interior of Somalia. According to Hersi (1977:117), in the tenth and eleventh centuries, Zeila in the north was widely described by Arab sources as an Abyssinian Christian city, and Mogadishu was a Muslim town at the same time. During the fourteenth century, there was a substantial immigration of Hadrami and Yemeni Muslims to Somalia (Cassanelli 1982:98). Islamisation of interior and northern Somalia is said to be linked to the Darood and Issaq clan-families. These two clan-families lay claim to an Arab forefather, "and not just any Arab, but one of Muhammad's [the prophet's] early followers" (McGown 1999:28). What is obvious, then, is that Islam in Somalia is rooted in history, and it is interesting to note that the penetration of Islam in Sudan also started in the same period.[13]

Despite claims to the contrary, Somalis are not a homogeneous stock, although Islam provides an overarching source of identification for them.

13. The penetration of Islam in Sudan started with the pact, in 632 A.D., between the Christian kingdoms of Sudan and the Arab ruler of Egypt, even though some historians argue that there had been Muslim enclaves in Sudan, along the Red Sea coast, earlier. See Hassan (1985).

Membership in different competing clans underlines difference and fragmentation within the Somali diaspora (Griffiths 2000). Somalis came into a society in Norway where there is already an established Muslim presence, represented by the Pakistanis who comprise the biggest Muslim community. Politically the Somalis are not visible, even if they are the most visible in other aspects.[14] However, the presence of Somalis as a Muslim community in Norway is clearly felt in relation to women's dress and attendance in mosques, especially during Friday prayers. Although Somalis share Islamic facilities (notably mosques) with other Muslims, they have their own Islamic centres and mosques in Oslo.[15]

Somali organisations in Oslo

My entry into Somali organisations in Oslo was through the Somali Welfare Union (*Somaliske velferdforening*), which represents northern Somalis or those from the Republic of Somaliland. The Republic of Somaliland was established in May, 1991 as an independent state following the collapse of Somalia. It comprises a coalition of northern Somali clans but the Isaaq is the dominant one and power wielder. The premises of the organisation are a sort of meeting place or club for northern Somalis, and the place is full all the day around; some coming in others going out. But it gets crowded during the evenings when many Somalis come to listen to the BBC Somali Service, which broadcasts news in the Somali language and focuses on Somalia. The Somali Welfare Union is one among many other Somali organisations in Oslo.

At the time of writing this chapter there are 16 Somali organisations in Norway; all of them are located in Oslo. Three of these are women-based organisations which are concerned with the welfare and the advancement of Somali women's condition. Many of these organisations are cultural bodies, and they function as a link between Somalis and their homeland. The locations of these organisations are meeting places for people, especially those organisations whose premises are in the centre of Oslo (areas around Storgata, Grønland and Tøyen). They are also arenas where Somali politics is played out. Financial support for these organisations is provided by the Norwegian

14. Such aspects include gender relations and the role of Somali women (*Aftenposten*, October 2000), the dependence of Somalis on welfare assistance and a pastoral mode of behaviour (*Dagbladet*, July 2000), and unemployment (Djvue and Hagen 1995).

15. Al-Tawfeeq Al-islami Centre in Oslo is the biggest religious centre for the Somalis in Norway.

government through the Municipal Authority for Refugees and Immigrants (*Flyktning- og innvandreretaten, Oslo kommune*). While all these organisations are apparently "Somali", they often tend to represent specific groups or categories more than representing Somalis in general. For example, the *Ogaden Støtteforening* is obviously a political body that supports and advocates the case of Ogaden Region in the western part of Somalia, where there has been a long standing conflict between Somalia and Ethiopia and where the two countries fought a devastating war in 1977. During the deliberations of the Third Islamic Conference in Oslo (4–7 August 2001), a pamphlet was distributed to the audience, containing the latest news about the struggle against the Ethiopians in the Ogaden. Along with these organisations, the development of web-sites by Somalis and the use of emails have helped to maintain links across a wide spectrum of Somali spaces and connect Somalis to their homeland.[16] Sudanese in the diaspora also have many internet forums and websites.[17]

How *efficient* these different organisations are is a different question that cannot be answered here. What concerns me here is the fact that they somehow act as symbols of Somaliness and are arenas where "Somali identity" is played out, however dubious such a phrase may be. It must be emphasised that many of these organisations are clan-based/dominated collectivities. The *Somalisk Velfredsforening* and *Ogaden Støtteforening* are obvious examples, where members of a specific clan dominate in both organisations. The fragmentation along clan lines is seen by some scholars of Somali studies as the culprit behind the lack of pan-Somali organisations (see Griffiths 2000). But then the realities which are still unfolding in the aftermath of the collapse of the state in Somalia in 1991, and the declaration of the Republic of Somaliland in the same year, are signals or caveats against anticipating any pan-Somali organisation that would encompass or bring together the different Somali factions in the diaspora. The dynamics of the Somali diaspora, therefore, might better be conceptualised and understood in terms of these different organisations or bodies than through looking at something pan-Somali, which does not exist. Before moving on to discuss the Sudanese community, a few words in conclusion about Somali clans in Norway must suffice here.

16. Some of the well-known Somali cyberspace web-pages include <www.somalianet.com>, and <www.somaliland.com>. For more about diaspora and cyberspace interaction see B. Conrad in this volume.

17. Two of the well-known Sudanese web-pages are <www.sudan.net> and <www.sudaneseonline.com>.

It is not difficult to recognise that the clan is still alive, long after Somalis left Somalia and resettled in Norway. Looking at the different Somali organisations in Oslo reveals the extent to which the clan is resilient. It is important to mention the role played by the clan in easing difficulties faced by Somalis during their early stages as refugees. Relatives, friends and clan members play pivotal roles in helping each other at times of crisis and emergency.

Nonetheless, the question of clan is intriguing. Claims of the centrality of clan in the lives of Somalis in the diaspora cannot easily be made explicit. We can say that the role of the clan in the Norwegian context is instrumentalist and not primordial. We can also say that the clan in Norway is undergoing some kind of transformation as a result of many factors. One salient factor here is that conditions responsible for producing violent clan ideology do not exist in Norway. A Somali informant recalls at the beginning of the 1990s, when many Somalis were still fresh arrivals from Somalia, there were simmering tensions between members of different clans. But such tensions are fading away. The direction of transformation in the Somali clan system is however, difficult to point out at this point in time.

Sudanese: Ethnic/religious categorisation and politics

There are about five hundred Sudanese in Norway. 70 per cent of them are categorised as refugees. The pattern of migration of Sudanese represents a contrast to that of the Somalis in many ways. Like the Somalis, however, the majority of Sudanese in Norway did not come directly from Sudan. Many came through other European countries and in some cases, a person comes to Norway already having refugee status in another European country. Reasons for seeking asylum are complex and ramified and cannot be discussed in this paper, but suffice it to say here that the stream of refugees reflects the crisis in Sudan; a war that is in its fifth decade and a concomitant economic crisis that has pushed over 90 per cent of the Sudanese below the poverty line (Sahl 1999; Ali 1994). Individual migration is one major characteristic of Sudanese refugees and, in contrast to Somalis, where the process of family reunification plays an important role in replenishing the Somali community, the majority of Sudanese in Norway are single persons, and with the exception of one family that is composed of five brothers and one sister, kinship networks are yet to develop in the Sudanese community. Before discussing the lot of the Sudanese in Norway, I shall provide some background information about the process of categorisation and identification in the Sudan.

There are different levels of identification and categorisation in which individual Sudanese are placed, but the primary basis of identification in Sudan is tribal. Tribal identification in Sudan is not constant. It is shifting and contextual as well as subject to political manipulation (Ahmed 1979; O'Brien 1998; Harir 1994). How someone is identified frequently depends upon the social and cultural context of a given situation. For example, a person from northern Sudan might be identified as an Arab when in southern Sudan, but in the north a specific tribal identity might be more important. That tribal identity might even be one that is not considered Arab. Even though Arabs have sometimes been thought of as people who speak Arabic as their native language, many Sudanese who are native speakers of Arabic are not considered Arabs in some situations.[18] Similarly, the identification of someone in northern Sudan as a southerner has real social implications, but in the southern region a person's identity would have to be given in tribal terms. At the political level, however, the rich tribal and ethnic diversities in both the north and the south are usually reduced to two broad categories vis-à-vis northerners (Arabs and Muslim) and southerners (Africans and Christian).

The plurality[19] of the Sudanese society qualifies it to be described by many scholars as representing a "microcosm of Africa" (Abdel Rahim 1985). Sudan is unique among the African countries because "it is at one and the same time both Arab and African" (ibid., p. 228). But such uniqueness, argues Mazrui (1985:240), confronts Sudan with a multiple political marginality, as neither Arab nor African, Muslim nor Christian. This multiple marginality is brutally reflected in the internal politics of Sudan and has put the country in an awkward position where its dominant elite, mostly from the riverine Arab north,

> desires it to be Muslim and Arab and its southern elite desires it to be African and de-Arabised. These two contradictory, even exclusivist, desires have been at the very heart of the political conflict that lies in the centre of the decay of the

18. For example, the Berti and Tunger tribes of western Sudan are native speakers of the Arabic language but they are not considered Arabs in many situations.

19. There are about 570 tribes in Sudan (Gore 1989:279) who have been grouped into 56 ethnic groups on the basis of linguistic, cultural and other ethnological characteristics they have in common. It is also said that 595 different languages are used by these tribes, even though Arabic is the lingua franca (Bell, quoted in Harir 1994:18). This diversity is further reduced in the 1955/56 census by regrouping the 56 ethnic groups into eight major categories. These include Arabs 39%, Nilotic 20%, Westerners 13%, Nuba 5%, Nubians 5%, Eastern southerners 5% and Foreigners 7%.

> Sudanese state. In the continuous and relentless pursuit of making Sudan an appendage to "something" Arabic, African or Islamic, both elites have failed to build "something" Sudanese as its uniqueness, expressed in being Arab and African at the same time, required (Harir 1994:11).

Like the case in Somalia, members of the northern riverine dominant elite consider Arabic and Islamic culture as representing the Sudanese culture. An "identity crisis" is at the heart of the Sudanese recent political history. Categories such as "Arabs", "non-Arabs", "Muslims", "non-Muslims", etc., underline the Sudanese political crises. Although this type of categorisation is simplistic in the sense that it reduces the otherwise complex plurality, it nevertheless, resonates with political cleavages and how power politics has been played out since Sudan got its independence in 1956. In the aftermath of the 1989 military coup and the promulgation of Islamic laws, this categorisation gained a new momentum with the involvement of religion in the Sudanese polity. Although this process actually started in September 1983 when president Nimeiri introduced Islamic laws and declared himself an *imam*, the incumbent government's policies with regard to the Islamisation of the Sudanese public space are unprecedented. The problematic and often controversial religious orientation of the Sudanese government and its attempts to militarise the entire country triggered large scale migration by young Sudanese. At the heart of the government's orientation is a project of *taaseel*[20] (authenticity). This project is aimed at reviving religion and subverting secularism, which is believed to have gained a foothold in Sudan. It is also a platform for mobilising popular support in the face of threats from the rebels who are considered infidels, traitors, and imperial pawns. According to this authenticity project, being a good Sudanese is defined on moral grounds, supposedly different from earlier secularised constructs. Those who are not supportive of the government are consequently excluded from the new construct. Similarly, Sudanese living outside Sudan, or Sudanese wishing to leave Sudan, are denigrated and deemed not authentic. Nonetheless, such policies have triggered return migration (even though on a very small scale) by those who are particularly called upon to come.

But the implications of this project have far-reaching consequences. The ambiguity surrounding the term "authenticity" resulted in its notorious abuse by power wielders and the government's supporters who are "authentic". Those who are not supporters, even if they are Muslims, are automatically catego-

20. It means going back to the roots and those roots, from the point of view of the incumbent government, are Arabic and Islamic.

rised as not "authentic enough" and consequently discriminated against in the public sector's job market, however qualified they might be. The criteria of recruitment for public office were thus based on things other than qualification. Many qualified civil servants and professionals were sacked from their jobs for *al-salih al-aam.*[21] Muslims and non-Muslims alike suffered as a result of these practices. The combination of war and these unfortunate policies, and the resulting generalised insecurity,[22] are the main reasons for the Sudanese to seek asylum.

The Sudanese problem is very complex and intriguing, and I cannot go deeper into it in this chapter. What concerns me here are the implications of the above aspects for the Sudanese diaspora, especially when diasporas are seen as national communities within the boundaries of other nation-states. The Sudanese in Norway mirror the rich ethnic and tribal diversity of Sudan described above. They are also the product of a complex political history that is characterised by an identity crisis. For the purposes of this chapter, I shall treat the Sudanese community in Norway as composed of two main categories: southerners and northerners.[23] Like the case with the Somalis, it is difficult to get the actual number of members belonging to each of these categories. Like the Somalis and other immigrant groups, the Sudanese are heavily concentrated in Oslo. In terms of work and other opportunities, Oslo is seen as the best place for immigrants in Norway.[24] To have a better picture of the Sudanese politics and divisions in Norway, a brief description about this community is provided here.

As is the case with Somalis, the Sudanese are also newcomers to Norway. Their earliest instance of migration goes back to the 1970s. But the great majority of them came to Norway during the 1990s and later. The Sudanese in Norway are differentiated along ethnic, religious, and political lines. This differentiation takes its cue from the rich diversity characterising the Sudan. People of different religious and political hues are found in Norway. This

21. It means "public interest" but in this context is an excuse to get rid of somebody who is suspected of being an opponent or *taboor khamis* (fifth column).

22. See Fuglerud's (1997) account of Tamil refugees in Norway, where he emphasised the need to look into the plight of refugees and asylum seekers in terms of "generalised conditions of insecurity" and not on the basis of individual or personal persecution.

23. The political game of the Sudanese diaspora in Norway is actually played along these two lines, even though the active members of both categories operate under the umbrella of NDA (National Democratic Alliance), a loose political organ that brings together southern and northern opposition groups against the government of Sudan.

24. For immigrants' concentration in Oslo see Brox (1998) and Djvue and Hagen (1995).

differentiation affects the way people interact and relate to each other. But religious and political categorisations are the most salient features of the Sudanese community in Norway. Within the community of northern Sudanese, there are three main categories: (i) those who are categorised as religious or "the mosque category"; members of this group are actively involved in religious activities in terms of observing religious codes and organising different religious functions in collaboration with others (e.g. Somalis); (ii) those who are categorised as the group of "liberals". This group comprises many of the old-timers and its members are seen by the mosque group as the people of *dhalal*;[25] and finally, (iii) those who do not belong to the above two groups, or the rest of the Sudanese community. It is important to note that other characteristics overlap and cut across these three categories; for example reasons for coming to Norway, work, male or female, and, importantly, being a refugee, etc.[26]

The group of southern Sudanese also manifests interesting characteristics, but they appear more united than their northern counterpart. Within this group, tribal belonging affects interaction with others who are not from one's own tribe, especially for those who are politically active. Those who are not active politically maintain relationships across tribal and other forms of belongings, and these relationships extend beyond the boundaries of being a southerner. This is very clear in Bergen where the Sudanese community is cohesive compared to a fragmented one in Oslo. In terms of political engagement, those who belong to the Dinka and Nuer (the main two tribal groups in southern Sudan) are active. But then the relationship between them is tense, and each group runs its own organisation separately, although both organisations are registered as "southern". Division along tribal lines in southern Sudan seems to have been transferred to Norway, and more importantly the dichotomy of southern/northern is vividly reconstituted as well.

In the year 2000, a group of Sudanese met in Oslo in an effort to establish a body that would represent the Sudanese community in Norway and eventually contribute to solving the problem back home. The NDA (National Democratic Alliance) was thus formed in Norway. In the beginning people were enthusiastic about the idea but shortly the enthusiasm waned and the old dichotomies (northern vs. southern, Muslim vs. non-Muslim) started to take their toll. Divisions among the group of northern Sudanese and the

25. It means going astray or getting lost. But in this specific context this word is used to characterise those who do not observe religious codes.

26. For more details on these categories see Assal (2004:165–7).

religious factor also played an important role in thwarting the effort. From the start, the mosque group were sceptical about, and thus not supportive of, any political engagement that would bring Muslims and non-Muslims together. For them, such an engagement is non-Islamic, even though many of them are not supporters of the incumbent Sudanese government. Ironically, the establishment of the NDA has further weakened the already divided and fragile community, and at the time of writing this chapter the Sudanese in Norway are just individuals who lack any corporate body that would bring them together, like other immigrant communities. The three southern-based organisations are ineffective and with the exception of those who are formally responsible for them, nobody knows about them and many Sudanese are astonished when I mention these organisations. I am not romanticising or overemphasising the political game within the Sudanese community in Norway. Many Sudanese are actually not active politically and some would prefer a form of collectively that is apolitical. For those who espouse such views, politics can only divide and will bring no good for anybody. Two of the Sudanese in the third category claim that there are no serious divisions in the Sudanese community:

> There are no divisions and tensions within our community. What exist are groups which manifest different and sometimes contradictory interests; some go to the mosque, others to the pub. Yet others are just concerned about their work. In this country everybody is so immersed in their own problems and life-situations, and we think that formal bodies and organisations bring problems only. But if we must talk about categories, then there are two of them: one supporting the government back home and the other repudiating it. One arena which was hoped to be a place for the Sudanese was the club, but because it was a business (it was owned by a Sudanese), it was closed down. We tried twice to make something that would bring people together but both attempts failed. What we were left with is the Sunday football match only.[27]

Females' views about intra-group relationships within the Sudanese community merit looking at. One woman argues:

> There are a lot of things that should be considered when we talk about the relationships between the members of our community. First of all you cannot talk about good relationships between people in a situation where there is a serious rift between people, and where there are many groups each claiming it is the right one. That is why I prefer distance when dealing with others. Secondly, there are some people (especially men) who stick their noses in other people's affairs and I do

27. Interview with Badawi Adam and Abbakar Hassan, Oslo, 14 July 2001.

> not like that. Related to this is a deep-rooted Sudanese habit of judging others according to some arbitrary moral standards that may not exist at all in reality. For such reasons I prefer to have some distance. Of course I have good relationships with some people but the way I see it, it is better to not to bother with others.[28]

The Sudanese in Norway have very different backgrounds and histories, and many do not seem overtly interested in knowing about each other in a meaningful manner. There are no channels for communication that are shared by all. Trust or rather mistrust is an important issue here. Mistrust, in the case of the Sudanese, manifests itself in accusations of lack of morality, fanaticism or even paranoia. Thus, those who deem themselves religious see other categories as hopelessly immoral, while others for their part see those religious people as harassing or puppets of the government back home. Those who had the experience of being repressed in Sudan are particularly sensitive and selective in establishing relationships with others. Mistrust is not easy to put into words, however. For many Sudanese, mistrust is overwhelming to the extent that when I asked about it they would deny it.

Bringing the different threads together: Is "diaspora" a good analytical tool?

In what sense can the different issues discussed above, in relation to the intersection of religion, ethnicity/clan and politics, be conceptualised as diasporic phenomena? Is it useful to deploy the concept of diaspora to talk about deterritorialised ethnicity? And why is ethnicity said to be deterritorialised? Do Sudanese and Somalis in Norway qualify to be looked at as diasporic communities? Some prominent critics of the diaspora concept have it that

> the concept of diaspora, whilst focusing on transnational processes and commonalities, does so by deploying a notion of ethnicity which privileges the point of 'origin' in constructing identity and solidarity. In the process it also fails to examine trans-ethnic commonalities and relations and does not adequately pay attention to differences of gender and class (Anthias 1998:558).

The characteristics that qualify a certain community or others to be diasporic are listed by many scholars (cf. Clifford 1994; Safran 1991; Cohen 1997; Manger 2001b; see also Manger and Assal in this volume) and I will not repeat them here. I will instead try to follow up the critique presented by Anthias (1998) in light of my above material on Somalis and Sudanese. My impression

28. Interview with Maria, Oslo, 27 August 2001.

when reading literature on diaspora is that the attention is focused on the concept itself more than on the actual or empirical processes for the analysis of which the concept is deployed. To me, this resonates with the prevalent focus on, and critique against, other concepts that are accused of reification and essentialism, e.g. the culture concept. Such a problem is also attendant in Anthias' otherwise powerful critique in which she pointed out the weaknesses and problems of the diaspora concept. Concepts are nothing but what we make of, and by, them. Generally 'diaspora' is an enabling concept to use, and, following Behar (1996:144), I use it as a refusal to submit to the tyranny of categories. Diaspora embraces all the different categories, without necessarily collapsing them into one. Nonetheless, I have problems with the phrase "deterritorialised ethnicity" (Anthias 1998) and the ambiguous ways in which it is used. Is it used to describe ethnic groups operating outside their "natural" or "autochthonous" homelands? What is an ethnic group anyway? The phrase *deterritorialised ethnicity* blatantly presumes a primordial link between a certain group and a homeland, and talking about deterritorialised ethnicity is certainly talking about primordial attachments. Here there emerge two possibilities: i) either primordialism is so important for the groups which are characterised as diasporic that researchers cannot do away with it; or ii) it is a figment of our scholarly imagination, in which case we are doing nothing but inventing traditions. Ethnic groups do not operate in spaceless space, and those ethnic processes which are of interest to us as researchers can only be actualised within definite territories. Those political and religious processes within Sudanese and Somali communities take place in a definite territorial space (it does not matter whether these communities are ethnic groups or something else), which is Norway even if such processes are affected by a compound of other aspects that are beyond the boundaries of Norway. To be very specific, the actualisation of the processes I am talking about takes place in Oslo and Bergen. If my intention is looking at such processes as "deterritorialised ethnicity", I must, first, assume that Norway as a territorial space is the natural homeland for "Norwegians", which means that others who are not Norwegian must essentially be categorised as deterritorialised groups that do not belong to Norway or otherwise consider the majority of native Norwegians as not constituting an ethnic group. A further implicit presumption in the phrase "deterritorialised ethnicity" is that ethnic groups become territorialised when they return home, which is again essentialising such groups and portraying them as primordial and given. It is hollow to think of ethnicity as always involving a search for identity on the basis of origin. In the case of my two groups, ethnicity relates both to the homeland and to the society of settlement (Norway). It is also reconfigured and reconstituted within a diasporic space, since Somalis and Sudanese relate to other nodes apart from their respective homelands and Norway.

The relationship that binds the Sudanese and Somalis in Norway to their respective homelands is contested and therefore talking about home without problematising it will be analytically disabling. Problems plaguing the Sudan make it a contested homeland and unless we view it as an essentialised site on the map, we cannot talk about it as something to which the Sudanese in diaspora will eventually return. If home is a place where one thrives and feels safe, and not an essentialised point on the map (Deleuze and Guattari 1987; Malkki 1992; Massey 1994), then going to a place from where one fled as a refugee is not going home. Furthermore, the Sudanese political project may be heading towards splitting the country, which will further complicate realities for both the displaced and emplaced populations. The case of Somalia also presents a challenging and intriguing situation. For the moment, there are two Somalias (the mainland and the Republic of Somaliland established in 1991). Although a relative peace and stability have been maintained recently in Somalia, there is no guarantee that these will be lasting, and one basic worry for many Somalis I talked with is that nothing is certain in Somalia and that as long as people continue clinging to their clans, nobody can guarantee anything. Since its declaration of independence in May 1991, the Republic of Somaliland has survived many problems but has so far failed to impress other governments with the need to be recognised. The political, religious and ethnic processes of both Sudanese and Somalis may not resonate with the political projects and games played back home, even though such processes somehow mirror those taking place in the homeland. In the early years of immigration, the expectation of return combined with other factors that keep immigrants or refugees as disadvantaged groups makes homeland politics more relevant than the affairs of the host country (Norway). Homeland politics is normally exercised through the formation of cultural, social and, where allowed, political associations. Engaging with politics is one thing that people resort to in the diaspora, and it is one way of keeping alive memories and links to the homeland, even though such engagement may be far from the realities of the homeland. Homeland politics is not something uniform. It can take many forms.

One possible form is setting up enclaves that would further or advance the interests of the homeland, through supporting national governments. But even this does not usually take a specific form. The support can be political, economic, etc. (see Griffiths 2000). On the other hand, refugees' resentment at having to leave their country of origin for economic or political reasons may give rise to political associations, again where allowed, that work for change in the homeland. Both these two situations obtain in the case of Sudanese and Somalis in Norway, although in varying degrees. Whereas refugees are normally expected to live peacefully in the host country and are discouraged from pursuing political goals, political activities that are opposed to homeland regimes do exist, although again this takes different forms and is subject to political and diplomatic considerations in the host countries. It is important to note that these political processes are not only transnational, they are transethnic too. During my fieldwork in Oslo in the autumn of 2001 (specifically on 24 August), a delegate representing the Republic of Somaliland in Sweden visited Norway, to negotiate with their counterpart representatives in Norway how to end a recent dispute in the Republic of Somaliland. Equally, there is a well-coordinated chain of political activities by different Sudanese diasporic communities in Europe. How effective such activities are, however, is an empirical question. The Sudanese opposition has no official recognition in Norway, but it does have representation and its leaders' views on what is going on back in Sudan appear frequently in newspapers. In the case of Somalis, homeland politics is exercised along clan lines, but it is a bit different and organised in the case of the Republic of Somaliland, which has an informal representation (the Somali Welfare Union).

The relationship between minorities and their host society, however, is itself problematic and affects the ways identity politics is played out. This is especially interesting in the case of Norway where there was a heated debate on immigration policies and the situation of immigrant minorities in the 1990s, between what Andersson (2000:4–6) designates as group A and group B debaters. The different debates on the lot of immigrants, not the least Somalis, corroborate jarring challenges for both the immigrants and the host society, and this, in turn, feeds back on how immigrants view themselves vis-à-vis others. Unni Wikan, who leads group A, which is critical towards certain dimensions of immigrants' culture, accuses immigrants of appropriating a reductionist model of them:

> Why would immigrants reappropriate a reductionist model of them? The answer is complex. Suffice it here to note a peculiar fit between the self-interest of many, especially men, and official policy in the new home country. Blinded by what they can gain, personally, materially and/or politically by presenting themselves

> as culture driven, many immigrants are naturally willing to do so. The government encourages the strategy. Committed to a policy of 'respect for their culture', immigrants are perceived as uniform carriers of culture conceived as a static object. this paves the way for eloquent spokesmen to enter the arena and proclaim -in truth- what is the culture. Thus government agencies and immigrants collude in perpetrating a version of culture and a view of 'man' that works to the detriment of the welfare of especially weaker members of ethnic minorities but also of immigrants in general (1999:58; emphasis original).

While many of the critical utterances made by Wikan are well taken, she reifies cultural difference and, in addition, treats *Norwegian culture* as natural and given. Moreover, I find it very problematic that she denies immigrants the right to *krav på respekt*.[29] The Somalis represent one group that is not favoured in the Norwegian society, and some glimpses of this reality appear every now and then in the media.[30] Mistrust is one issue here. In the autumn of 1999, the Norwegian Ministry of Justice launched a DNA analysis project in connection with family reunification applications from Somalis. The purpose of the project was

> to ensure that residence permits would be granted to those persons who needed them. A general requirement in family reunification cases is that familial relations must be documented. The Ministry of Justice selected Somalis for this pilot project because obtaining reliable written information on familial relations in Somalia has been particularly difficult for a long period of time (UDI 1999:29).

Another area where Somalis have problems is the housing market. But they are not alone in this. Other immigrant groups also face serious problems in finding a place to reside in. An investigation by the Norwegian Central Bureau of Statistics in 1996 revealed that 60 per cent of the Somalis who were asked reported that they had been refused to rent housing. The same report also showed that 20 per cent of all immigrants who were included in the investigation reported they were discriminated against in the housing market on the basis of their immigrant background. Among the reasons why Somalis face housing problems, size of the family is often cited (see Harring 1999). The image created by the media also makes it difficult for Somalis to compete not only in the housing market, but also in the labour market.

29. For Wikan, this claim for respect is totally unfounded and unrealistic: "in no society that I know can you come *uninvited* and demand respect" (ibid., p. 61; my emphasis).

30. See for example the article by Jan Haakonsen in *Dagbladet*, 31 July 2000.

The Sudanese also face problems when it comes to housing. But because their number is far less than that of the Somalis, the problems they face are less visible. During my fieldwork in Oslo (July–September 2001) a Sudanese refugee was beaten by the police and sustained an injury to his arm as a result.[31] While such an incident may fall under the daily and routine life experiences of immigrants, and can happen to anybody else, it nonetheless says something about the contested relationships between refugee or immigrant groups and the Norwegian society. The incident was interpreted by the victim and other Sudanese as racist, and that he was beaten because he was "black". Another tension that obtains between refugees and the host society is related to the lot of immigrant women. The issue of female circumcision brought to light by a 21-year-old *Somali-Norwegian* girl in October 2000 is a case in point. Although it started as something that was within the Somali community, it was dramatised by the media along religious lines, by their portraying it as something that is peculiarly *Islamic.* Thus religion was brought into the picture. While the Norwegian debate on immigrants and refugees is local in nature, it must be related to the general debates on diaspora and transnational subjectivities (Assal 2004). Some of these general debates are discussed below.

The problems and challenges Somalis and Sudanese face in Norway show that while the question of intersectionality (Anthias 1998) must be attended to in diasporic studies, such attendance must not be allowed to divert our attention from looking at the relationships between immigrants and the host society (Fuglerud 1999:3–4). The excess in revealing such intersectionalities will serve to conceal the disadvantageous position many diasporic groups sustain, and may again bring us back to processes of "boundary management". While Anthias is critical of diaspora studies on the ground that they tend to be heavily skewed towards ethnicity, she can be criticised on a similar ground. One issue here is Anthias' advocacy of class analysis. To avoid missing the mark in Anthias' advocacy of class analysis in diasporic situations, it is important to point out some of the pitfalls in such advocacy. What is lacking in Anthias' argument is a differentiation between what Marx designates as '*klasse-für-sich*' and '*klasse-in-sich*', where the former refers to a class whose members perceive themselves to constitute a class, and the latter as an analytical category based on individual differential positioning in a system of stratification, regardless of whether they themselves acknowledge this or not. In my situation, "class" does not appear in the emic discourse among Sudanese

31. See *Verdens Gang,* July 2001.

and Somalis. Thus, the relevance of class analysis is doubtful for a number of reasons chief among which are the sense of egalitarianism entertained by Somalis and Sudanese, and the similarity in the material conditions of people. In addition to this, the term "class" itself is actually not in the vocabulary of people and nobody talks about it. This in a sense resonates with the ethos of the Norwegian society, *likehet/likestilling* (equality), even if the realisation of this may be open to contestation.

While Anthias (1998, 2001a) is not clear about how to go about studying class empirically in studying class in diasporic communities, Friedman (1995) and Werbner (1999) look at the issue of class through transnational and cosmopolitan subjectivities, thus supporting, and taking a further step in, Anthias' advocacy for class analysis. Transnationals[32] and cosmopolitans are two emerging *classes* in the evolving global ecumene. For Friedman (in Werbner 1999:18), such subjectivities are manifestations of class formations:

> One might also suggest that there has emerged a global class structure, an international elite made up of top diplomats, government ministers, aid officials and representatives of international organisations such as the United Nations, who play golf, dive, take cocktails with one another, forming a kind of cultural cohort. This grouping overlaps with an international cultural elite of art dealers, publishing and media representatives, the culture industries,... producing images of the world and images for the world... .

Moreover, Friedman (1997) argues that the celebration of hybridity by diasporic cosmopolitans is a self-interested strategy, which is divorced from working class immigrants' predicaments and concerns. For the troubled immigrants or refugees other identities prevail, leaving little room for hybrid identifications of the sort pleaded for by cultural elites. This resonates with Anthias' claim that cultural identifications are a matter of social position. Thus, "diasporic elites are in reality as socially and culturally encapsulated in their cocktail-sipping worlds as are ghetto dwellers in theirs" (Werbner 1999:18).

But I am not talking about cosmopolitans here. I am talking about transnationals, in the manner defined by Pnina Werbner.[33] Nonetheless, by using the term 'transnationals' I am not in any sense trying to homogenise Sudanese

32. Werbner (1999:19) defines transnationals as "people who move and build encapsulated cultural worlds around them".

33. Werbner (1999:18) argues that "even working class migrants may become cosmopolitans, willing to 'engage with the Other', and that transnationals – Hannerz' term redefined to encompass migrants and refugees as well as occupational travellers – in-

and Somalis in Norway. Quite the contrary, the material I have presented in this chapter attests to the fact that the two groups are heterogeneous. Such heterogeneity questions the analytical usefulness of class category, beyond a heuristic level. The sort of classifications people use are based on, among other things, length of stay in Norway, clan or ethnic affiliation, naturalised or still retaining native citizenship, Muslim or Christian, working or relying on the welfare system and, of course, male or female. These classifications crosscut any notion of class and to focus on class alone as an analytical category will miss looking at such classifications and obstruct eliciting their effects on the lives of diasporic communities. It is important to note that in a very recent contribution Anthias (2001c:841) alludes to the problems of class analysis:

> When one looks at processes for the production of unequal outcomes … then one cannot use the class category alone, unless it becomes merely a shorthand for all those processes that lead to outcomes of unequal resource distribution. These problems do not imply abandoning class but treating it as an heuristic device rather than about actual groupings of people, i.e. for sociological purposes rather than for auditing purposes.

The issue of gender is also no less intriguing than class, particularly when it intersects with Islam. The status of Somali women in Norway is closely linked to such issues like *kvinnelig omskjæring* (female circumcision), *tvangsekteskap/arrangertekteskap* (forced/arranged marriages), etc. The image created through focusing on these issues victimises the Somali women and portrays Somalis in general as people who ill-treat their women. For the Somalis, the issue of gender is just a sidetrack that is meant to divert the attention from their subordinate and disadvantageous position in the Norwegian society and an issue that is directed against Islam.[34] Thus, from whose perspective can diasporic gender be addressed? Against whose yardstick? Such questions must be addressed expeditiously before talking about gender as one field of intersectionality in diaspora studies.

evitably must engage in *social* processes of 'opening up to the world', even if that world is still circumscribed culturally".

34. This is the view of the former leader of the Somali Welfare Union.

Conclusion: Beyond boundary maintenance and diaspora

The answer to the question whether Sudanese and Somalis in Norway should be considered diasporic or not must be clear by now. But if I must be explicit, then they are. However, what count are the empirical realities experienced by people. While the two groups I am discussing are immigrants/refugees or something that does not belong naturally to Europe, I believe what I am doing falls within "an anthropology of Europe" framework, and my criticism of the notion of "deterritorialised ethnicity" was an anticipation for such a position. The presence of different "others" is now a basic component of the realities in Norway, and portraying such a presence as something less than this would miss an indispensable basis for constructive scholarship. This being said, I must make it very clear that being part of the reality in Norway, or Europe in general, and yet retaining the identity of being part of something else, are not mutually exclusive situations. Home is where somebody makes it (Graham and Khosravi 1997). Many immigrants are nostalgic but at the same time pragmatic and keep their options open. They do not do away with the possibility of moving to yet a third country, especially if there are some relatives or friends there. Many Somalis have family and kinship connections in more than three countries, in Europe and elsewhere.

I look at my material on Somalis and Sudanese as posing difficult questions that relate to how I can make intelligible the condition of being part of Norway and at the same time part of Sudan and Somalia, or of yet something else. Is it by deploying concepts like "diaspora"? Or is it by resorting to the old-fashion "boundary maintenance stuff" that seems to be out of favour for the moment? Well, the answers to these two *simple* questions are not easy to cultivate, and maybe they lie somewhere in the dialectics of the two options, or probably somewhere else which I do not know. The processes of politics, ethnicity, religion and the ways Sudanese and Somalis relate to their homelands may tempt us to direct our attention to analysis of particularistic identity formation, yet, at the same time, to universalistic analysis when it comes to claims making. In forming those various types of cultural organisations discussed above, both Sudanese and Somalis, and other immigrant groups also, will advance their respective particular identities. In doing this, they cultivate the generosity of an abstract discourse, of the host society, that celebrates "cultural" difference and emphasises equality. This discourse is codified, in the sense of being part of the government bureaucracy and the mass media, and it is appropriated by different actors, including immigrants themselves. Yet, the same discourse which celebrates difference tends to problematise immigrants' identity and cultural practices, and often portrays these cultural practices as pathological. The example of the *kvinnelig omskjæring* (female circumcision) affair is a case in point. Obviously neither boundary maintenance nor diaspora can be analytically adequate to unravel the complexities posed by these unfolding realities. The way ahead, as I see it, is to focus on specific positioned cases and let the material direct our analysis. This is not an advocacy for methodological and theoretical anarchy, however. It is one way of saying that concepts often fall short of capturing reality.

References

Abdel Rahim, Muddathir, 1985, "Arabism, Africanism and self-identification in Sudan", in Hassan, Yusuf Fadl (ed.), *Sudan in Africa*. Khartoum: Khartoum University Press.

Adam, Hussein M., 1995, "Somalia: A terrible beauty being born?" in Zartman, I. William (ed.), *Collapsed states: The disintegration and restoration of legitimate authority*. Boulder and London: Lynne Rienner.

—, and Richard Ford (eds), 1997, *Mending ribs in the sky: Options for Somali communities in the 21st century*. Lawrenceville: Red Sea Press.

Africa Watch, 1990, *Somalia: A government at war with its own people. Testimonies about the killings and the conflict in the north*. New York: Africa Watch.

—, 1993, "Seeking refuge, finding terror: The widespread rape of Somali women refugees in north eastern Kenya", in *Africa Watch Women's Rights Project*. London: Africa Watch.

African Rights, 1993, *The Nightmare continues: Abuses against Somali refugees in Kenya*. London: African Rights.

Ahmed, Abdel Ghaffar, 1979, "Tribal elite: A base for social stratification in Sudan", in Diamond, Stanely (ed.), *Towards a Marxist anthropology*. The Hague: Mouton Publishers.

Ahmed, Ali Jimale (ed.), 1995, *The invention of Somalia*. Lawrenceville, NJ: Red Sea Press.

—, 1996, *Daybreak is near: Literature, clans and the nation-state in Somalia*. Lawrenceville, NJ: Red Sea Press.

Ali, Ali Abdelgadir, 1994, *Structural Adjustment Programmes and Poverty in the Sudan* (in Arabic). Cairo: Centre for Arab Research.

Andersson, Mete, 2000, *All five fingers are not the same: identity work among ethnic minority youth in an urban Norwegian context*. Report no. 1, IMER, Centre for Social Research, University of Bergen.

Anthias, Floya, 1998, "Evaluating diaspora: Beyond ethnicity", *Sociology*, 32(3):557–580.

—, 2001a, "New hybridities, old concepts: The limits of 'culture", *Ethnic and Racial Studies*, 24(4):619–641.

—, 2001b, "The material and the symbolic in theorising social stratification: Issues of gender, ethnicity and class", *British Journal of Sociology*, 52(3):367–390.

—, 2001c, "The concept of social division and theorising social stratification: Looking at ethnicity and class", *Sociology*, 35(4):835–854.

Assal, Munzoul A.M., 2004, *Sticky labels or rich ambiguities? Diaspora and challenges of homemaking for Somalis and Sudanese in Norway*. Bergen: BRIC/University of Bergen.

Behar, Ruth, 1996, *The vulnerable observer: Anthropology that breaks your heart*. Boston: Beacon Press.

Bell, Herman, 1989, "Languages and ethnic identity in the Sudan and the Soviet Union: A comparative study", in Hurreiz, Sayyid and Abdel Salam, Elfatih (eds), *Ethnicity, conflict and national integration in the Sudan*, pp. 186–195. Khartoum: Institute of African and Asian Studies.

Brons, Maria, 2001, *Society, security, sovereignty and the state in Somalia: From statelessness to statelessness?* Utrecht: International Books

Brox, Ottar, 1998, "Policy implications of the settlement patterns of immigrants: Some Norwegian experiences and viewpoints", in *Immigrants, integration and cities: Exploring the links*. OECD proceedings.

Cassanelli, Lee, 1982, *The shaping of Somali society: Reconstruction of the history of a pastoral people, 1600–1900*. Philadelphia: University of Pennsylvania Press.

Castles, Stephen and Altastair Davidson, 2000, *Citizenship and migration: Globalisation and the politics of belonging*. Basingstoke: Macmillan Press Ltd.

Clifford, James, 1994, "Diasporas", *Cultural Anthropology*, 9(3):302–38.

Cohen, Robin, 1997, *Global diasporas: An introduction*. London: UCL Press.

Deleuze, Gilles, and Félix Guattari, 1987, *A thousand plateaus: Capitalism and schizophrenia*. Trans. B. Massumi. Minneapolis: University of Minnesota Press.

Deng, Francis, 1993, *Protecting the dispossessed: A challenge for the international community*. Washington: The Brooking Institute.

Djuve, Anne and Kåre Hagen, 1995, *Skaff meg en jobb: Livekår blant flyktninger i Oslo* (Get me a job: Living conditions among refugees in Oslo). Oslo: Fafo.

Evans-Prichard, Edvard, 1940, *The Nuer*. Oxford: Oxford University Press.

Farah, Nuruddin, 2000, *Yesterday, tomorrow: Voices from the Somali diaspora*. London and New York: Cassell.

Friedman, Jonathan, 1995, "Global system, globalisation and the parameters of modernity", in Feathersone, Mike, Scott Lash and Roland Robertson (eds), *Global modernities*, pp 69–90. London: Sage.

—, 1997, "Global crises, the struggle for cultural identity and intellectual porkbarrelling: Cosmopolitans versus locals, ethnics and nationals in an era of de-hegemonisation", in Werbner, Pnina and Tariq Modood (eds), *Debating cultural hybridity: Multi-cultural identities and the politics of anti-racism*, pp 70–89. London: Zed Books.

Fuglerud, Øivind, 1999, *Life on the outside: The Tamil diaspora and long-distance nationalism*. London: Pluto Press.

—, 1997, "Ambivalent incorporation: Norwegian policy towards Tamil asylum-seekers from Sri Lanka", *Journal of Refugee Studies*, 10(4):443–461.

Graham, Mark, and Shahram Khosravi, 1997, "Home is where you make it: Repatriation and diaspora culture among Iranians in Sweden", *Journal of Refugee Studies*, 10(2):115–133.

Griffiths, David J., 2000, "Fragmentation and consolidation: Contrasting cases of Somali and Kurdish refugees in London", *Journal of Refugee Studies*, 13(3):281–302.

—, 1997, "Somali refugees in Tower Hamlets: Clanship and new identities", *New Community*, 23(1):5–24.

Gore, Paul Wani, 1989, "Contemporary issues in ethnic relations: Problems of national integration in Sudan", in Hurriez, Sayyd and Elfatih Abdel Salam (eds), *Ethnicity, conflict and national integration in the Sudan*, pp. 269–299. Khartoum: Institute of African and Asian Studies.

Harir, Sharif, 1994, "Recycling the past in the Sudan: An overview of political decay", in Harir, Sharif and Terje Tvedt (eds), *Short-cut to decay: The case of the Sudan*, pp. 10–68. Uppsala: The Scandinavian Institute of African Studies.

Harring, Thore H., 1999, "Somaliere på boligmarkedet i Oslo: Hvorfor har somaliere større problemer på boligmarkedet enn andre innvandrergrupper? (Somalis in the housing market in Oslo: Why Somalis have serious problems in the housing markets than other immigrant groups?)" Oslo: Høgeskolen i Oslo.

Hassan, Yusuf Fadl (ed.), 1985, *Sudan in Africa*. Khartoum: Khartoum University Press.

—, 1967, *The Arabs and the Sudan from the seventh to the early sixteenth century*. Edinburgh: The University of Edinburgh Press.

Hein, Jeremy, 1993, "Refugees, immigrants and the state", *Annual Review of Sociology*, 19:43–59.

Hersi, Ali Abdurahman, 1977, *The Arab factor in Somali history: The origin and development of the Arab enterprise in cultural influences in the Somali peninsula*. Ph.D. Dissertation. Los Angeles: University of California.

Kapteijns, Lidwien, 1994, "Women and the crisis of communal identity: The cultural construction of gender in Somali history", in Samatar, Ahmed I. (ed.), *The Somali challenge: From catastrophe to renewal*, pp. 211–232. Boulder and London: Lynne Rienner Publishers.

Laitin, David and Said Samatar, 1987, *Somalia: Nation in search of a state*. Boulder: Westview.

Lewis, Ioan, 1998, *Saints and Somalis: Popular Islam in a clan-based society*. London: Haan Associates.

—, 1994, *Blood and bone: The call of kinship in Somali society*. Lawrenceville: The Red Sea Press.

—, 1982, *A pastoral democracy: A study of pastoralism and politics among the northern Somali of the Horn of Africa*. London: Oxford University Press.

Malkki, Liisa, 1992, "National geographic: The rooting of people and the territorialisation of national identity among scholars and refugees", *Cultural Anthropology* 7(1)24–44.

Manger, Leif, 2001a, "The concept of diaspora and the theorising of identity". Paper presented at the conference on *The Concept of Diaspora and the Theorising of Identity*, Univerity of Bergen, 5 September 2001.

—, 2001b, "The Nuba mountains- battlegrounds of identities: Culturalk traditions and territories", in Johansen, Maj-Brit and Niels Kastfelt (eds), *Sudanese society in the context of civil war*, pp. 49–90. Copenhagen: Centre for African Studies.

Massey, Doreen, 1994, *Space, place, and gender*. Minneapolis: University of Minnesota Press.

Mazrui, Ali, 1985, "The multiple marginality of the Sudan", in Hassan, Yusuf Fadl (ed.), *Sudan in Africa*. Khartoum: Khartoum University Press.

McGown, Rima B., 1999, *Muslims in the diaspora: The Somali communities of London and Toronto*. Toronto: University of Toronto Press.

Mukhtar, Mohamed Haji, 1995, "Islam in Somali history: Fact and fiction", in Ali Jimale Ahmed (ed.), *The invention of Somalia*, pp. 1–27. Lawrenceville: Red Sea Press.

O'Brien, Jay, 1979, *The political economy of development and underdevelopment*. Khartoum: Development Studies and Research Centre.

—, 1998, "Power and the Discourse of Ethnicity in Sudan", in Mohamed Salih, M., and J. Markakis (eds.), *Ethnicity and the State in Eastern Africa*. Uppsala: Nordiska Afrikainstitutet.

Safran, William, 1991, "Diasporas in modern societies: Myths of homeland and return", *Diaspora*, 1(1):83–99.

Sahl, Ibrahim, 1999, "Crossing the Poverty Line: The destiny of the Sudanese middle-class public sector employees", *Social Sciences Research Report Series*, No. 11. Addis Ababa: Organisation for Social Science Research in Eastern and Southern Africa.

Salih, Mohamed and John Markakis (eds), 1998, *Ethnicity and the State in Eastern Africa*. Uppsala: Nordiska Afrikainstitutet.

Samatar, Ahmed I. (ed.), 1994, *The Somali challenge: From catastrophe to renewal?* Boulder and London: Lynne Rienner Publishers.

—, 1994, "Introduction and overview", in Samatar, Ahmed I. (ed.), *The Somali challenge: From catastrophe to renewal?*, pp. 3–20. Boulder and London: Lynne Rienner Publishers.

Samatar, Said, 1990, *Somalia: A nation in turmoil*. London: The Minority Rights Group.

Statistics Norway, 1996, *Levekår blant innvandrere (Living conditions among immigrants)*. Oslo: Statistisk Sentral Byrå.

Sørensen, Jens Magleby, 1996, *The exclusive European citizenship: The case for refugees and immigrants in the European Union*. Aldershot: Avebury.

UDI (Norwegian Directorate of Immigration), 1999, *Annual report on the implementation of the immigration, refugee and integration policy*. Oslo: UDI.

Werbner, Pnina, 1999, "Global pathways. Working class cosmopolitans and the creation of transnational ethnic worlds", *Social Anthropology*, 7(1):17–35.

Wikan, Unni, 1999, "Culture: A new concept of race", *Social Anthropology*, 7(1)57–64.
Wohlgemuth, L. and Mohamed Salih (eds), 1994, *Crisis management and the politics of reconciliation in Somalia*. Uppsala: The Scandinavian Institute of African Studies.

ANNEXES

Table (1) Numbers of Somalis and Sudanese in Norway (January 2002)

Category	Men	Women	First Generation	Second Generation	Total
Somalis	6120	5149	8723	2546	11269
Sudanese	477	195	418	59	477

Source: <www.ssb.no/emner/02/01/innvbef/tab-2002–09–05.html>

Table (2) Somali and Sudanese refugees in Norway (January 2002)

Category	Refugees with Norwegian citizenship	Refugees without Norwegian citizenship	0–15	16–29	30–49	50–66	67+	Total
Somalis	2238	5117	1776	2638	2676	235	30	7355
Sudanese	68	235	46	98	149	9	1	303

Source: ibid.

Table (3) Somalis and Sudanese asylum seekers during 1989–1999

Year	1989	1990	1991	1992	1993	1994	1995	1996	1997	1998	1999
Somalis	362	313	731	444	259	251	189	180	552	938	703
Sudanese	3	9	34	29	40	15	23	32	34	44	55

Sources: UDI (1999b) and SSB (Central Bureau of Statistics).

The standard definition of *flyktninger* "refugees" adopted by the Central Bureau of Statistics is that "the term refugee refers to persons resident in Norway, who have come to Norway because of flight (family included). *Children born in Norway to refugees are not included*," while the Norwegian Directorate of Immigration (UDI) gives the following definition: "in the legal sense, the term 'refugees' applies to resettlement refugees and asylum seekers who have been granted asylum. This is also a common term used about a person who is fleeing, for example because of war, unrest, human rights violation or environmental catastrophes. In connection with refugee assistance in Norway, the term 'refugee' is used for resettlement refugees and asylum seekers who have been granted asylum or residence on humanitarian grounds" (1999:50). Both definitions do not specify for how long a person will continue to be labelled "refugee." The same source defined an immigrant as "a person born abroad, permanently resident in Norway, but whose parents were both born abroad". From this definition, *innvandrere* (immigrants) will continue to be immigrants for the rest of their lives. But according to the Norwegian regulations, foreign citizens can apply for Norwegian citizenship after residing in Norway permanently for seven years. Citizenship can also be obtained after four years of marriage with a Norwegian citizen. This applies for both *innvandrere* and *flyktninger* (immigrants and refugees).

The contributors

Roqaia Mustafa Abusharaf is Senior Research Associate at the Pembroke Center for Teaching and Research on Women and a fellow at the Francoise-Xavier Bagnoud Institute for Health and Human Rights at Harvard University School of Public Health. Her latest publication is *Wanderings. Sudanese Migrants and Exiles in North America* (2002).

Munzoul A.M. Assal teaches anthropology at the University of Khartoum, Sudan. His recent publications include his published PhD thesis from Bergen, *Sticky Labels or Rich Ambiguities? Diaspora and challenges of homemaking for Somalis and Sudanese in Norway* (2004) and *Darfur; an annotated bibliography of social research* (2006). He is also the co-editor of *Anthropology in the Sudan* (2003).

Anne K. Bang is Postdoctoral Research Fellow at the University of Bergen. Her main publication is *Sufis and Scholars of the Sea. Family Network in East Africa, 1860–1925* (2003).

Sindre Bangstad is affiliated to the International Institute for the Study of Islam in the Modern World (ISIM) in Leiden, where he pursues a PhD study on "The impact of social and political change on Cape Muslim communities in Cape Town, South Africa".

Bettina Conrad is currently completing her PhD study on the Eritrean Diaspora at the Institute for Political Science in Hamburg. In 2005 she co-edited a special issue of the *Eritrean Studies Review*: "Eritrea Abroad. Critical Perspectives on the Global Diaspora".

Leif Manger is Professor of social anthropology at the University of Bergen. His latest monograph is *From the Mountains to the Plains. The Integration of the Lafofa Nuba in Sudanese Society* (1994). He has co-edited a book on the Red Sea, *Survival on Meagre Resources. Pastoral Adaptation of the Hadendowa in the Red Sea Hills* (1996) and edited the volume *Muslim Diversity. Local Islam in Global Contexts* (1999).

Index